# No More Masks

# No More Masks

## Journals & Letters on a Bowing Pilgrimage

by

**Heng Sure Ph.D.**
**and**
**Heng Ch'au Ph.D.**

## Volume Three

Buddhist Text Translation Society
Dharma Realm Buddhist University
Dharma Realm Buddhist Association
Burlingame, California U.S.A.

# No More Masks
## Journals & Letters on a Bowing Pilgrimage. Volume Three.

Published and translated by:

**Buddhist Text Translation Society**
1777 Murchison Drive, Burlingame, CA 94010-4504

© 2007  **Buddhist Text Translation Society**
**Dharma Realm Buddhist University**
**Dharma Realm Buddhist Association**

First edition 2007

16  15  14  13  12  11  10  09  08  07    12  11  10  9  8  7  6  5  4  3  2

ISBN 978-0-88139-908-0

Printed in Malaysia.

Note: Contents previously published under the title "With One Heart Bowing to the City of Ten Thousand Buddhas"

Addresses of the Dharma Realm Buddhist Association branches are listed at the back of this book.

Library of Congress Cataloging-in-Publication Data

Heng Sure, 1949-
 No more masks / by Heng Sure and Heng Ch'au.
   p. cm. -- (Journals & letters on a bowing pilgrimage ; v. 3)
 ISBN 978-0-88139-908-0 (hard cover : alk. paper)
1. Spiritual life--Buddhism. 2. Heng Sure, 1949- 3. Heng Ch'au. 4.
Buddhist pilgrims and pilgrimages--California. I. Heng Ch'au. II.
Title. III. Series.

 BQ5625.H466 2007
 294.3'43509794--dc22

2007002696

# *Contents*

---

# Preface

Three steps, one bow – three steps along the side of the highway, then a bow to the ground, so that knees, elbows, hands, and forehead touch the earth, then rise, join the palms together, and take three more steps, then begin another bow. Hour after hour, day after day, for two and a half years, this was how they made their pilgrimage. In China, devout Buddhists sometimes undertake the arduous and prayerful practice of three steps, one bow, for the last few hundred yards of a journey to a sacred site. But this was California, and these two pilgrim-monks were young Americans. Dressed in their robes and sashes, carrying no money, armed with nothing but discipline and reverence, they walked and bowed 800 miles along the narrow shoulder of the Pacific Coast Highway. Progressing a mile a day, they bowed from downtown Los Angeles north along the coast, through Santa Barbara and along the Big Sur, through San Francisco and across the Golden Gate, then 100 miles farther north to the City of Ten Thousand Buddhas, a newly founded religious and educational center in Mendocino County. As they bowed, their prayer was that the world would be free of disaster, calamity, and war.

The silent monk in the lead was Heng Sure. Originally from Toledo, Ohio, he had found his way in 1974 to Gold Mountain Buddhist Monastery in San Francisco. There on a side street of the Mission District, an eminent Chinese monk, the Venerable Master

Hsuan Hua, was living in obscurity as he carried out his pioneering work of transplanting the Buddhist monastic tradition to the West. Moved by Master Hua's virtue and wisdom, Heng Sure joined other young Americans in taking a monastic name and the full ordination of a Buddhist monk.

During his subsequent studies, Heng Sure read of a bowing pilgrimage made in the 1880's by the Venerable Hsu Yun ("Empty Cloud"), who was the most distinguished Chinese monastic of his generation. Master Yun had bowed every third step across the breadth of China; it had taken him five years. Heng Sure knew that Master Yun had been patriarch of the Wei Yang Lineage of the Chan School, and he knew that his own abbot and teacher, Master Hua, was the current patriarch, having received the lineage transmission from Master Yun in 1949. Inspired by this close connection, Heng Sure asked Master Hua if he could undertake his own pilgrimage of three steps, one bow. Master Hua approved, but said, "Wait."

Heng Sure had to wait a year. What he needed, Master Hua said, was the right companion and protector. It was to be Heng Chau. Originally from Appleton, Wisconsin, Heng Chau had come to Berkeley to study martial arts, and he had become an adept in several traditions. When his tai-chi teacher finally told him, "Chan is higher than any martial art," Heng Chau crossed the Bay to study at Gold Mountain Monastery. He soon heard about Heng Sure's vow, and he asked if he could bow with him. Within a week Heng Chau took novice precepts and made a formal vow to bow beside Heng Sure, as well as handle the logistics of cooking, cleaning, setting up camp, and talking with strangers.

Thus the pilgrimage began. Master Hua saw them off as they left Gold Wheel Monastery in Los Angeles on 7 May 1977. To Heng Chau, the martial artist, he said, "You can't use your martial arts on the pilgrimage. Heng Sure's vow is to seek an end to calamities, disasters and war; so how can you yourselves be involved in violence? If either of you fights – or even indulges in anger – you will no longer be my disciples." For protection from the dangers of the road, Master Hua instructed them to practice instead the four unconditional attitudes of the Bodhisattva: kindness, compassion, joy, and equanimity. It was by no means the last time that the two bowing monks would need their teacher's advice.

On the road, the two pilgrims followed their monastic discipline strictly – eating one vegetarian meal a day; never going indoors, sleeping sitting up in the old 1956 Plymouth station wagon that served as their shelter. In the evenings after a day of bowing they studied the Avatamsaka Sutra (Flower Adornment Sutra) by the light of an oil lamp. They translated passages into English and attempted to put into practice the principles of the text in their day-to-day experiences on the road, as their teacher had encouraged them to do. The monks guarded their concentration by avoiding newspapers, by leaving the car radio silent, and by keeping to a strict meditation schedule. Heng Sure held a vow of silence for the entire journey, and it became Heng Chau's job to talk with the many people who stopped along the highway with questions. Occasionally the visitors were hostile, and some threatened violence, but the greater number were curious, and often the curious became the monks' protectors, bringing them food and supplies until the monks had bowed their way out of range.

Everything important that happened on the highway – the mistakes and the growth, the trials and remarkable encounters, the dangers and the insights, the hard work with the body and in the mind – the pilgrims reported in letters to Master Hua. He would answer in person by visiting them from time to time, giving them indispensable spiritual guidance, admonishment, humor, and timely instructions – both lofty and mundane. These letters are the contents of this volume. They were not written with the thought that they would be published. Rather, they were a medium in which the two monks attempted to speak to their teacher as openly and sincerely as possible about their experience on the road. As such, the letters preserve an unadorned account of an authentic spiritual journey.

# The Venerable Master Hsuan Hua

## A Brief Portrait

"I have had many names," he once said, "and all of them are false." In his youth in Manchuria, he was known as "the Filial Son Bai"; as a young monk he was An Tzu ("Peace and Kindness"); later, in Hong Kong, he was Tu Lun ("Wheel of Rescue"); finally, in America, he was Hsuan Hua, which might be translated as "one who proclaims the principles of transformation." To his thousands of disciples across the world, he was always also "Shr Fu" – "Teacher."

Born in 1918 into a peasant family in a small village on the Manchurian plain, Master Hua was the youngest of ten children. He attended school for only two years, during which he studied the Chinese Classics and committed much of them to memory. As a young teenager, he opened a free school for both children and adults. He also began then one of his lifelong spiritual practices: reverential bowing. Outdoors, in all weathers, he would make over 800 prostrations daily, as a profound gesture of his respect for all that is good and sacred in the universe.

He was nineteen when his mother died, and for three years he honored her memory by sitting in meditation in a hut beside her grave. It was during this time that he made a resolve to go to America to teach the principles of wisdom. As a first step, at the end of the period of mourning, he entered San Yuan Monastery, took as his teacher Master Chang Chih, and subsequently received the full ordination of a Buddhist monk at Pu To Mountain. For ten years he devoted himself to study of the Buddhist scriptural tradition and to mastery of both the Esoteric and the Chan Schools of Chinese Buddhism. He had also read and contemplated the scriptures of Christianity, Taoism, and Islam. Thus, by the age of thirty, he had already established through his own experience the four major imperatives of his later ministry in America: the primacy of the monastic tradition; the essential role of moral education; the need for Buddhists to ground themselves in traditional spiritual practice and authentic scripture; and, just as essential, the importance and the power of ecumenical respect and understanding.

In 1948, Master Hua traveled south to meet the Venerable Hsu Yun, who was then already 108 years old and China's most distinguished spiritual teacher. From him Master Hua received the patriarchal transmission in the Wei Yang Lineage of the Chan School. Master Hua subsequently left China for Hong Kong. He spent a dozen years there, first in seclusion, then later as a teacher at three monasteries which he founded.

Finally, in 1962, he went to the United States, at the invitation of several of his Hong Kong disciples who had settled in San Francisco. By 1968, Master Hua had established the Buddhist Lecture Hall in a loft in San Francisco's Chinatown, and there he began giving nightly lectures, in Chinese, to an audience of young Americans. His texts were the major scriptures of the Mahayana. In 1969, he astonished the monastic community of Taiwan by sending there, for final ordination, two American women and three American men, all five of them fully trained as novices, fluent in Chinese and conversant with Buddhist scripture. During subsequent years, the Master trained and oversaw the ordination of hundreds of monks and nuns who came to California from every part of the world to study with him. These monastic disciples now teach in the 28 temples, monasteries and convents that the Master founded in the United States, Canada, and several Asian countries.

Although he understood English well and spoke it when it was necessary, Master Hua almost always lectured in Chinese. His aim was to encourage Westerners to learn Chinese, so that they could become translators, not merely of his lectures, but of the major scriptural texts of the Buddhist Mahayana. His intent was realized. So far, the Buddhist Text Translation Society, which he founded, has issued over 130 volumes of translation of the major Sutras, together with a similar number of commentaries, instructions, and stories from the Master's teaching.

As an educator, Master Hua was tireless. From 1968 to the mid 1980's he gave as many as a dozen lectures a week, and he traveled extensively on speaking tours. At the City of Ten Thousand Buddhas in Talmage, California, he established formal training programs for monastics and for laity; elementary and secondary schools for boys and for girls; and Dharma Realm Buddhist University, together with the University's branch, the Institute for World Religions, in Berkeley.

Throughout his life the Master taught that the basis of spiritual practice is moral practice. Of his monastic disciples he required strict purity, and he encouraged his lay disciples to adhere to the five precepts of the Buddhist laity. Especially in his later years, Confucian texts were often the subject of his lectures, and he held to the Confucian teaching that the first business of education is moral education. He identified six rules of conduct as the basis of communal life at the City of Ten Thousand Buddhas; the six rules prohibit contention, covetousness, self-seeking, selfishness, profiting at the expense of the community, and false speech. He asked that the children in the schools he had founded recite these prohibitions every morning before class. In general, although he admired the independent-mindedness of Westerners, he believed that they lacked ethical balance and needed that stabilizing sense of public morality which is characteristic of the East.

The Venerable Master insisted on ecumenical respect, and he delighted in inter-faith dialogue. He stressed commonalities in religious traditions – above all their emphasis on proper conduct, on compassion, and on wisdom. He was also a pioneer in building bridges between different Buddhist national traditions. He often brought monks from Theravada countries to California to share the duties of transmitting the precepts of ordination. He invited Catholic priests to celebrate the mass in the Buddha-Hall at the City of Ten Thousand Buddhas, and he developed a late-in-life friendship with Paul Cardinal Yu-Bin, the exiled leader of the Catholic Church in China and Taiwan. He once told the Cardinal: "You can be a Buddhist among the Catholics, and I'll be a Catholic among Buddhists." To the Master, the essential teachings of all religions could be summed up in a single word: wisdom.

* * *

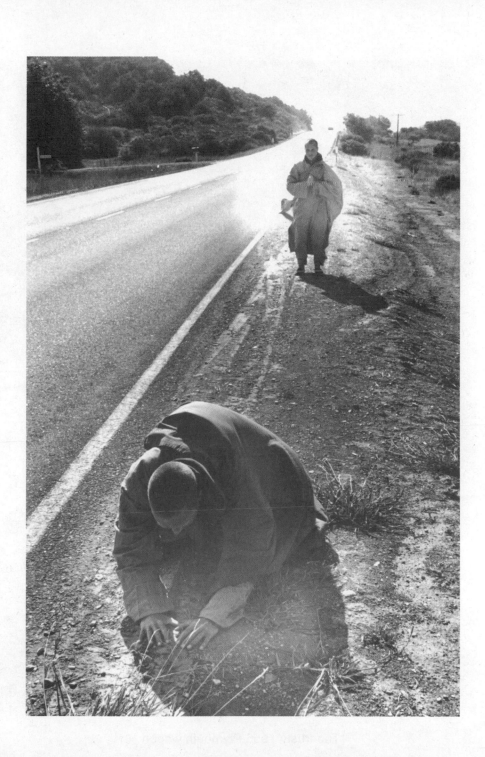

The trusty 1956 Plymouth wagon

# No More Masks

* * * * * * * * *
October 1977

**Heng Chau** • October 25, 1977
First I lost my temper, then I lost my finger

Scars.

Everybody has a scar, probably. Some of us are missing teeth or limbs. Some of us have burn scars or limps from falls and accidents. Why?

> Living beings' bodies are all different.
> They come from adherence to different thoughts.
> So, too, of the many kinds of Buddhalands
> None does not come from karma.

The Avatamsaka Sutra<br>Chapter 5

When we were putting a cart together for the pilgrimage in a wood workshop on the waterfront in San Francisco, I noticed the carpenter was missing a finger. "Hey, Alan," I asked, "How did you lose your finger?"

"First I lost my temper, then I lost my finger," he replied matter-of-factly. "It's called karma." He went on to relate how he came to work full of angry thoughts towards his father because his father was sick and wouldn't take care of himself. Full of fire and not concentrating, Alan pushed his hand right into a high RPM skil saw and sliced off his finger. "I have a constant reminder now of where anger gets me," he said.

I am beginning to see the scars of my greed, anger, and delusion all around me as we bow up the West coast. Every new freeway and plastic shopping plaza is the scar from my thoughts of "more and better for me." The military bases, missile test sites and veterans' cemeteries are the scars of my anger and hostile thoughts. The billboards promoting cigarettes, Vodka, and gambling are the scars made by my stupidity and upsidedown mind.

All the disasters and suffering in the world, the pollution and depletion of the environment, our own unsettledness and worried souls, come from the karma created by thoughts of greed, hatred, and delusion. It's just like Alan's sawed off finger, only bigger and more developed, that's all.

Morality, concentration, and wisdom leave a trail, too, but we don't notice it as easily. Why? That trail is natural and in keeping with the Middle Way. It is like the old saying, "You never miss the water until the well runs dry." We notice the hand with the missing finger.

Happy families where the children live with both parents and are free from fear and worry are the "unmarked" marks of morality. Places where crops are plentiful, where there is a good rainfall and no disasters are the "unmarked" marks of concentration. Wisdom allows things to come and go according to their natures, and where it's practiced, deaths from drug overdose and alcohol are few. Here, old people die naturally and not in old folk's "rest homes" depressed and pumped full of drugs.

The natural way to live, the Tao (Middle Path) is simple and in harmony with people, earth, and heaven. There are no wars and calamities, no missiles and triple-locked doors. There is returning to our "perfect and complete" nature, the Buddhanature. When we purify our minds, our karma is purified. Keeping to this natural way, we "get to see the Tathagata according to our wishes." The Tathagata is a person who perfected purity and became a Buddha.

"The Tathagata does not compose his body by means of marks, but only with the unmarked, still, tranquil Dharmas. His body's marks, his awesome manner, are altogether perfect and complete. Beings in the world see him according to their wishes.

Avatamsaka Sutra<br>Chapter 5

Scars are made from the mind and erased with the mind. When the mind is pure, the nature appears. It is without marks and within it everywhere is peaceful, everyone is happy. Hold your temper, keep your fingers, leave all marks, see the Buddha!

Everything is cultivation; everything speaks the Dharma. Heng Ju came by on his way to L.A. and oiled, sealed, watered, replaced, taped, and tightened the Plymouth. "Gotta do it regularly or they return to the elements," he said.

If you get stuck, you fall apart. All things change and flow. This is the principle of non-attachment: "Seek movement in stillness and in stillness seek movement." Let the gears of a car get attached and the car dies. Let your mind get attached and you die.

With the car, use oil and grease. For us, it's bowing with a "single mind." It's said, "When you concentrate, movement and stillness are one."

We are camped on a plateau overlooking a valley. The road we are bowing on twists and winds for miles ahead and behind. There's a man crouched on the ridge next to us scanning the hills with binoculars. His name is Wesley. He's looking for wild boar.

"Wesley's my name. Pleasure to meet you. Lots of folks around here have been wondering what you represent." He's wearing a rough-rider cowboy hat and has a weather wrinkled face from years outdoors. Wesley's a wild pig hunter from Indiana. He likes the idea of bowing and trying to help folks. "Now that's what we need a lot more of," he exclaims about the City of Ten Thousand Buddhas. "Folks will be mighty pleased to hear what I got to tell them about you Buddhists."

He goes to his camper and returns with an offering and his high-powered rifle. "It isn't much, but I don't keep much that doesn't have meat in it." I return the Pork 'n Beans. "Oh, yeah, guess pork is considered meat, eh?"

Passion is yin; compassion is yang. Giving is yang; taking is yin. Self is yin; our true nature is yang. Support is yang; criticism is yin.

There are hundreds of noisy, fluttering blackbirds perching on the power lines overhead. The leader moves to flight and in a blink they all follow and disappear, just as if there was only one bird. All quiet, empty line.

There are hundreds of noisy, fluttering false thoughts in my mad mind. Find the source, the one first thought and put it to rest. All the others follow in flock, like there was only one thought. All quiet, empty mind.

Truly, "everything is ok." If not, I've only got my self to blame. Heart at rest, it's all the same; no winds can stir extinguished flames.

We were taking a rest after bowing a long isolated stretch of road. I let my mindfulness relax and was spacing out "at the sights" in the fields and hills around us. A man and woman pull up in a yellow car. Weird vibes immediately. The woman steps out and walks toward us. She's wearing white and has whitish hair. Suddenly I remember a dream I had about a white seal or fox. I remember the seal swim toward me and bite me on the hand. Something connects inside, and both Heng Sure and I without a word feel a danger and brace. The woman is flattering us. We both look at her for an instant and then turn away and excuse ourselves because something isn't straight. It's like she isn't for real.

In a few minutes I'm curled up with cramps and stomach pains. That night Heng Sure has a dream in which he wrestles with a demon and wakes up in a sweat. I woke up just before him, reciting the Great Compassion Mantra after dreaming of being surrounded by danger and dark shadows. Strange things happen sometimes.

"Cultivators of the Way can't be even a tiny bit casual or sloppy," the Master warned us last month in L.A.

What is real and what isn't? We are just beginners and because our false thoughts and hang-ups are so huge, we don't see clearly and recognize things for what they are. "Ultimate understanding" is the Buddha, and because the Buddha has no self, everything is reflected perfectly and seen "as it really is."

> What is real, he sees as truly real.
> What is not real, he sees as unreal.
> In this way, his understanding becomes ultimate.
> Therefore he is called the Buddha.

> Avatamsaka Sutra
> Chapter 14

---

**Heng Sure** • October, 1977
Rely on the Dharma, not on ego

Talk From The Heart.

When talking, use Dharma. Talk real, from the heart. If you want people to understand what you understand, quiet your mind, respectfully pray for the assistance of the Triple Jewel, and then talk the way you talk when you want to save living beings. Rely on the Dharma, not on ego; you are the vessel, not the source. Stick to the teachings you have absorbed from the Master and then speak them through your experience of their light and truth. If you want to make it live, people will hear you, and the Dharma will connect from heart to heart.

**Heng Chau** • October 26, 1977
America is the Western Land of Ultimate Bliss!

"Who do you bow to?"

"We don't bow to get or seek, we bow to lose some of the weight of selfishness."

"Why?"

"Because selfishness is the cause of all the messed-up things in the world. If we bow away some of ours, then there's that much less in the world."

"There's still a lot left, but I think what you're doing is right on, anyway, so good luck."

Bright Star.

We are camped on a small plateau just below a pass off Highway One in the Santa Yves Mountains south of Lompoc. Biting cold gusts of wind from the North whistle through the car as the full moon rises in Taurus, lighting up the hills and valleys for miles.

Tonight Heng Sure read from the Worthy Leader Chapter of the Avatamsaka Sutra:

"Another light is released called 'saving and taking across.' This light is able to awaken all the masses and cause them to universally bring forth the mind of great vows and to take across and liberate all beings from the ocean of desire."

Where does this light originate that is called "saving and taking across"? Tonight after meditation, I stepped outside and thought of our destination, the City of Ten Thousand Buddhas. Someone has called it a "bright star in a troubled world."

Heng Sure had made his vow to do a bowing pilgrimage to the City of 10,000 Buddhas to try to turn back some of the suffering and disasters in the world and to curtail the creation of destructive weapons. Too many people have been killed in wars, and bad karma is filling up everywhere. I had just made a vow to go along to help and protect him. In both of our minds, the City of Ten Thousand Buddhas is the hope for America and the world. This is where a "great reversal" will begin that can turn back the imminent disasters and despair we all face. This is where the search within, "the returning of the light" will start. The path we all seek and can never find to the "worry-free city of liberation", is finally opening up in the West. We are bowing to make a small contribution to its success.

> "If one is able to make universal and great vows, and to rescue and liberate all beings from the ocean of desire, then one is able to pass through the four violent floods, and reveal the path to the worry free liberation city."

The four violent floods are: 1) desire, 2) attachment to existence, 3) ignorance, and 4) wrong views. The world is covered with the four floods. The City of Ten Thousand Buddhas is the way to "pass through", and we know that path began right in our own minds. The path to the city of liberation is to be found in purifying our own hearts of greed, hatred and delusion.

Guo Li said "You know, America is the Western Land of Ultimate Bliss! It is the Pure Land!" There is a saying, "When the East goes to the West, then the West goes to the mind." (i.e. Within, "return the light").

His words really made a connection for Heng Sure and me. This comment was made as Guo Li, Heng Sure and I were driving back from the City of 10,000 Buddhas one time. As we drove across the Golden Gate Bridge back to Gold Mountain Monastery, the pieces all started coming together and then I remembered this account: the Sixth Patriarch appeared to the Master when he was cultivating by his mother's grave as a young man and told him that in the future the Master would spread the Dharma to the West.

> "Great Assembly, the worldly person's own physical body is the city… The Buddha is made within our own nature. Do not seek outside the body. Confused, our nature is a living being. Enlightened, our nature is a Buddha."
>
> Sixth Patriarch Sutra

Tonight I could feel a light called "saving and taking across" coming from the City of Ten Thousand Buddhas. It was shining out in all directions from the City of Ten Thousand Buddhas, calling living beings everywhere home, revealing "the path to the worry-free city of liberation." The impact and importance of the City of Ten Thousand Buddhas is going to be very big and very bright.

Time: A woman stops and says, "Hey you're making good progress." She watches us as she commutes 60 miles back and forth to work everyday. She does in an hour what we do in about two months.

---

**Heng Sure • October 1977**
I feel ready to make the vows

Vows.

Vows are the key, after faith and before practice. In the Ten Grounds Chapter, the Bodhisattva on the Ground of Happiness makes vast vows and realizes ten kinds of minds (beneficent, improving etc). Shih Fu explains that these states of accomplishment were unavailable to the Bodhisattva before he made the vows. "Deep faith, firm vows, and actual practice are the ingredients."

I feel ready to make the vows of a Bodhisattva. Today while bowing, the vows I wish to make came right out of my heart. I verbalize what I really want, hope, wish to do right now and forever: Making offerings to all Buddhas; serving them, praising them; attending all Buddhas' Dharma Assemblies; cultivating all the Bodhisattvas' wisdom, practices, and expedients; leading a great gathering of former disbelievers and old believers to attend the Dharma

Assemblies of all Buddhas; taking across all beings; manifesting bodies in all worlds to teach and transform beings; getting born and dying and going to Nirvana provisionally in all paths of existence in order to lead beings to make a commitment to Bodhi, to perfect all merit and virtue, to perfect all compassion, to perfect all dhyanas, liberations, and samadhis, to perfect limitless hands and eyes, to obtain unobstructed function of great dharanis, to perfect spiritual penetrations, and to perfect the Ten Perfections, the Ten Grounds, all vows, expedients, and conducts, forever throughout all time and space.

Immediately, I felt so happy and light, so real and resolved that I know the time is right. I will let them come up, contemplate each vow in my heart, find the simplest, truest expression of it, and when they are complete will announce them before the great assembly. Paramita. Suo puo he.

---

Heng Chau • October 27, 1977
The old plastic pail

The cultivation and foundation is within, on the mindground. If the center is solid, then no matter what comes, "everything's ok." If you're not solid at home, in your true heart, then no matter where you are, you'll make mistakes.

True cultivation at all times in every pore of your mind and body is the only way to slice it. Total sincerity and right practice forge the markless Dharma sword that lets you cut all the crust and cobwebs. Then you never get stuck, but become smooth, pure, gliding and "eternally bright."

Always bowing, always bright.
Mind stops bowing, always night.

In the Dharma mirror, you check out your heart. If you're clean to the core, then the image is flawless and bright. If there's a flaw even the size of a grain of sand, it will show up as big as Mount Sumeru in the bright light of perfect wisdom. Every time I look at the Master's face and eyes, it is like looking into this mirror.

> It's just like a pure bright mirror:
> Depending on what object stands before it,
> The different images each appear.
> The nature of karma is the same.
>
> Avatamsaka Sutra – Chapter 10

After listening to the cries of a young deer being eaten alive by a pack of dogs, I made a vow to fast on the 15th and 30th of each lunar month, to recite the Bodhisattva precepts, and to observe silence. The sounds of suffering in the world are deafening. They come from bad karma "created by body, mouth, and mind based on greed, hatred, and delusion." I am hearing the echoes of my own misdeeds, and I want to change.

The sound of all suffering is one sound. We all speak it; we all hear it. The source of all Buddhas is one source. We all have it; we all will become Buddhas. The "source of all Buddhas" is the Bodhisattva precepts. Whoever diligently holds them will become a Buddha. I vow that all living beings will receive and uphold these precepts and fill the Dharma realm with the sound of joy and peace.

Back in Santa Barbara, we found an old plastic pail in a ditch and used it for dirty clothes. It had paint splotches on it, but it was strong and practical.

Walking along the highway today, I saw an identical white pail in some bushes on the side of the road. I thought to myself, "Ah! This one's better and cleaner than the crummy one we've got now!" That was greed.

I grabbed for the pail. Ouch! The bush was nettles! I was covered with swelling stings all over my face, neck, and hands. Nettles for meddles. I got a real good lesson on how all my problems and "disasters" come from greed and seeking. The world isn't dangerous and confused. I am.

**Heng Sure** • October, 1977
Walk the proper path

A symbol that came to me back at Gold Mountain Monastery returned again today. One of a series of previews of this trip that are proving accurate.

The Chinese character is composed of the element "to argue" above the element "sufficient," which also can depict "feet." Meaning: holding my tongue is important. No talking. Watch eating carefully. Be mindful of tongue-to-roof-of-mouth dharma and do it as often as possible.

Feet: plant feet solidly on the earth. Walk the proper path. Practice. Know sufficiency. Know when to stop. End stingy greed.

**Heng Chau** • October 28, 1977
Howl! Swoosh! Do the dishes!

We are two or three miles south of Lompoc. It's cold. Our writing, like our words, feels empty and shallow.

We've been playing around with our breathing while bowing and found some interesting things: 1) concentrating on inhaling and exhaling in a fixed pattern isn't natural and brought on a lot of unusual states and flashes. They were interesting and "trippy" but wild goose chases of the ego. 2) When you need to inhale, inhale, and when your body wants to exhale, exhale. Don't force it or even *think* about how you are breathing. *Concentrate* the mind, and everything else will line up and harmonize naturally, without effort.

> Perfecting pure white Dharmas
> And amassing merit and virtue
> Happen within all wisdom
> And are not apart from the concentrated mind.

Avatamsaka Sutra – Eulogies in the
Tushita Heaven Palaces, Chapter 24

Part of the Gold Mountain Monastery creed reads:

> Starving, we do not beg.
> Freezing, we do not scheme.
> Dying of poverty, we ask for nothing.
> We accord with conditions, but do not change;
> We do not change, yet accord with conditions...

A man commented about how we get our food, clothing, and shelter, "So you just kind of take it as it comes, eh?" That's really the heart of it. And how "it comes" depends on how "it went." If good things come our way it's because in the past we did good. If we get nothing and hassled to boot, it's what we deserve. In the past we gave nothing and obstructed people with our greed and anger.

"Do not change" means we do not abandon the precepts, a single mind, and wisdom. It does not mean that we never fail to seek, always looking for bargains for ourselves. "According with conditions" means not attaching. It's the principle of revealing "mind that dwells nowhere." As things come up, we respond without leaving the nature. If nothing comes, we don't go out and look for it. Not getting angry or craving something is non-attaching, not climbing on conditions.

Easy to write; hard to live.

Eat and fast; fast and eat, and soon it becomes clear how much of eating is need and how much is greed. If we overeat, we under bow. Eat past need; you're feeding greed.

> "Being apart from all inversion is called proper Enlightenment."
>
> Avatamsaka Sutra<br>Chapter 24

Food habits are what psychologists call "primary reinforcers." This means they don't respond to common sense and are hard to change. Changing what's hard to change is cultivation. Cultivation is getting rid of all your bad habits and faults. When you've cleaned house of all your hang-ups, enlightenment is revealed.

Eating, talking, and writing too much are like the antics of a mischievous monkey – a lot of action, but still chasing peanuts inside a cage.

> Just as the rising wind
> Sets all things drumming and fanning together,
> Yet those objects do not know of each other,
> So, too, are all Dharmas the same.
>
> Avatamsaka Sutra
> Chapter 10

After lunch Heng Sure and I started to write Dharma verses for children. I knew it was playing, but I thought, "Oh, just a little bit won't matter."

Whoosh! Up came a wind and blew all the food over. We ignored it, and continued to write. Howl! Swoosh! Crash! Bang! Another strong gust blows the water jugs and bottles off the top of the car, shattering them into a hundred slivers. "Ok, ok!" I say to myself and hustle out to do dishes. It was the wind speaking the Dharma.

"Hey, my friend, my friend," came this friendly, happy voice behind me on the road. I turn around.

"Hey, Mike!" It's Mike from the little rundown gas station back in Gaviota.

"Yeah, it's good to see you again. You're really out here now," he says, scanning the mountain range and valleys to the East.

He looks real good. He is smiling and has a little light and glow about him. "Yeah, well, I, ah, just came out to pick up some chickens and well, uh, here…" he says a little awkwardly, quickly slipping a money offering into my hand. "Well, I gotta run and you gotta work…"

"You're looking good, Mike. Nice to see you so happy," I said. As he walked back to his pickup truck, beaming and lighthearted, I thought, "Is this the same guy who tried to trick us out of nine dollars a few weeks ago, and then turned around with an offer of homemade soup and pulled us out of a ditch for free?" Yes, it was, and yet it wasn't. I was so quick to judge Mike at first. I thought I knew something: he was so worldly, and I was so wise. In the end he taught me.

> Living beings falsely discriminate:
> "This is Buddha; that is worldly."
> One who penetrates to the nature of dharma
> Knows that there is no Buddha and nothing worldly.
>
> Avatamsaka Sutra
> Chapter 24

Cold, windy overcast October weather. Frani Roemer and a man named Rodruigez stopped again with another offering. "I'm Jewish and Rodruigez is Catholic, and we both think it's really nice what you're doing." They stop every day on their way home from work to make an offering and wish us well.

---

**Heng Sure** • October, 1977
I wore no gloves and no kneepads. Why?

Competition?

When Heng Ju and Heng Yo came to visit, I found myself showing them my callused hands and wornout shoes. I was happy to tell Heng Ju that I wore no gloves and no kneepads. Why?

Am I competing with my comrades for status as a strong man? If so, that ought to get uprooted and junked. Do Heng Chau and I compete? Not openly, and often I'm happy to follow his lead. The other night he broke out of a bizarre slumber samadhi to go do *tai ji* basics at 9:00 p.m. in a high wind. It saved my life and it felt great, but I never would have gone out there by myself. Real Dharma Protector! We mutually encourage and stimulate each other, I think.

Bowed past a group of men stringing barbed wire for a rodeo on Saturday and I saw the work of swinging the wisdom sword as real, honest work: something that a cultivator does. Other people can't do it until they do what has to be done to learn the method and lay the foundation to do the practice. It's a job and it's a good one. Real work. Sometimes I can't get it going – strong thoughts and ego resistance – almost fearful because the ego knows it's getting chopped out and it's fighting for it's life. Other times something will happen and the sword starts swinging almost by itself, everything clears in my mind and some piece of Dharma-truth will rise up, liberated.

One thing certain: each inch of progress brings on "demons" and hassles. Each degree of pressure and heat brings a counterattack by the ego in the form of old memories, crazy pictures, tunes, smells, and lots more. Be ready and don't casually take on new practices without preparing for a fight. Even skipping food one day can increase the thought-response by double. We're walking a tightrope, and if you increase the load on the left, you better get stronger on the right.

---

**Heng Chau** • October 29, 1977
Like a turning ring of fire, with no beginning or end

There is no self. Nothing confirms "me." Everywhere I look for validation, there is a sign "no vacancy." Behind everything I take for real and lasting is thin air and empty space. Family, car, wife, and clothes say, "sorry, no vacancy." Success, failure, parties and funerals, say "sorry, you are only dreaming; this is a recording."

Eventually we all start seeing these "no vacancy" and "out of order" signs. They show up unexpectedly and uninvited like, say, when you're at a wedding, driving home from work, waiting in a line, or on the toilet. Hard to say. Sometimes they show up in the mirror. I saw one in the mirror I shaved in front of this morning. It was in my own face.

But where once seeing the emptiness of self and all things (dharmas) would send a shudder up my spine and freak me out, now there is a little patience and evenness of mind. It is said that when one truly sees things as they really are, then one obtains, "irreversibility from patience with the non-arising of dharmas." Far from a freakout, this vision brings peace and delight. "This is the realm of the one who delights in still extinction, the one who has much learning." (Avatamsaka, Chapter Ten). I've got a long way to go before "fear and trembling" is replaced with delight, but each day of bowing leaves things a little clearer and my heart lighter.

The Avatamsaka Sutra is such a fine friend and advisor during these little psychic crises. These passages turned a potential cosmic collapse in front of the mirror this morning into a smile. How did I ever come to think I was so important anyway?

> "Discriminate and contemplate within yourself this way: 'Who am I inside?' If you can understand in this way, then you will realize that the self does not exist. The body is falsely set up. Its dwelling place has no fixed position. When one truly understands this body, then within, there is nothing at all to attach to.
>
> "Contemplate the body well and see it all clearly. Be aware that all aspects of it are empty and false. Do not use mental effort to make distinctions among them. Who is it that gave you your life? Who is it that takes it away? It's just like a turning ring of fire, with no beginning or end."
>
> Avatamsaka Sutra
> Chapter Ten

I've got a long way to go before I "see it all clearly." As we were bowing around dusk, a huge flying, silent thing flew over my shoulder, hovered above me and then enveloped me. I jerked and spasmed in fear. I felt my guts pole vault.

What was this creature? It was my nylon sash. A brisk tail wind had blown over my head. Now who is it that is afraid and of what? A long way to go before I'm really "aware that all dharmas are empty and false." The guts tell the true story.

Bowing is a trick. It's like hide-and-seek, only after a while you forget to seek. You try to bow so single-mindedly that you trick yourself and disappear. Bowing is a trick to get free and benefit others.

The Avatamsaka Sutra

The Avatamsaka is very special. As the bowing progresses, we come to places inside that are too new and raw to understand. These states and changes seem too "far out" to even try to clarify or share. We learned early on that it was best to keep a lot of thoughts and inner experiences to ourselves.

But then Heng Sure will read a passage from the Avatamsaka (the King of Kings of Sutras) and zap! There it is! That's exactly what was in my heart today. The feeling of isolation and weirdness breaks open. The Avatamsaka is like having another sun in the world.

There's a bone-chilling stiffness before sunrise in these mountains. When the sun rises, it sets everything vibrating with warmth and light and melts the ice coverings. The Sutra does the same for the mind/heart and all its states. The Avatamsaka is a very special friend. To be without it would be like losing the sun. Here's the verse Heng Sure read:

> "Another light comes forth called wisdom lamp. This light is able to awaken the masses, and cause them to know that the nature of living beings is empty and still, and that all dharmas do not exist.

> "This light proclaims that all dharmas are empty and lack a host. They are like an illusion, like a flame, like a moon's reflection in water. They are also like a dream, like a shadow, like an image in a mirror. For this reason this light comes about."

**Heng Sure** • October, 1977
The breath should be even and natural

Breathe.

Why did it take us this long to incorporate mindful breathing into the bowing? It's been there on the fringes of consciousness all along. The Abbot instructs the Forty-two Hands that way and in his Dharma talks he says that breath should be even and natural. It makes a real difference in concentration when the breath is rhythmic. I don't nod while sitting if my breath is even and mindful. Yesterday the proper breathing became a bridge between bowing and seated meditation. They merged into one practice because the breathing was the same.

**Heng Chau** • October 30, 1977
There is no other Buddha

Some friendly people from Lompoc stopped with offerings and warm words of welcome. Plain and simple and very real. They weren't "marked" or pretentious like me. It is said when all marks of self are gone, this is to "open the knowledge and vision of the Buddha." What is the Buddhas' knowledge and vision?

"You should now believe that the Buddha's knowledge and vision is simply your own mind, (for there is) no other Buddha."

The Sixth Patriarch
Great Master Hui Neng

This is the heart of it.

Started to practice the Forty-two Hands. I was feeling hard, mean, and uptight. I did number 42 and after felt soft and subdued. I happened to look up at that point and saw a strange cloud passing overhead identical to the ones in the pictures of the Forty-two

Hands in the Dharani Sutra. It was the only cloud near us for miles and clearly different from all the others.

Duk Khai and her two sons drove out this A.M. and bowed into Lompoc with us for a few hours. We shared a meal offering in a small, deserted park on the outskirts of Lompoc.

Some surfers stopped with money and food offerings. A few kids ask the usual questions, wish us luck, and ride off to jump driveways and gopher holes with their bikes.

As we were cleaning up after lunch two cars sped into the parking lot and squealed to a stop on either side of us, boxing us in. They were full of high-spirited, half drunk high school kids full of mischief and out doing their own version of "trick or treat." There were two of us and ten of them, and nobody else in sight. Sort of a tense scene.

We didn't run or get angry and threatening, and they didn't know quite what to do then. One by one they slowly lifted their Halloween masks and started asking questions.

"We saw you since yesterday. Come all the way from South Lompoc – that's not very far for only two days."

"We started in South Pasadena last May. We are on our way to the City of Ten Thousand Buddhas – about 110 miles past San Francisco."

"Hey they're for real you guys!"

"What's in it for you?" (sarcastic)

"We're doing it for others, not for ourselves."

"Yeah, like who 'others'?" (hostile)

"Like our parents. We haven't been very good to them, and we're trying to set that straight."

"Oh." We parted with hand shakes and good lucks.

**Heng Sure** • October, 1977
On a train

In this work, it's like we're on a train. As long as we keep chugging, it feels like we're on a level track. As soon as we stop, we suddenly realize we were climbing a hill as we dive backwards. (Heng Chau's analogy).

**Heng Chau** • October, 1977
Beginning to appreciate her world

"It takes all kinds, I guess," says a gas station attendant to a woman filling up her car as they watch us slowly bow past.

"The realm of living beings within the Dharmarealm ultimately has no distinctions."

Avatamsaka Sutra

"But originally we are all one," I thought. "All kinds" come about because of karma and the phony distinctions we put between us. All things, "all kinds," have the Buddhanature, just like the waves in the sea, though each is different, they are all the same water. The things that separate us are paper thin. What we share is beyond reckoning and "levelly and equally it courses through the world." Between us and the gas station attendant is a few feet of empty space and a fake thought. At root we are brothers.

Robes and Silence.

Our monk robes and sashes must seem strange to many people. But where I grew up, brothers, priests, and nuns in long robes were a common sight. You saw them in stores, the hospital, at school, running the bases, and in your home.

Our family lived only a few blocks from the rectory, church, and convent. So I always had the "opportunity" to get up two or three mornings a week at 4:30 a.m. to serve the early mass for the sisters in their convent. It was a real drag to a get up that early and trudge out into a dark, 20-degree Wisconsin winter morning by myself.

But it was special, too. Everything was so quiet and without shape or rules. The only sounds were the crunch of the frozen crusted snow under my feet and the snowwind whirlpools caught in doorways.

I also got a glimpse of a nun that never talked and was seldom seen. I never knew her name. She was petite and quite young. I would ring the strange-sounding door bell and wait, listening for her footsteps coming down the long dark corridors to open the door. Without a wasted gesture or uncertain step she would lead me through the convent to the sacristy where a clean white starched surplus and cassock were neatly laid out. The priests always came at the last minute and wore sandals even in the winter.

Bowing behind Heng Sure through the streets of Lompoc this a.m., I remembered these things. Even though many people felt this nun to be living a dull and restrictive life, I knew differently. Light, strong, and at peace with herself, she was always happy. Her silence came from a place of understanding and not from fear or a martyr's role. Talking less and bowing more, I am beginning to appreciate her world and the freedom and purity she tasted. Leaving one world, free to wander in many. Pure karma begins with a pure mouth.

> "You should contemplate the mundane sphere, for within it are humans and those in the heaven, who accomplish the fruition of pure karma. They are happy and delighted all the time."
>
> Avatamsaka Sutra
> Chapter 5, Part 3

The Lompoc police knew we were in town and why. All clear.

A middle-aged businessman swerved his car to the curb and after watching us for a while, approached. "I'm really fascinated how two young men came to do something like this." We had a real straight talk. His wife was nervous and kept motioning for him to come back to the car. "No, no, Mildred, this is really interesting!" he shouted to her. He made an offering, shook hands, and wished us luck.

> "The Bodhisattva first makes a commitment to enlightenment because he wants to know, within a single thought, all vast, great worlds without obstruction."
>
> Avatamsaka Sutra
> Ten Dwellings Chapter

A young man in a van who had been observing our progress for months finally stopped to ask, "I can't understand the drive behind it."

"It's the same 'drive' all living beings have and share — the drive to get to the source and heart of things. Nothing zany or mysterious, just the basics."

"How do you accept Jesus Christ?"

"We try not to accept or reject anything."

"Hmm. Interesting stuff. Good luck, brothers."

"Oh, you're Buddhists! I've heard of them. That's what Muhammad Ali is."

A mother with three kids and a big smile, "My, oh my, such dedication. God bless you both!"

A man who spends a good part of his life working for world peace and nuclear disarmament offered to take care of our food and lodging while in Lompoc.

"Peace and getting rid of destructive weapons is just common sense and the only sane thing to do," he said.

\* \* \* \* \* \* \* \* \*
# November 1977

**Heng Sure** • November 1977
This work takes time

It's like a kid with limitless ice cream. He's going to get sick after gorging himself a few times until he learns how to appreciate it.

The basic lessons are always before me after a fall: Don't be greedy. A little greed causes a loss every time. This time it was greed for trying to progress too quickly in cultivation. What are you forcing? You don't know. Don't attach to *any* state, good or bad. Be patient. This work takes time.

**Heng Chau** • November 1, 1977
Robbing a bank on Halloween

Lompoc, California.

Early a.m. a young man earnestly and straight out said, "What can I say? Your dedication and courage in the Way has really touched me deeply. I was seriously thinking of dressing up like a mummy on Halloween and robbing a bank yesterday. Then I saw your pictures and read about you in the paper. I am very grateful. Thank you."

An old lady with a bag of apples: "Thank you for your concern."

A mailman on his route stops with a money offering and, "I wish you a good journey."

A young couple: "You'll be needing money for gas" and an offering.

An old woman, bent over and shaking, came up and, squeezing some dollar bills into my hand, simply said, "Bless you."

"Will you accept these (groceries)? I am a Catholic, so I can understand your message and what you are trying to do." from a middleaged mother of five.

Young, slick salesman from Realty office wearing sunglasses and mod clothes: "Hey what's happening there Bart buddy? Got some good news for me? You have a good one now, you hear?"

Gang of kids on bikes with offerings of carrots and good wishes. "We're Catholics, no school for us today."

A heavily made-up woman in tight pink slacks, silver high heals, and a blonde wig steps out of an old Cadillac, "A hundred and ten miles past Frisco?! Wowee, you got a long haul baby!" she says chewing on some gum without pause and looking down the street at Heng Sure with her hands squarely on her hips. "Yes siree, a long haul! Whoiee. Good luck, honey." Smiles and drives away.

We are camped in some sand hills behind a grove of eucalyptus trees between Vandenberg AFB, Purisima Concepcion Mission, and the Lompoc Federal Prison.

**Heng Sure** • November, 1977
Ashamed at my selfishness

When I cry, it is because I feel so ashamed at my selfishness. When I am happy, it is because I am allowed to repay my debt to all living beings.

**Heng Chau** • November 2, 1977
The words are black and the paper is white

> After listening to the Sutra, Bodhidharma asked, "Dharma Master, what are you doing?"
>
> "I am explaining Sutras," the Dharma Master replied.
>
> "Why are you explaining Sutras?"

"I am teaching people to end birth and death."

"Oh?" said Bodhidharma, "Exactly how do you do that? In the Sutra that you explain, the words are black and the paper is white. How does that teach people to end birth and death?"

Sixth Patriarch Sutra.

The Buddhadharma is meant to be experienced, not simply read about. Our writing is already a step removed from the direct experience. Reading it is two steps away. Words make differences where divisions don't originally exist.

As the Avatamsaka says it, "All the world's words are discriminations."

TV and movies are a huge dream world. The more we watch, the more confused we get. It's so easy to become what we behold – to start seeing the world as if it were a novel or TV serial. In cultivation, one tries to gaze on the world and the mind first-hand. I am very ashamed of my writing. "The words are black and the paper is white," how can anyone benefit from this? Yet when I read the Sutras and listen to my teacher speak Dharma, these words, though still words, light up the Way.

"Within language is revealed the independent self-mastery of all Buddhas. Proper enlightenment surpasses language. Language, though false, is used to speak of it."

Avatamsaka Sutra<br>Chapter 24

Writing and talking have their place. When you are enlightened, you turn them. When you are a common person, like me, they turn you. Almost every time I speak or use a pen, I come to regret it.

Last month in L.A. I was frantically taking notes as the Master discussed the bowing trip with us. Right in the middle, he stopped, reached over, and picked up the paper I was writing on. He held it up and examined it as if it were a rare document, slowly and with absorbed curiosity. "Oh," he said, "What's this?"

"Ah, ah, those are my notes, Master, I'm taking notes." I answered nervously.

He paused and examined them minutely saying, "Hmm, ok." All the while he held them upside down! Then smiling, the Master handed them back to me. I got the point. Says the Master: "Americans write down everything they hear."

Main Street, Lompoc. Faith.

"Thank you for all this divine energy you brought with you to our town. A lot of people can really feel it!" young mother.

"I am also a vegetarian and I said if I ever saw you, I would give you something because I understand what you are trying to do and I want to help." Well-dressed businesswoman.

During the noon day meal an elderly farmer in a straw hat slowly walks up and peeks in the car door. "Eating lunch, eh?" he says with a kind of smile. Then he stretches out his arm and hands in some folded money like no one is supposed to know and strolls away.

Mother out shopping: "I just wanted to say that even though I don't understand yet about the Buddha and where your hearts are to be able to do this, I hope to someday. I need to tell you this because I have been moved by what you are doing and when it's my good fortune to, I will join you."

A local high school science teacher drove out to give us a helpful roadside lecture on wild edible and poisonous plants in the area.

"Now that there between those two signs – the bright green one, right, is wild tobacco. About as bad for you as tame tobacco. No benefits!"

"We never touch the stuff."

"Good. Now if you boil the brown out of the acorn nuts they're ok – no leavening, but an edible flour. They take forever to boil."

"I think we'll skip those and use the time for bowing."

"Good. Now that cattail, especially this time of year, has a deep root…" and so on he went for a good forty-five minutes.

He made a special trip out and went running all over the fields and along the dry creeks by the Santa Yves bridge for samples to illustrate. People give in all sorts of ways. He was making an offering of his skill and time. The same excitement and light was in his eyes that everyone shares who gives from the heart. It's called faith.

People want to believe in wholesome things: that there can be peace and an end to disasters in the world. They want to be able to benefit others and have their own faith renewed that all of us can reach the other shore. In faith, they come out to make offerings and to say, "It's for real, isn't it? We all can make it. I feel good in my heart."

> "Faith is the source of the Path and the mother of merit and virtue. It nurtures and raises all wholesome dharmas. It cuts through the net of doubts and leaves the flow of love. It opens up the highest road to Nirvana."
>
> Avatamsaka Sutra
> Chapter 12, Part 1

---

**Heng Sure** • November, 1977
Now I'm just feeling uptight

Naturally Uptight and in the Center of It.

Heng Chau called me on some obvious outflows of self: stiff posture, energy high in the shoulders, fussiness over the body, etc. He said, "I know that we both opened a great deal this last weekend at Gold Wheel and now we're holding on, trying not to retreat."

I wrote in reply, "I expanded to a new level at Gold Wheel. Now what I learned is contracting naturally, and it will return to a new center when it's ready. It's okay."

I'm just watching myself go naturally uptight; letting it go, and not trying to hold on to yesterday's openness. That would be an attachment and not true. The truth is, I really am uptight and kind of enjoying watching it happen. I'm not uptight about feeling uptight. I'm not afraid of losing anything anymore. It's all out of my conscious control. I think that's the covering that got broken off and opened up, and now I'm just feeling uptight.

As for retreating, the middle is not a static place that you advance to or retreat from. It's the dynamic, total center of wherever you are working. Attachments keep you from really working, and that is no longer the middle.

Vows motivate the working center one way or another; precepts give it form and strength, substance, fuel, and clarity; and faith gives birth to it each day.

And the teacher? He lets it all live long enough to transform itself. If it hangs together long enough as a working unit that's moving straight and true within the rules, then it will find its center in the work and be of use.

This is a brand new understanding and the openness never really leaves, the uptightness is always there. They take turns moving me, two sides of one circle, until I break out of it.

---

Heng Chau • November 3, 1977
Come to Gold Mountain and put it down

Last night three or four families drove out with money and food offerings. "Please accept this" and "just a little to help you out." A poor family offered a big box of food. You knew they meant it.

They were all so happy and light! Why? Because like Heng Sure and me, they were "entering the Buddhadharma." Together we are all discovering that Buddhism is for real; that it is the teaching and nature of all beings. It is not negative. The principles of the Buddhadharma are the best and highest in the hearts of all of us. There is no discrimination and arrogance. There is no anger or criticism or rejection. The Buddhadharma accords with the wishes of living beings and doesn't beg or try to convert. It says, "We want only for all living beings everywhere to be able to awaken to their original and enlightened pure nature, to end all suffering, and to obtain the peace and happiness they seek. Let all beings live in harmony and treat each other with respect and compassion." It is like there is a little light in all of us, call it faith, that recognizes without a moment's thought these principles and we are drawn to them like iron filings to a magnet.

> "Faith has no turbidity and no stain. It purifies the mind; it eradicates arrogance; it is the basis of respect... With faith, one can give, and the mind will not be stingy. With faith, one can happily enter the Buddhadharma."
>
> Avatamsaka Sutra
> Chapter 12, Part 1

It has been so long since this kind of bright light has been seen that all of us at first are stunned and even suspicious. But faith is strong, and slowly it starts to thaw our frozen hearts and light up our cloudy minds.

> "Faith's power is solid; nothing can destroy it."

Jim Bone, the deputy from the Sheriff's Department stopped to check on us. He has been reading about Buddhism and had some practical questions about life on the road. "How do you guys survive without violence? I mean this area is full of weirdo's and bizarre crimes, not to mention the local cowboys who are probably going to really give you hassles." We explained that not killing, stealing, or engaging in sexual misconduct, not having a loose tongue, and avoiding intoxicants is our self-defense.

"Obviously it works. The guys in the Department can't figure out how you manage to stay in one piece."

Jim said he knows for himself that Buddhism is "it", but, "I can't put down girls."

"Anyway, we'll be keeping an eye out for you. You have any needs or problems or anything just call, and I'll be there," he said.

(Later in a car ride with the Master to L.A. I related this exchange. When I mentioned Jim's line about knowing Buddhism was "it" but couldn't "put down girls" the Master commented with a smile, "He can't put down men. Putting down men and women is the same. You can't see through the emptiness of others, because you can't see through the emptiness of self. So your self attaches and grasps at others… Tell him to come to Gold Mountain and put it down.")

Food and sex are the root, primal ego supports. Learning to turn them and not be turned by them is the key to the "great reversal." It's really difficult, the hardest and most wonderful work I've ever done or imagined. When the six roots of eyes, ears, nose, tongue, body, and mind are gathered in and "returned," things start to open up and get interesting.

It finally happened. I was late so much I didn't "earn" lunch! Results: The ego went into a rage. I never thought it could be so hard. All afternoon I was false thinking about food and looking outside and grasping. I even picked up a broken piece of car mirror on the roadside and looked at myself "just checking, am I still here?" Squirm, screams, and tantrum.

Every pore and ounce of skill and strength I can muster is being used to subdue the self. At the end of the day, total exhaustion. What an experience! Maybe I am using too much force and not enough patience?

An old van pulls up. Bennie, a stocky muscular man who looks and talks like a boxer and has a heart of gold, steps out and says, "I've seen you guys all the time – but we were always on different sides of the road. Pure mind! That's what it takes… pure mind! You set your mind to it, and you can do anything."

Bennie has the energy of a nine year old. As he talks, he's dancing and moving around full of excitement.

"I know this. This is where it's at (pointing to his head). You got it! You guys are going to make it, see. I know you will. I respect that. Anybody can use his mind like that, I respect." Bennie reaches out to shake hands. He's clean and real and having fun.

"Yeah, this sure is something. You're going to make it all the way." He announces jabbing a right hook with his fist into the air and a wink, "You hang in there! I'll be seeing you again. I'll bring some food next time."

A man who had bicycled down from Oregon stopped to share road information and gave us a "special vegetarian" nut and seed mixture he swore would help us get to the City of Ten Thousand Buddhas in top form. "That's quite a commitment!" he added.

---

Heng Sure • November, 1977
A significant absence of sexual desire

Gold Wheel Weekend.

Sense of violent bouncing back and forth in and out of control, i.e. working or not working. While bowing or reciting or meditating, I make progress and feel clean. I take rest in the work.

While talking, or reading, or eating, I lose concentration, drift from the work, and the self returns. Had a moment of clarity in the car riding back. Felt the Master totally relaxed and all there, waiting for me to quit being uptight in my life and to come and join him. His words are astounding, "One of my disciples now has heads on top of heads, like Guan Yin Bodhisattva, all of them with their eyes open. That takes samadhi power to sustain and a significant absence of sexual desire." Wow!

**Heng Chau** • November, 1977
These are your Dharma Protectors

A kind little old man stopped this a.m. He was worried and "thought about us all night" because of the road we are on. It's all hills and tight curves with no shoulder for the next ten miles. "It's just too dangerous," he finally said. "I think what you are doing is 100% right and wonderful. I strongly urge you to take this other road. It's much safer."

A little while later two men stop with similar advice. These people had something special and different about them from the other people who stop. It's in their eyes and vibes. Their eyes are clear and deep and their vibes familiar and at ease. Unusually so. (The Master, hearing of these encounters, commented, "These are your Dharma Protectors. You should listen to them. They have come to help you.")

An elderly white-haired woman walked up with two apples and a fresh, big, clean smile. "Peace my friends."

"I think it's far out what you're doing. It takes a lot of... I don't know. I think it's far out." (Young woman on Highway 1 north of Lompoc.)

On our right is a quiet grove of eucalyptus trees and smiling people from Lompoc coming out to wish us well and make offerings to the Triple Jewel. On our left is barbed wire fence behind which is the "bam, thud, boom" of exploding shells from Vandenberg AFB.

> The way of people is harmony,
> With merit and error interspersed.
> On virtuous deeds you rise, offenses make you fall,
> It has nothing to do with anyone else at all.
>
> The Ten Dharma Realms
> Ch'an Master Hua

Surprise! The Master drove all the way out from Los Angeles with some laypeople to pick us up and take us to Gold Wheel Monastery. Seeing the Master, with his bright robes and sash and wise and awesome deportment at the gas station we had just bowed past a few days ago, is a mind blower! The laypeople were rushing around with Shramanerika Guo Jing getting the cars arranged, as we bowed to the Master next to the gas pumps. Two young attendants were dumbstruck and staring. A happening all of us will remember for who knows how long? That's the way it is in the presence of the Master! Whatever happens, happens deep and is not soon forgotten. And always expect the unexpected!

"Without any distinctions made and without any fuss, in an instant's thought he pervades everywhere like the moonlight that falls on all places. He transforms the flocks of beings with measureless expedient means."

Avatamsaka Sutra
Chapter 12, Part 1

**Heng Sure** • November, 1977
Reaching for an apple on a rickety ladder

Saturday morning at Gold Wheel. I pass through a major attack of the yin drips and chills. Feels like a purge. Heading toward health. I really do nearly stop cultivating when my feet hit this soft carpet and my ears hear conversation, especially Chinese language. It brings out the old self and I forget the high ground and sink into the valley. What happens? Who is it?

I know there will be an end to it; it waits ahead of more work. There will be a time when I will rest unmoved by any state. These monthly checkups with our cultivation Doctor are bitter/sweet. I keep working, keep to the time just a little longer each visit, but the melting of my yang clarity happens every time.

I really do want to purge my sticky spot. I detest these chains that keep me apart from life. Now there is new life underneath the old crust, and I want to break through and throw it off. Worst is being chained by the old habit energy between women and men. The defiled response has got to go. I believe I can return to purity and be free of the old dirt – it must be so.

Turning fear to faith, turning juice to crystal, daring to open the heart, chipping and melting old limits and crusts, building new soft clean strength. Intention true, heart true, away from narrow self to ocean-wise, universal scope and practice. All changes come from the practice of the Dharma.

Back to Basics.

I just caught one of my very worst old habits. It's called "reaching for an apple on a rickety ladder" or "trying to fly before you learn to walk" or "overlooking the near, while straining to see the distant."

I am just learning how to bow for real. My palms should be together, no holes between them, and then my mind can be single, unified, no holes. My bowing should be bowing down, lowering my self to the ground as low as I can get, paying homage to the Triple Jewel, the Flower Adornment Sutra, and the Flower Adornment Assembly, paying back my debt to all that lives. This is real bowing. There is no room for skywriting in my head if this work is to be real.

Recitation comes from the heart. The Sutra is wonderful, the assembly is where I want to be, so I praise them from the heart.

There can be no forcing, no struggle in this work. That's not real.

What is the bad habit? Broad and superficial, not concentrated and deep. I've taken on a whole landscape of practices before I've even truly practiced my basics in bowing. As a result, I am as phony, as much an actor as ever, only now in robes. I've even taken on externalist "skinbag" practices that actually hurt my work on the real ones. Crazy and ignorant, greedy, hateful, stupid and not in the middle.

What kind of Buddhist disciple does not stand erect? Does not look at people directly? Is not happy at heart? A false kind of disciple does these things. All the glamour and flashy words are as thick as paint.

The real core is within real work. Do one thing well. Then do another. Don't look ahead. Don't look back.

How to Handle Tests.

Apply what you learn in your work to every state all the time. Don't leave your method for an instant. Real work.

---

**Heng Chau** • November 5-7, 1977
Use whatever works for you

Gold Wheel.

The Master rubs our heads and sends us back to do "our stupid thing." As we left, the Master gave us this instruction, "Pure mind. Continue, continue. Be mindful and single-minded. Don't have that second thought. I don't have a thought in my head all day. I don't think about this and then ponder that."

"We have lots of false thoughts, Master."

"Until you realize the fruit you will occasionally have defiled thoughts. Everyone does. You've got to come up with a way to subdue them. Use whatever works for you."

Heng Sure and I related some of the difficulties in our cultivation that were hard to subdue. We keep repeating the same old mistakes, and both of us were getting really down and "bummed out" about it.

Master: "Don't worry about anything at all. Basically there is no problem at all. If you are attached to some kind of difficulty and say, 'Bummer, bummer,' then suddenly it becomes a bummer." The Master *never* leaves you feeling down or bad. The Master only gives and never seeks.

**Heng Sure** • November, 1977
Pretty small and defiled

Measure of Truth in States.

Next time you work through what feels like an important understanding or a big step forward in progress, ask yourself whether or not it takes you off center to applaud the state. Ask yourself whether the self hasn't already taken over the state. Ask yourself, "Could I offer this state, this understanding, as is, to the Buddha?" Or would it look pretty small and defiled sitting up there on the altar?

**Heng Chau** • November 8, 1977
The water is left running a little

You've got to really "let go" right down to the bone. Once you truly decide that, then each day is easier and lighter. It's indecision and weak faith – trying to hold on and let go at the same time – that rips the heart and mind apart. Indecisiveness destroys us. "Don't have that second thought."

During the coldest weeks of a Wisconsin winter, the water is left running a little so the plumbing won't freeze. Water that isn't moving breaks the pipes. Stopping and hesitating with second and third thoughts is the same way. How much of my life have I spent in worry, doubt and tension because I didn't flow with the first true thought – the thought that comes from the heart and doesn't even slow down long enough to be put into words? In all directions, in all places to the ends of empty space, let go and merge with the Way! Flow or freeze. Woman with offering from her garden, "I really admire and respect what you are doing. I understand! Really!" she says, "and I think it's very fine."

---

**Heng Sure** • November, 1977
Self is created to attach to states

Rules for Eating.

Eat enough of what is offered, then stop. Don't eat for flavor. Don't eat for pleasure. Observe the Five Contemplations and the Three Wishes. Waste as little as possible.

Self fears loss of life. Self is created to attach to states, to stop the mind from turning freely, and to steer it in familiar ways. This is not true to principle. There is nothing to lose and nothing to gain. Fear is not needed. Only practice is real.

---

**Heng Chau** • November 9, 1977
Catching the fire energy

The Master gave us some herbs for "fire" and some for "cold." "All cultivators are prone to catching fire energy from time to time." As the Master said this, I was thinking about how my "fire energy" rises right before lunch. For some reason I haven't been able to figure out yet, I fear not having enough food. I fear we'll run out of food, and I won't get my fill. I was about to say, "Master, we really don't need these herbs..." but just as I started to open my mouth the Master smiled and turned saying, "...besides you can eat them when you're hungry and run out of food." Blush.

When you catch "fire," a crowd always gathers. Burning with greedy food flames just before lunch in an abandoned field next to a shopping center, I witnessed five or six women come up within fifteen minutes of each other. Some were seductive and giggling, and one had a hot cheese pizza with "just a little garlic." "Everything's a test to see what you will do..." They were followed by a crazy man mumbling nonsense and staring at us, "If the Marines kill them, then where are you going... a football," he said as he rocked back and forth on his feet. Fire is like this. Fire comes from greed and spills out into anger. On fire, you're covered with hooks and edges, and everything you touch sticks and tears. A lot of trouble is caused this way. The Bodhisattva is no longer burning with the fire of ego. His mind achieves "what is called self mastery." In other words, he is "cool and clean."

> He makes no mistakes.
> His mind is vast, big, pure.
> He is happy, blissful,
>     apart from all wrong and vexation.
> His mind and his will are soft and flexible.
> All his organs are clean and cool.

> Avatamsaka
> Ten Transferences

While we were bowing this afternoon, a man stopped and just straight out said,

"I'm an electronic technician at the Base. I've been working nights for years. Next week they are going to put me on days. I'm not competent at my work, and I'm afraid."

Monk: "What are you afraid of?"

Man: "If I work days, they are sure to know. I won't be able to hide my mistakes like on nights. I don't know what to do. Can you suggest anything?"

Monk: "Not really. The thing we try to do is to treat people like our parents. You wouldn't sell your parents a lemon used car; you wouldn't cheat them or cause them to take a loss or slander them in any way."

Man: "No, that's true."

Monk: "It's the same with your work. You wouldn't want your parents to ride in an airplane or car you tested if you knew it wasn't safe, wasn't up to code and safety standards."

Man: "But the embarrassment…"

Monk: "If you treat others like your family, then you'll be treated that way and there won't be any hurt or big damage. It's when we just think of ourselves that we get big troubles."

Man: "Is it true you're dedicating your work to everyone? I mean, what's your reward? Or is that it?"

Monk: "We're not after rewards. We do it for our family."

Man: "You mean like *everybody* is your family? Hmmm. Well, thanks and good luck. I've got some thinking to do."

Highway 1 north of Lompoc is too dangerous. The narrow shoulder is soft sand. Local people and the Highway Patrol advise alternative: cut over on Burton Mesa Rd. through Vandenberg Village and up 520 through the Air Force Base. 520 is rolling sand dunes and scrub oak. Today is slightly overcast, relieving some of the heat.

Meditation changes: Sitting is hard, yet it is the only thing that feels real. Reading, writing both feel like skipping stones on the water – irrelevant and superficial. There is a new lightness, but also a bone-chilling cold followed by a strong urge to sleep. Reality is a bizarre mix of past, present, future, with no clear divisions or differences. Dreams of being rejected by old friends and family. Strange and heavy.

The importance of a good teacher is essential to cultivation. The Master's instructions pull us through these states and unfamiliar places. "Chan is sitting in Dhyana meditation, cultivating the Path that has no superiors… Use your spiritual skill of patience. No matter what karmic obstacles arise, they won't hold you back when you are set on enlightenment."

**Heng Sure** • November, 1977
Repent, and pay no attention

When Desire Thoughts Arise Do This:

>Repent
>Pay no attention
>Be patient
>No emotion in turning place
>It all comes from you
>All dharmas are equal
>Keep working
>Maintain
>Don't talk inside
>Recognize it
>Pull back the light
>End it
>One fewer is one purer
>Chop it off
>Who's doing it?
>It's false and empty.
>Vows.

**Heng Chau** • November 10, 1977
There is nothing to debate or dispute

We are camped on a back road outside the prison. Strange vibes here. Will try to find a different site tomorrow.

The car was loaded with offerings when we returned to it at the end of the day. A man and woman drove out from Lompoc with fruit, nuts, and juice. They were really happy. "This may be the last time we get to come out," they added, regretfully. Straighten the mind, purify your every thought. Get out every little wrinkle and return to the "forgotten city." The City of Ten Thousand Buddhas is the "forgotten city" – our own nature and original limitless pure mind. As I write this I have a strong deja vu. It includes the whole bowing trip to minute detail. Too fast and thick to write down or look at, it rushes through. How can this be? How can we remember things we are just now doing? Did we do them before? Or did we just see the previews? Or is *now* a dream, and a long memory? I don't know. There's so much that no one can explain or know, so much.

A hot-under-the-collar roadside preacher poured out the "word" to us as we bowed along 520. He was crying, yelling, threatening, pleading, and wailing to the sky and hells. On his feet, kneeling, jumping, and running along side while we kept bowing. There wasn't anything to say. He stayed for an hour and drove off hoarse and sweating. There is nothing to debate or dispute.

> "…in this way he tends towards true real principles, and he gains entry into the profound place that is without wrangling."
>
> Avatamsaka
> Ten Transferences Chapter

A single mind clears up 10,000 problems. A single thought causes 10,000 problems.

---

**Heng Sure** • November, 1977
No charm will win this prize

Catching the Kid Onstage.

After we rejoined Highway 1 above Gaviota, something changed. Between that time and reaching Lompoc, I recognized my inner ego-child, the actor, the mark of self that had run my life for so many years. He is a cheater. He is a performer, a child who wears masks to "protect" his heart. He lives for strokes, for glamour, for recognition. He loves fame and praise. His mouth is his tool, he is very fast and sharp.

At bottom, he hates acting. He is very frightened of life and wants affection – mother-love and father-strength, most of all. He acts in order to "earn" it.

On the hill up to Rancho San Julian, Heng Chau gave me feedback on the photographer who shot four rolls of me bowing. He pinned down my search for glamour in Buddhist robes and my basic lack of real resolve to leave the world.

These are some of the notes that came out of the next three weeks.

Heng Chau and I always went to the top of whatever social scene we were in. Once we won the prize, we pooped out on the work. The game was over; it was time to find a bigger game. This attitude carried me through 28 unsatisfied years. I always quit in the face of real work. I always knew that I was a quitter, a cheater, and that I did not live in my real heart. Actor.

Now, as a Bhikshu, the stage is as big as life. The biggest prize lies ahead of the cultivator, but it is not of the world. The Dharma is world-transcending and there is no room for individual fame or glory. There are no "stars" among cultivators. Real gung fu is not visible.

No charm will win this prize. No words will help. Only direct experience and total giving up will take me across. If it's not really from the heart, it's still phony!

Stress principle: banish self. Only pure faith and hard work will succeed. Self-seeking in spiritual life is self-defeating. Penetrate self, transform stingy greed, and give birth to a new being, transformed from the Dharma.

This is the sticky spot!

---

**Heng Chau** • November 11, 1977
We are both fasting

The fifteenth of the lunar month. We are both fasting. Heng Sure is reciting the Great Compassion Repentance and I'm reciting the Bodhisattva Precepts. Flat tire this a.m. We are bowing outside the prison and entering Vandenberg AFB.

---

**Heng Sure** • November, 1977
Do not cause beings to lose their faith

Short Flashes.

Does your mind move when a person approaches? It comes from you, not from them. What do you want that you keep leaking out? Mother love!

Resolve to "bring out the heart." Uncover your true heart. Let it beat as one with the Patriarchs' heart. The heart repays the debt; the head feeds the self.

Watch the gates. Pull your light back from all six sense gates. Back to the center, fuse it, send it up.

Watch lunch carefully. Dangerous time. Take time and watch before you eat a lot of food. Eating is not important. Preserving samadhi is important. This is protecting transcendental Dharma.

All dharmas are the same. All people, men and women, are the same. We're all confused until we work to enlightenment. The Sixth Patriarch earned enlightened wisdom through his own effort.

Make one good, complete bow without having any false thoughts at all. Stand and do it again. Use the method to hold your mind still.

False thinking is yin, cloudy. No thought and cutting off thoughts are yang and bright.

Have a strong feeling that what the Master does is give us a stage to cultivate on that we can manage. When we have almost finished that act, he "lifts a curtain" to reveal the next stage far off in the distance, and he gives us cheer and energy to start out after it. If, when we had just begun, we had seen how far it was to the end, we probably would have been discouraged or caused to disbelieve. "Do not cause beings to lose their faith." So we cling to our little victories, our step-by-step states of progress, and we release the tenacious grasp on our fragile selves bit by bit, blind to the whole truth, over-concerned with details, tense and self-important, but still walking, still working. Our eyes are starting to turn in. The distant goal is not far, it is *deep*.

---

Heng Chau • November 12, 1977
God on our side

Lots of offerings the last few days from ranchers, teachers, children, servicemen and their families from the Air Force Base.

Al is an older "lifer." "I was in two wars," he related from his motor scooter as we talked on the road shoulder. "They are ugly and horrible! We are working for the same thing, I feel – peace. We just do it in different ways." He looked up watching for a response and then said nervously, "Sometimes we have to fight for peace." It was more of a question than a conviction.

Al isn't as sure about getting peace by fighting as he is about the need for peace. Who wants to feel they did something "ugly and horrible"? Yet in every war, good people find themselves committing acts of destruction and killing. Why? How?

All countries have "god on our side" when they go to war and they all fight "to end all wars" and "bring lasting peace." Where does such upside-down reasoning begin? It starts with a single thought of discrimination. First there's "me" and "you" then there's "we" and "they." Separate your heart from the oneness of all things, and your natural seed of compassion and kindness dries up. When the seed of compassion withers, factions, parties, countries, and armies come along. The undivided family of all beings and things is split into a thousand little pieces (discriminations). After that, killing and war come quickly and easily. "Ugly and horrible" things come from thoughts based in greed, anger, and delusion. It begins with "I," and we haven't seen yet where it could end. Al has, and he is worried and afraid for humankind.

He came back later with a food offering and said he and his wife would be happy if we stayed at their place for the night. Al said the base is huge and that tomorrow a.m. he will scout out the best bowing route to follow North of the main gate. Al inspired us both to work harder. I have so many selfish thoughts.

Doubt, we are discovering, is just another state of mind and part of cultivation. This p.m. I got a heavy dose of doubt. Nothing seemed real or solid outside. Inside nothing mattered. Our evening ceremonies, food, the sutras, Buddhas, me, others – all just went flat and empty. A real winner!

I went outside to meditate and somehow at the bottom of this pit of doubt was an opening and beyond it a warm, relaxing light and state beyond words. A line from the Sixth Patriarch came close to describing it: "There are no dharmas, just expedients to get unattached by."

Doubt is just a trick. It's a test to see if you are sincere in your resolve and willing to put it all down. We are learning that anything can happen, and, no matter what happens, nothing changes.

> All dharmas are apart from words and language.
> Their nature is empty, still, extinct, and uncreated.
> Because he wants to completely and clearly
>     fathom the doctrine,
> The Bodhisattva makes
>     his initial commitment to Bodhi.

> Avatamsaka
> Ten Dwellings Chapter

**Heng Sure** • November, 1977
Does the spotlight still throw a shadow?

No More Masks.

Why are lay people's visits so hard for me to navigate? Well, it's because they push all the buttons that feed the Self. I go on stage, even in silence, and listen for applause. "Fear of loss" is basic to my nature. It leads to acting, to falseness, and to hiding behind masks. The masks need energy to maintain them. The energy falters and out comes the light in a "leak." Fear follows.

The energy is given away through tension because the mind and the muscles are tight in defense against being real. Cultivation of the method works on the root – the fearful self – at the same time it spotlights the false masks and makes them uncomfortable to maintain. When the fear is understood then there is no need to act. There is no tension because there is no energy wasted in holding up masks. Thus there is no energy leak, no giving away the light. Then, because the dharma method is at work, I look and feel constantly real.

When the laypeople come, don't be afraid. Think of ways to take them across. We are all one substance – four elements and five false skandhas and the Buddhanature within. What is there to fear? Remember your heart's vows to save all beings. Feel out ways to give to them. Breathe naturally and return the light always. Watch the actor-self carefully. Accept no strokes and hear no praise. Give no repartee inside or outside. Let the mantra or the holy name relax the body and the mind. Where else will you look to find joy?

When people bow to you, does the spotlight on you still throw a shadow? That's the measure of your remaining ego.

**Heng Chau** • November 13, 1977
Are you sure?

One of the lay people and her family came out to bow. As I came upon all of them bowing with Heng Sure, I was really moved. It made a deep impression. The experience reconfirmed in my heart the value of "constant bowing" as a dharma of true humility and selfless giving. I have much to be ashamed of and much to be grateful for. Bowing works on both.

The car was covered with groceries, sugar cane, money, and offerings again today from the people of Lompoc and from the base.

Around sunset as a cold wind came down from the North, two young women in a van pulled alongside:

"Hey you guys want to smoke a joint?"

"No. We don't smoke."

"Are you sure?"

"Positive."

"Want a beer?"

"We don't drink."

"Are you sure?"

"Positive."

"What else is there in life? We're just trying to help you out."

"We're fine."

"Are you sure?"

"Positive."

**Heng Sure •** November, 1977
Food is love

Losing Fear of Loss.

Food offerings fill the car. I felt uptight that there were so many. Why? Because I knew some would go bad before I could cram them in my greedy mouth at lunch. Lunch is a big hustle to juggle the soonest-to-spoil with the best of flavors. Why the trouble? Well, food is love. Mother feeds you love through the mouth and you take all you can get, never wasting a drop. For someone who is working to leave the world, that food reinforces all the opposite energies.

None of the food has my name on it. Ultimately, I can only eat my fill, and then I must stop, no matter how much there is to eat up. I have left home now and I no longer hang out gathering dividends on mother-love. I don't belong to my parents any more, nor to food, nor to my body, nor to life itself. That is the key to birth and death.

What was my face before mother gave birth to me? It was a monk's face. Then, as now, I belonged to the Buddha, the Dharma, and the Sangha – to the Triple Jewel I return my life in worship and in reverence.

**Heng Chau •** November 14, 1977
I am a monk on the inside now

> "Within each and every thought are produced measureless numbers of Buddhalands…"
>
> Avatamsaka Sutra
> Chapter Five, Part Three

Got a new universal joint on the Plymouth in Lompoc. For the first time since leaving home back in May, I was struck by the fact that I was a monk on the *inside* now not just in appearance. This trip to town and standing under the grease rack in a sash put me at a loss for words... Something had changed gears inside. It was like falling asleep in one world and waking up in another.

How many different kinds of worlds are there? The gas station is one, the used car lot salesman across the street is another. Heng Sure is back in an abandoned field bowing in one world, and the person in the back of the ambulance speeding by is in another. The bookkeeper counting the cash behind the locked door is in one world, and in another part of the world, people are asleep and dreaming. They are dreaming of worlds upon worlds. How many worlds are there? How many thoughts are there? They all come from the mind.

> Buddhalands in variety beyond thought;
> Worlds without limit.
> Splendid adornments, fine and greatly varied,
> All come from the power of the Great Immortal.
>
> Avatamsaka Sutra
> Chapter 5, Part 3

---

**Heng Sure** • November, 1977
Taking the ego-child across

Repaying the Debt.

Because I have a big debt to all living beings, I have resolved to cultivate the Way. Therefore I practice:

    — being true all the time

    — uncovering my true heart

    — bringing forth a total resolve for enlightenment

    — subduing my ego/child/actor with personal virtue and compassion and unmoving, constant resolve to take him across.

    — pulling back and gathering to the center all the energy that runs out the six gates,

    — purging all emotion from the turning point

    — letting my mind be like empty space

    – turning my fear to faith

    – cutting through all thoughts

    – relinquishing all states

    – staying in the middle and not wandering

    – emptying the top, rooting the bottom

    – asking who I really am

I will succeed in this work and make all of it an offering to the Buddhas.

You cannot force your ego-child to stop play acting. He will fight back. You have to use compassion and expedient means to subdue him and take him across. Tell him to be true. The old play is over, and no one wants to see it again.

Give him an example of virtue. You be true and real all the time, and then he will watch and listen and bow along with you. Have faith. Take across fear and doubt with pure faith. Bow and pray.

---

**Heng Chau** • November 15, 1977
Lots of mistakes, but no blues

"Me, me, me; I want more, more, more" is the single biggest obstacle to world peace. While this thought drives and pushes inside of me, I can never know peace. World peace comes from peace of mind. World wars come from the war inside. In my heart there are countless thoughts of greed, anger, and jealousy. In my mind, a never-ending stream of false thoughts and desires wage all-out battles. How can you find "what you're looking for" if you cannot find yourself?

Dream of demon hawk with metal vice-like talons suffocating me. Woke up trembling and sweating. Did a mantra and went back to sleep.

The Blues.

All of us get the blues. We accept it as part of the game, part of living. The blues are a kind of melancholy, moody "down" state. Sad and dreamy, feeling sorry for ourselves, and wallowing in the dumps. It's said, "nobody knows where the blues comes from." That's not true. The blues come from turning your back on your true nature and uniting with the dust. The blues come from taking the easy way and getting lots. Every half-hearted move that wasn't 100% "right on" and true brings in the blues. The blues come from cheating and not following the rules – from not having the guts to be honest with yourself and check out the motives behind your moves. Sneaking by, pulling a quick-one – not checking out the thoughts (are they defiled or pure?) The blues go when you put down the fake and pick up the true.

Heng Sure and I used to get the blues. Since leaving home, we don't get the blues anymore. We make lots of mistakes, but there's no blues.

---

**Heng Sure** • November, 1977
Your own womb

Back to the Source.

Pursued the idea of all desires as various ways to return to mother-love, wealth, sex, fame, food, sleep, and fear, pride, doubt, jealousy – are the high and low sides of the same need. Ordinary people want to return to their physical source: the womb.

Sages return to their spiritual source: the 0, the golden thread of the Buddhanature that pervades everywhere. First, find the thread. Then make offerings to it, so it becomes important to you. Hold precepts so that it purifies and runs straight. Do good so that it grows yang. Establish faith, which is the small inner voice. Study so that it connects with worldly knowledge. Begin to cultivate so that you collect and return all the light/energy from your senses and actually enter into your own womb – your energy center – and go back home.

Ordinary people seek the fetal position, curled up and yin – completely dependent and ignorant. The cultivator seeks the full lotus of the Buddha – straight and yang, completely independent, light, and aware.

---

**Heng Chau** • November 16, 1977
Turn catastrophes into auspiciousness

Outside of Vandenberg AFB main gate a speeding van slides and squeals, just missing Heng Sure. Close call. Just this a.m. We read in the Sixth Patriarch's Sutra how a hired assassin made an attempt on the Patriarch's life. He couldn't kill the Ch'an master because it wasn't his time to die. The Patriarch said, "I don't owe you my life, I only owe you this gold," referring to a debt from a previous life. The assassin's sword couldn't cut the Master's flesh.

How and when we die isn't easy to know, but it's not chance. When it's time, it can't be avoided. If it isn't time, it won't happen. Either way, it's useless to worry. How our life goes, and our death comes, has to do with our karma – what we do is what we get.

Nothing is fixed. Bad karma can be eradicated, and good karma increased. It all depends on what we do. In every thought and every deed we determine our lives. Maybe Heng Sure's sincere bowing to erase "bad karma created by body, mouth, and mind, based on greed, anger, and delusion" turned a near-fatal accident into just a few tire skid marks and a cloud of road dirt? The power of repentance and reform is hard to conceive of.

The Master lately instructed us, "All the time you must concentrate your mind and will, when you bow. Then you can turn catastrophes into what is auspicious, turn calamities into good fortune. You can't meet danger now."

The kids from Vandenberg AFB:

A very young girl: "I've studied a little bit about Buddhism and although I don't believe in all of it, I really admire your dedication and sincerity." She was sincere and trying to act mature in the midst of a noisy gathering of "little kids" on bikes.

"How should we address you, sir?" stiffly asked a little boy representing a group of 20 or so kids watching from a safe distance.

"How do you address your friends?"

"Well, uh… 'Hi!'"

"Hi!"

With that he gave the high sign to his friends and we were surrounded and laden with fruit from lunch pails, and wheat germ ("This is really good for you"), pats on the back and a lot of "good lucks."

We are halfway across the base and being closely watched by the military police. Empty hills and missle sites ahead.

**Heng Sure** • November, 1977
Awaken the Buddha seeds within

Find the Golden Thread.

This principle makes clear the importance of producing the thought for enlightenment which is just the time when one discovers the golden thread within. Most people eat and sleep through billions of life times before they discover their Buddhanature. The Venerable Abbot has vowed that the sound of his voice or one look at his face will awaken the Buddha seeds within. Bad karma covers it over and shrinks it down. Good deeds make it grow. It survives birth and death: "good roots" are just the thread. Some are born with it thick and deep and easy to find, others actually decrease it during a life time through creating bad deeds and exhausting blessings.

The Avatamsaka explains the many ways one first recognizes the connection to the Buddhanature.

---

**Heng Sure** • November 16, 1977
He sat in full lotus, reciting a mantra

Dear Shr Fu,

Sometimes the practice of the Bodhisattva Path is very "conceivable". We're perched on a sandy field of scrub oak and dry, dry grass. The Lompoc Federal Prison is over the hills to the West, and Vandenberg Air Force Base lies to the north. A more cheerless, bleak, November landscape is hard to imagine. The bowing is over for the day and the wind which has been whipping the hilltops since noon now has some real teeth in it. I've lit the oil lamp to write these lines that occurred to me just moments ago as the sun fell, red and windswept.

A Bodhisattva's work is never done; there is no 9 to 5 day in the job of cultivation. There is no Monday to Friday workweek, no retirement with bonus at age 65. The Avatamsaka Sutra tells us that living beings have no end, they are infinite and boundless, yet the Bodhisattva has vowed to save them all. Therefore, his work does not end. A Bodhisattva saves himself, too, and by cultivating the Proper Dharma, he gains wisdom, compassion, and expedient power. This wisdom allows him to get involved in the gritty, muddy middle of the mundane world and work to save others right where they live and suffer most. However, the Bodhisattva has broken all attachments to his self. He no longer has desires, so his work for others gives him more happiness and satisfaction than a lifetime of leisurely vacations and selfish pleasure-pursuits. The Bodhisattva rests in his work and works while he rests. Life is work and work is bliss – a truly wonderful state of mind.

Just as I wrote the last line, out of the darkness came a knock on the car window and a tight voice said, "Uh, hey, we're stuck in the sand, can you give us a tow?" Heng Chau did not hesitate, but stepped outside, and found two unhappy men. He said, "Sure, be right there." We repacked the lamps and meditation gear and drove through the ruts and flying sand to extract a pickup truck and put it back on the road. Reciting the Great Compassion Mantra has become automatic whenever we aren't bowing or reciting ceremonies. Its strength lifted the truck out with ease, our Plymouth providing solid muscle as well. We walked through the headlights back to the car.

"Thanks, you guys, a real lifesaver," said the men greatly relieved.

"No problem," replied Heng Chau.

A small matter and easily accomplished, but it added cheer and light to this desolate central California coast.

At other times the events that occur in the practice of the Way are truly inconceivable. We see so little of what is actually going on in the world behind the facade of the senses. We just piece together bits and echoes of the actual reality. Bowing along on a Friday afternoon I suddenly sensed the Venerable Abbot's presence right in my heart. He sat in full lotus, reciting a mantra, apparently, and this image calmed my mind profoundly. Suddenly, fifty yards ahead I heard the sounds of screeching tires and a huge cloud of dust billowed up. Heng Chau later described the scene: apparently a driver fell asleep at the wheel and ran off the road. His car climbed six feet up a sharp embankment then turned, still speeding along, and zoomed straight down towards two cars and a truck that crowded the lanes below. Somehow, unbelievably, the car slipped between a van and a truck, missing both by a hair and continued on down the road, leaving several ashen-faced drivers badly shaken, but happy to be alive. Had the cars collided we would have been right in the middle of the scene – King Yama would have had a busy day receiving new souls from Highway 1. As it turned out, the Master's image faded from my mind moments later. What is really involved? Who saves all these lives from four hundred miles away, invisibly, without expecting a thank you or any recognition at all for the effort? I have no doubts that it was the Venerable Abbot's presence manifesting in the nick of time that prevented the collision on the road. Prove it? There's no other way to explain how the falling car shoehorned its way back on the road. How many times have things like this happened in the lives of disciples: narrow escapes from certain death, when Guan Shi Yin Bodhisattva appeared before people at the critical moment and then disappeared again after all was safe?

As we work to make our hearts a pure place, I've found myself always returning to the basics. For instance, the first thing a new Buddhist learns is how to put his palms together in respect. Joined palms indicate singleness of thought. As the work of cultivation is on the mind-ground, singleness of thought is most important. I noticed that my joined palms mudra has grown rather sloppy, with gaps between fingers and thumbs. Standing next to the Master last week at Gold Wheel Temple before he spoke Dharma, I watched him bow to the Buddhas. I was deeply moved. When the Master joins his palms there is a totality about it – a perfection that can only come from singleness of mind. I tried my new, improved, palms-together while bowing and the mindfulness to the external form *did* quiet my mind inside. The false thoughts were easier to subdue when my palms were fully joined, without gaps or leaks. Back to basics.

Witnessing the Master's bowing is a humbling experience, a good medicine for arrogance and a model for people and gods. His bowing is a completely magical transformation: when the Master bows he disappears. His total lack of ego is revealed, he seems to become one with the Buddhas he bows to. I don't know the Master's state when he bows or at any other time, but something very pure and special happens when he bows before the Buddhas. There is just bowing. It looks as if there is no bower and no one bowed to, it is simple and profound reverence; wonderful to watch. Back on the road I am learning to bow correctly, from the beginning. Lower the ego to the ground as far as you can, with heart fixed on the Eternally Dwelling Triple Jewel, and then rise up and put your palms together with a single mind on the way to the City of Ten Thousand Buddhas.

Disciple Guo Chen (Heng Sure)
bows in respect

Heng Chau • November 16, 1977
This is home

Dear Shr Fu,

I am in Lompoc at a gas station waiting for the car. Open, empty country is ahead with no towns and few gas stations for "bowing miles". So I am in town getting supplies and needed repairs for the weeks ahead. Heng Sure is bowing in an isolated field-plateau in the hills overlooking the Federal Prison on the fringe of Vandenberg Air Force Base. This is where we camped last night. The mechanics have advice and humor on the roads ahead and wish us luck.

Shr Fu, it's funny, but lately on this pilgrimage I am finding it more and more natural and honest to be quiet. It isn't that there are no thoughts or feelings. I am happy and full, but not of conversation words. So it is difficult to write because this is a new and unfamiliar place. The words of the Sutras, especially the Avatamsaka, are what I like best to hear and repeat. They echo in our hearts all day and are part of this quietness. Other noises and sounds come and go, but the sounds of the Sutras stay, speaking directly to our experience and circumstances. The sounds of the Sutras are natural and blend with the stillness of the wind and trees.

There is a subtle, peaceful merging of these principles and our minds. As we read to each other from the Sutras our faces and eyes light up, saying, "Hey! Yeah! That's it. That's the way it is!" heads nodding, faces smiling in agreement. It often feels as if we have another person with us – a wise and infallible friend who understands our deepest thoughts and feelings - the Avatamsaka Sutra.

What we experience, the Sutra explains; what the Sutra explains, we experience. When we get to a place in cultivation neither of us has been before, invariably in the evening the Sutra glows, explaining and expounding on that state. Inconceivable! And there is so much to enter and explore!

As we bowed through the small town of Vandenberg Village at sunset Tuesday, a crowd of some thirty people gathered around – watching, discussing, wondering about us. A little old man stepped out of his house, respectfully walked up and made an offering. With a kind smile and a gesture of his arm to the north he said without words, "Hope this helps you on your way. Keep going. Good luck." Suddenly the tense and uncertain crowd that had quietly watched this dispersed. In a matter of minutes they came streaming back laden with money and food offerings. Old people and young, little kids and grandparents, all smiling, giving, and wishing us well. The power of giving and gathering in by one person turned a practically hostile crowd into happy well-wishers.

Driving back from the gas station I found Heng Sure smiling and full of light and peace, bowing in a wind-blown, empty field off Highway 520. As we quietly sat inside the old Plymouth eating a lunch of bread, fruit, nuts, and vegetables, I realized we had bowed ourselves into another world – a crystal pure, and happy place – and we were only beginning. My mind went to Gold Mountain and shortly the Master and entire community. Face after face manifested, squeezed together in the car, all happy, all leaving the Saha dust together. This was home: the eternally dwelling Triple Jewel without a place or limit.

Someday every face we have seen while bowing once every three steps – the police, the kids, mechanics, deer, ants, the old people and prostitutes, reporters, wind, rocks, and clouds – will be one face. All will return and rely on the eternally dwelling Triple Jewel within our true self nature. All living beings have the Buddha-nature. All will become Buddhas. A very happy day, today.

A woman runs across four lanes of high-speed freeway traffic, slips and slides down a steep embankment to offer homemade cookies and $5 – full of smiles all the way.

Much peace in the Way,
Disciple Guo Ting (Heng Chau)
bows in respect

**Heng Chau** • November 17, 1977
We are only passing through

> Just like the many kinds of fruits
> Which grow in great variety from the orchard's trees
> So too, in the variety of Buddhalands
> Do the many kinds of living beings dwell.

Avatamsaka
Chapter 8, Part 3

We are camped in a little clearing that serves both as a dump and a picnic spot on Vandenberg AFB. Just after dark a man and his young son drove up in a camper. They were out looking for "mountains to climb" said Carlos, the little boy.

"That's funny," said Joe, the father, looking directly at me, "You are there and I am here and yet we both are here, now, right next to each other." (Different words yet "all of these together move around" – Avatamsaka).

"How is that funny?" I ask.

"I mean, I'm a G.I. and live just over there, and you are a monk and you are living just right over here. Right now! Really amazing:"

We talked about being a monk and being a G.I., about the military and the monastery, and Joe was interested in our vows of no sex.

"Somebody's got to do it, right? I mean what would the world be like without sex?" he asked.

I told him about my father taking two weeks off from being a father and working man to do a retreat at a monastery in an island on Lake Michigan. "When he returned he was different and he said something I'll never forget." I related.

"What did he say?" asked Joe.

"He said, 'We are just passing through this world. We shouldn't get so attached to things. We are only passing through.'"

"You know," said Joe after a silence. "Somewhere inside I know that is true and right. Sometime I will need to face that. Who knows? Maybe some crazy hunter will come over that hill in a minute and shoot me full of holes?" Carlos shines the flashlight at the hill no doubt looking for "crazy hunters."

Heng Sure brought over some fresh orange juice and Joe threw away his beer. He and Carlos shared the juice. "I'd like to offer you something but I only have beer," he said apologetically.

"So you look into that stuff, birth and death, I mean. That's your work, huh?"

"That and helping others."

"That's ok." and then as an aside, "Kids are a hassle" as he hands Carlos the juice with a smile. He and Carlos are good friends but Joe knows sooner or later each of them will have to face "that stuff" for himself. He is impressed by Heng Sure's vow of silence.

Later while we are meditating he and Carlos come back with a box full of groceries, some candles, and a colored post card showing all the wild animals of the desert from Carlos. "Sorry to interrupt your meditation."

"No problem. You drove a long way on a cold, dark night to make this offering."

"Equally no problem," answers Joe smiling. "We wanted to offer something."

Faith.

Someone gave us these alfalfa seeds. They are tiny, dry and don't look like food. But put a few in a jar, cover them with water, and they all crack open sending out sprouts. Amazing!

When a lot of people first hear the sutras it's just like water hitting dry, withered seeds – "crack, pop" and out comes a sprout. They feel that for as long as they could remember these questions and principles were in their minds. They were subtle and hard to grab, but, they were true and equally hard to ignore. Often these ideas and feelings become a secret world within, not shared – almost as if to protect them and keep them pure and special.

Outside we lived our lives and crossed the street when the light turned green. But inside this mind kept looking and quietly watching. We dodged the false and sought the true, and waited and hoped for the water.

Picking and choosing, we could hear and see things as they really are. Inside the heart would say, "No. Close, but that's not it." or "Phoney, false, be careful." And then one hears the sutras, "Yes, that's it!" Home at last.

Faith is like a fine, luminous thread weaving through space and time without beginning or end. It connects the hearts of all living beings with the true source and returns to the root. It cuts through countries and the boundaries of years and life itself. It calls and leads all living beings back to their original self-nature. Now in India, then Ohio, Canton, Oakland, England, Los Angeles, and Singapore expanding without limit "to the ends of empty space." It doesn't change as it weaves and gathers us in.

I never really understood faith before. I found a note Heng Sure had written on the Avatamsaka calling faith "people's words" and "little voice." So that's it! Faith is just another word for what we call "true heart" or "intuition" or "something inside says…" Faith is what I have been going on for years without knowing it. Some "little voice" without words like a faint pulse says, "Keep going, you'll find it." Faith is a gyroscope that can't be touched – it's a piece of the thread. When your piece meets the thread they merge like water drops into a stream. Faith isn't blind, we are. If things seem dark, it's because I've neglected my eyes.

> "It's just like the sun which appears in the world, but does not hide or fail to appear because there are blind people who fail to see it."
>
> Avatamsaka
> Chapter 25

**Heng Sure** • November, 1977
Returning now back to my real original home

## Why Hang Around The Saha?

Miserable time trying to concentrate. Hornet sting on hand, huge resistance to correct breathing and returning the light – tight muscles and flowing out to everything. Thoughts flying like flocking crows.

Finally at 4:30 the sword begins to cut with this resolve established: "This disciple of the Buddha is not waiting around for pleasure through the senses any longer. Having a body is suffering and the world is truly a blazing house on fire. I am not holding on for any more mother-love, or sweet milk or strokes to please and support my egochild. I am returning now back to my real original home in the magic circle of the zero and I'm not following these false senses to my death any more."

I began to pull back on all the light that had been flowing into cars and rocks, thoughts and the weather and after the breathing was grounded, my eyes and concentration reversed and came together inside and the rest of the afternoon, although an uphill fight, was peaceful and good work.

**Heng Chau** • November 18, 1977
It's my mind that can't be filled

> "He, himself recalled all the good roots planted in the Buddhas' places in the past."
>
> Avatamsaka Sutra

Where are the Buddhas' places? In India? In heaven? In outer space?

"Is the Buddha down there on the sidewalk – is that why you are down there?" asked a child watching us bow. The Buddha's place is just our own mind cleansed of all greed, hatred, and stupidity.

Each pure thought and selfless act of patience, giving, morality, vigor, concentration and wisdom plants a Buddha root.

The Buddha's place is within us in our own nature, not outside. It can't be attained or lost. We either cover it over or we awaken to it, but it doesn't come or go. The Buddha's place is full of light. We gravitate toward it with kindness, compassion, joy, and giving. This is where our roots stretch and grow healthy. This is the Buddha's place, the unlimited mind.

All along our way we meet people who are looking for the "Buddha's place" – looking for a real and true place to plant and nourish their good roots. People are looking hard for a way to "put it down" and not feel afraid or ashamed to let go and do it like it really is. The Triple Jewel is water for these good roots and soon it's going to rain and there will be pots cracking open to enlightenment all over the place.

Where is the Buddha's place? Where is the Buddha? The Buddha's place is just your own body. Awakening to your own true self-nature is the Buddha.

> Bodies like those in the mundane world
> The bodies of the Buddha are also the same,
> To understand and know their self-natures,
> This is called the Buddha

Avatamsaka Sutra<br>Chapter 24

The Middle Way.

Fasting and bowing doesn't work. The body needs fuel to bow especially in cold weather. Over-eating and bowing doesn't work either. If you are too full of food you can't bend over. Not too much and not too little is keeping to the Middle Way. There is a time for everything.

> When living, sit, don't lie.
> When dead, lie down, don't sit.

> How can a set of stinking bones
> Be used to cultivate?
>
> Sixth Patriarch's Sutra

Fasting this last month left me weak and stumbling all over the road in a daze of fatigue. Bound and determined to subdue my greedy food habits, overnight or sooner, I bulldozed my way into a dead end. When it was time to bow all I had to cultivate with was a "set of stinking bones."

Then I got so hungry that I inhaled the food the next day bringing on diarrhea. And now today I was so afraid I wouldn't get my fill that I bit hard into a broken piece of glass in some rice and broke my tooth leaving a nerve exposed. Really dumb!

Food is in the mind. It is my mind that needs to be subdued not the diet. Fear of not getting my fill has something to do with fear of letting go – of having no attachment, nothing to control and hold on to as "mine."

Too much or too little, force or license, all sabotage cultivation. As usual I am learning the Middle Way the hard way.

Bottomless Pit:

> The mind of greed is just like a bottomless pit.
> Add some more, but it's hard to fill,
>     and anger soon appears.
> The five desires in confusion
>     turn thoughts upside down
> Ignorant and unaware the Dharma vessel topples.
>
> Venerable Master Hua

"Cultivation is easy, is it?" asked the Master last month in L.A. with a big grin. "Each day try eating a little less than full. Keep to the natural, the Middle," he suggested. How reasonable! It works, too.

So now we both try to eat a little less than our fill and find bowing and Ch'an meditation much improved. I don't false think about overeating or starving and the light can focus now on the real issue: it's my mind that can't be filled, not my belly.

We get a month's supply of Dharma in a time-capsule from the Abbot. We use it slowly. By the end of the month the last bit is understood and fits neatly into place like the final piece of a jigsaw puzzle. We are ready for more. Any way you look at it, this is really hard to conceive of.

> He is everywhere
> a good and wise advisor for living beings.
> He speaks the proper Dharma
> and causes them to cultivate.

Avatamsaka Sutra
Chapter 25

---

**Heng Sure** • November, 1977
Twentieth century asceticism

Expedient Asceticism.

Ascetic? Well yes in their own 20th century fashion. This includes bitter practices that others could not manage. On the one hand they work to put down their attachment to their bodies. On the other hand they continue their cultivation and prolong their suffering with the following medicaments: food for the body, fruit juice ditto, tea ditto, ginseng to reduce fire, white flower oil for toothache and tense muscles, ching liang balm for sprained ankle, alcohol for feet, ointment for sun-dried eyes, cream for flaking skin, salve for bleeding, cracked hands, toothpaste to clean their teeth, lip balm for cracked lips, foot powder for wet feet. And their journey continues.

**Heng Chau** • November 19, 1977
As soon as it is described it ends

Every once and awhile we are able to bow with a single mind. It's hard to say what that's like because as soon as it is described it ends. I wrote this about it: "Everything is light and easy. There is a soft, creamy texture and gentleness to the wind and rocks. The body feels supple, not stiff and tense, and blends naturally with the environment. Cool, clear, not hot or on edge: no gravity."

As soon as I finished writing this, the state finished too.

> All the world's words are discriminations
> There has never been a single dharma
> That, once obtained, provided entry
> Into the Dharma nature.
>
> Avatamsaka Sutra
> Chapter 10

Sitting Ch'an late at night. No sounds or lights. No noise or thoughts. The mind nowhere and everywhere just for a few seconds. Then I saw how encumbered and complicated I make things with all my desires, thinking, and grasping. The wonderful emptiness, the natural, I fill up and obstruct day after day with garbage and junk. Why? There it was, clear as day. There was no one else to blame. I take this wonderfully pure and blissful natural state and pollute it with my false thoughts and then cultivate and work to try to purify it. Why do I do this?

> Living beings from beginningless time
> Always have flowed and turned in birth and death
> And not understood the true real Dharma.
> This is why Buddhas appear in the world.
>
> Avatamsaka Sutra
> Chapter 28

**Heng Sure** • November, 1977
A mirror to each other's experiences

Giving Up and Going Home.

Heng Chau and I continue to mirror each other's experiences only in exact yin-yang opposition. He is experiencing a shattering of his yang confidence, he is being softened by a series of painful jolts that convince him he is not in charge of things. Heng Sure is experiencing a concentration of his yin fearfulness. He is being hardened by a series of situations that force him to take charge of his resolve and to make concrete his faith and his knowledge of the Dharma. He has to know for real that he can stand on his own for the Dharma, without help and without hiding behind anything. In this way he is being led to uncover his true heart. Heng Chau has to rely on principle instead of self and he also is learning to believe in the truth of the Dharma without needing support from the palace. In this way he is being led back to his true heart. Neither monk is allowed to force the growth. The wonder of it is that the more they both let go of thought and plans and concern for themselves, the more of this growth they experience. Their progress back to the source is truly a relinquishing, a giving up, a purging of what was learned and obtained before they met the medicine of the Proper Dharma.

**Heng Chau** • November 20, 1977
When in doubt, bow

Tooth shot – liquids only. Heng Sure pulled his back. The car needs to be repaired and is missing a tire. It's cold. The military police shadow our every move. All in a day's work.

The real work is on the mind ground not in the body. This is the Dharma door to understanding the nature and lighting up the mind. It's all too easy to forget this and get hung up on flat tires and back aches. When we bow with a single mind these mundane things take care of themselves. When we worry about them, they multiply and get totally out of hand.

Our motto in times of hassle and when nothing is going right is "When in doubt, bow." What is there, really, to rely on? So it says in the Avatamsaka:

> In one Buddhaland he relies on nothing;
> In all Buddhalands it is the same.
> Nor is he attached to conditioned dharmas,
>> because he knows
> That is the nature of these dharmas –
>> there is nowhere to rely.

*Avatamsaka Sutra – Ten Transferences, Part 2*

---

**Heng Sure • November, 1977**
Keep working all the time

**When Lay-people Visit**

> Faith without attaching to any state.
> Uncover your true heart.
> Watch your gate with an empty mind.
> Keep working all the time.
> Do not leave the center.
> Accept no strokes.
> Watch the actor.
> Maintain quiet.
> Seek no sweet milk.
> Break the masks.
> Use the method quietly, there will be nothing lost.
> There is nothing to know and nothing to get.

Imagine how thrilling it will be when the actor-kid finally gets real and starts to work on his own because he wants to earn the fruits of cultivation!

Heng Chau • November 21, 1977
The machine that projects past lives onto a screen

The Body.

"It is turbid, it is stinking and evil, it is impure, it is disgusting, it is contrary and undependable. It is mixed up and stained, it becomes a dead corpse and ultimately it is a heap of bugs."

Avatamsaka Sutra
Brahma Conduct Chapter

Sickness speaks the Dharma. I can't eat and it's difficult to drink. The blood rushes to my head in bowing and the pain throbs. The mad mind yells and panics "Go to the dentist or you'll turn into a 'heap of bugs.'" Then I false think up a storm of food thoughts followed by a question. When my body goes as it will have to, what remains? As soon as I get a little sick, panic sets in. "Oh, I'm going to die? What will happen? When will I go? I've got to save my body!" How can I be so hung up on my body? All around us we see impermanence of form – leaves, bugs, animals, people, and puddles coming into existence, dwelling a while, decaying, and returning to emptiness. The body, my body, is doing the same. It is unavoidable.

"If one contemplates it thus, then one will have no desires with regard to the body, no attachment to what is cultivated, and will not dwell in any dharma. The past is over, the future has not arrived, the present is empty and still."

Avatamsaka Sutra
Brahma Conduct Chapter

P.S. So it's back to the Middle Way: "not up, not down, not left, not right, not too much, not too little; just perfect," as the Master described it last month. What a compassionate teacher! Shih fu saw my state of mind last month and knew all this trouble with food and extreme practices was coming. But seeing I wouldn't have listened then, he let me go ahead and be stupid. But he gave a lecture and smiling instructions on the Middle Way to us before we left. Not until this a.m. were those prophetic instructions ready to be heard and to sink in – over three weeks later! This kind of teacher is inconceivable!

> "All Buddhas, Bodhisattvas and Arhats were born from the Middle Path. Heaven and earth as well. It is the most important path. All Buddhas walked it. Place yourselves right in the middle where it's balanced… Don't fall into emptiness; don't cling to existence. Don't be trapped by either one… When eating keep to the Middle Way. Don't eat too little or your car runs out of gas. Don't fight with yourself, subdue yourself."
>
> Master Hua, 11/5/77
> Gold Wheel Temple

Dream: The Master is meeting with a group of renowned people to discuss the development of the City of Ten Thousand Buddhas. Shih Fu's scope and range is blowing people's minds. He is suggesting schemes and initiating plans that seem impossible. The Master proposes to pack up and move the entire City, brick by brick, from one place to another. All these bright people are scrambling like mad to keep up with the Master's ideas. Shih fu is smiling and totally at ease.

Someone appears with a new invention. It's a machine like a EEG that can tap into the mind's memory storehouse on a physiological basis (electroencephalo waves or something?) and then it projects a persons' past lives onto a screen.

Shih fu is amused and says we can all "play" with it, but we have to do it while standing on our heads. "Basically that's where the machine is at," says Shih fu. "It's upside down, it's putting a head on top of a head." Shih fu is having fun and smiling. Everyone else isn't quite sure.

**Heng Sure** • November, 1977
It's okay to be quiet

Guest-Host Verse.

> Ninety-nine doubts exhausted,
>     rest your mad mind.
> In stillness consider:
>     who's in there so busy?
> Eighty-four thousand of them;
>     let them all go.
> An independent, going nowhere,
>     awakened nature king.
>
> Master Hua

On the road when you slip into that automatic pilot funk, hold your head up, drop your energy, and ask "What are you doing?" Practice the method. Nothing will be lost. It's okay to be quiet.

When you say "Keep bowing all the time," and "only work is true" what do you mean? The work of cultivation is on the mind-ground. Success will result from constant practice of the Dharma methods we have been allowed to use. When bowing we apply the method in mind and body. When not bowing it is the same work.

**Heng Chau** • November 22, 1977
Maybe on another planet

As Heng Sure reads from the Avatamsaka Sutra, sometimes strange states of mind happen. Pieces and flashes of another time and place where things were much like now come to mind. It is subtle but real. In the midst of one world we can see yet other worlds like the flashes of sunlight through a canopy of trees while riding in a car. Heng Sure, the land, the visitors who come with questions and offerings all open and unlock doors into other places where we have all been before or will be. Hard to figure – they come and go like the morning fog.

Maybe it's like the Avatamsaka says: "The past, the present, and the future are the same" and only in our minds do we make them seem different.

FORE AND AFT, the local high school newspaper came out for pictures and an interview but the camera wouldn't work and no one was quite sure what questions to ask.

When the Sixth Patriarch was about to die, he told his disciples, "The leaves return to the root." As we were bowing through all the dry, rustling leaves alone on the backroads of Vandenberg AFB, the Patriarch's words came to me. The leaves come from the root and return to it. So do all living beings. The self is false and clinging to it is the cause of all suffering. Letting go of the self is the way back to the root and real happiness.

A car pulls up and an older woman comes walking across the highway in the rain. Smiling, she makes an offering of money and leaves without a word. She is happy.

Doug, a young man from Virginia stopped to talk. He had left his friends and home and was living out of his old Volvo. "I've come to California, kind of the end of America, to try to find some peace of mind and some answers," he said.

"You know," he went on, "There is so much evil and suffering. There's got to be a better place. Maybe on another planet. With all these rockets, you'd think they could just fill one of them full with all the evil in the world and then shoot it as far away as possible – get rid of it that way. Did you know that 6000 people just died in a hurricane in India?"

Doug made an offering from his dwindling supplies. "We should all just give and help one another. But there is just so much hate and evil out there."

"All that 'hate and evil out there' is made from our own hearts and minds. You've got to start inside yourself to change the world." I said.

"Like this?" asked Doug referring to the bowing.

"That's one way of thousands. That's what Buddhism and a monastery is all about: you take one of the thousands of methods and look into these problems and questions."

"If I came would I get the answer?" pressed Doug.

"It depends a lot on you. If you work you get results. If you don't work, no results. Buddhism provides the methods but you've got to do the work."

"Hmmm. That rings true. You have an address or something for this City of all the Buddhas?"

As Doug was getting ready to leave he had a final thought. He said this like he wasn't sure it would be taken right but needed to say it anyway. "You know I've been trying to get clean of all the bad I've done to others and that's been done to me. I want to get free of that trip... you know, kind of turn it all around." We shook hands and Doug went his way.

"The Bodhisattva sets his will on the search for Bodhi...
He does not want the Five Desires or a king's throne. He wants not wealth or success or amusement or fame. He wants only to end for eternity the suffering of living beings. He makes his resolution to benefit the world."

Avatamsaka Sutra
Chapter 12, Part 1

Doug had left everything, "wealth, success, amusement, and fame" to try to find a way to end suffering and "benefit the world." If his will is set, he'll surely find what he's looking for and be able to turn it all around. I hope so.

---

**Heng Sure** • November, 1977
I am not bowing for food!

This is a long process because the self is not a single block, it is a salad of small pieces, tiny fragments of images and dharmas, a mountain made of motes of dust. You can't knock it down all at once. It would just regroup in another place, perhaps in another body. It is held together by the momentum of past karma and the glue of bad habits.

In cultivation, the gradual waking to the tricks of the self slowly erases it bit by bit like waves washing on a cliff. One bow is one mote of dust less in the mountain of self. Sometimes there are break-throughs, whole pieces fall away. Mere intellectual understanding of the basic illusory nature of the process and of the self will not make any big difference. What counts is the movement, the effort, the heating and the cooling of the works and the practice of good habits under close guidance by a wise teacher. Then one day you bow down a mountain.

Stay Out of the Kitchen!

Talk about the sublime growing from the mundane! The hardest practice these days aside from holding singleness of mind for longer than one bow is really staying out of what the Self wants to get involved in. Number One among these is the kitchen. I pull my little child-actor out of thoughts of food about once every fifteen minutes. If an offering comes in or food goes out I have to physically restrain my body from wandering over and diving right in. I've done it enough in the past – I am not bowing for food! The kitchen is Heng Chau's territory and I trust his judgement. The Number Two temptation is to get all involved in the business details and planning of chores and trips and contacts. Again, this is not my concern now. The wonder of this trip is that I have the space and time to go as far into my cultivation as I have the guts to go – I don't have to do anything else. People have dreamed of a chance like this and never gotten it. To blow the time on food and other false thoughts is just too selfish and stupid.

---

**Heng Chau** • November 23, 1977
The right road feels wrong

A woman stopped with an apple pie this a.m. for Thanksgiving tomorrow.

The men of the 659th Instrumentation Squadron at Vandenberg AFB chose Joe, John, and George to represent them in making an offering. They took a pool of the squadron and went and bought groceries, blankets, juice, and supplies and brought them out with a lot of "good lucks" and support.

Heng Sure is translating Shih fu's verses on the Seven Buddhas of Antiquity after our meal offering. They are better than lunch and really turn the center peg of the heart.

Heng Sure tried abstaining from water after noon to help with ending the drought and I have been fasting twice a month. Both practices were too extreme. We have to use patience and gentleness on ourselves without slacking off or losing resolve. It's a tight rope to walk. We have been on the wrong track for so long that the right road feels wrong and when we think we are on the right road, that's a cue that we are heading for trouble. What feels good isn't always good for you. If it hurts it's not necessarily bad for you either. Nothing is fixed and you've got to listen real close to your own heart to find the right way... real close.

Got some kind of itchy rash – poison oak probably.

Take away all the things I have collected to lean on and who is left? I am not my father or mother. I am not my friends. I am not my education or job. I am not my house. I am not the monk. I am not even my body. My body is just a "snot heap." I am not my mind. The mind is like the wind. What's left?

I'm not sure who I am but I know that *really* finding out means getting to the point I can put down, one by one, all the things I am not. Each dissolving and painful breakdown of an attachment is followed by an indescribable calm and joy. When all the things I am not are removed and set behind, what's left? Whatever it is, one who finds it doesn't try to kill it with words. There is just a smile and light in this one's eyes and you know it's all worth it. Seeing or hearing one who has attained the Way is such an eye and heart opener that you won't rest until everyone is there.

> "The Bodhisattva should diligently cultivate the practices of Great Compassion and vow to save all, so that without exception, all come to fruition. Those beings who see him, hear him, listen to him, receive him, or make offerings to him, all these will be caused to get peace and happiness."
>
> Avatamsaka Sutra
> Chapter 12, Part 1

I have a bad habit of being a watchdog for other's faults and bad habits while ignoring my own. It's just another way of being lazy and arrogant. This week I got on Heng Sure's case and started fault-finding to avoid doing my own work. Last night in a dream I was wandering down a long out-of-the-way side street with lots of houses. I was peeking in the front doors and scrutinizing things. Just as I turned from nosing into one house the Master appeared. "Oh! Shih fu! What are you doing here... I mean, uh." I was stammering and caught. The Master didn't say anything but I knew immediately the question was, "What was I doing there?" I woke up and stopped being a watchdog. This really cleared up a wrong road I had been heading down.

In another dream we were riding with the Master in a car. I felt as though I should be taking notes but then realized that it was just a substitute for practice. The Master gave us advice for the future: "If you don't separate from the true nature, don't lose the Middle Way, then everything will be ok. Whatever comes up, respond naturally; rely on true principles." A lot was going to be happening but there would be no problems if we "do not separate from 'this'." The Master went on, "The small and the big are alike. They are both empty. Be quiet and still. Watch and accord with conditions. Be without a view of self, others, living beings, or lifespan!" The talk was warm and gentle but not emotional. Lots of happy light. "Then everything's ok, right?" asked the Master with a smile.

---

**Heng Sure** • November, 1977
It feels like a burning house

It Only Feels Like Death.

I felt dead last Saturday – scared literally to death of the new shifting world I'm growing into. Nothing remains to hang onto, nothing real but the work, the work is not yet solid to sustain the energy. Result: outflows 'and fear. Not enough kung fu to cut through but a real new emptiness inside and out. Ego screams, "I don't want to die!" Dives backwards into old pictures of sex, fame, food, and fantasies of family and friends.

The Dharma is the shining beacon of faith that keeps the work inching forward on this tight-rope between emptiness and existence. I know the Master knows and I know that in the ends and in the middle it's really all okay. But out here in between and back and forth, it feels like a burning house.

Deep faith and a pure resolve to leave it all will win the day. Patience and hard work will cut the doubts and chase the fears.

Heng Chau • November 24, 1977
We just look poor on the outside

For the Sangha, everyday is Thanksgiving. Everyday is a kind of Christmas and birthday too. The Sangha is one of the gems of the Triple Jewel because their purity in holding precepts takes them out of the dust of the material world. So they shine and are models for all living beings.

One of the precepts is "Do not hold gold, silver, and valuable objects." And yet they don't beg or seek. Heng Sure and I are finding one needs very little to survive, and even less to be happy! All food, clothes, and shelter are offered to the Sangha as a "field of blessings." It's the same on the road. If what we need isn't offered, we don't need it. If something is offered, we need it. Why? Because it's the heart of giving that is being planted and nurtured. The world needs more giving so the more people that give, the better for everyone. We are just the field, the harvest belongs to everyone.

We are all one source, one heart, one substance to the ends of empty space. Wherever we are we are always at home. And we spend *all* holidays with our "family"!

Thanksgiving meal: peanut butter and jelly, nuts, canned beans, lettuce, fruit, and bean curd and left over apple cobbler. The best part was the verse from the Seven Buddhas of Antiquity:

> Seeing the body as unreal is the Buddha's view.
> Understanding the mind as illusory
>     is the Buddha's understanding.
> One who understands that the body and mind
>     are empty in their fundamental nature,
> How is this person at all different from the Buddha?

"We were sitting around eating our Thanksgiving dinner and my mom said, 'Those poor monks...' So here I am," said Matt, the editor of the local school newspaper. He made an offering from his family of bread and homemade preserves.

"Tell your mom the offering is well received and that we just look poor on the outside. Inside we're rich and happy."

"Ok!" said Matt. "Will do."

> Like one who gets a treasure store of jewels,
> And is ever after free of poverty's suffering,
> When the Bodhisattva gets the Buddhadharma,
> He leaves the dirt, his mind is purified.

Avatamsaka Sutra<br>Verse in Praise of Tushita Heaven

Ahead at bottom of this mesa are the brown rolling hills of the Casmalia oil field dotted with pumping derricks. The little town of Casmalia is in sight. It is quiet with just a sound of a few barking dogs, train whistles, and the lowing of cattle carried up.

---

**Heng Sure** • November, 1977
For nine months, no pumpkin pie

Humbled Pie.

A big little lesson today. In the past I have always been attached to pumpkin pie. It was my favorite food from earliest memories. It was connected with my birthday which fell during the season and holidays hallmarked by pumpkins. Pumpkin pies always meant happy birthday. Lots of ego strokes.

At Gold Mountain Monastery I intensified my attachment to pumpkin pie. I went through some greedy schemes to get pie that now make my ears burn to remember. For example after a three-week fast I let it be known that pumpkin pie was my favorite food and the pies began to roll in. Pumpkin bread came from home and like a big-eyed mouse I scarfed down more than I could hold. The result: A prolonged case of diarrhea.

As things happen at Gold Mountain, often one's biggest attachment is used as a teaching device – favorite dharmas suddenly turn into inescapable mind-turning tools. At a certain point pumpkin pie totally disappeared from Gold Mountain's desert board. For nine months not one pie came through. My greed for them grew so large and their absence grew so obvious that I could not avoid making the connection that something was being taught – if I had eyes to learn it. I resolved to end my desire for pumpkin pies and for all kinds of sweets and foods that I was attached to.

The resolve held and I forgot about pumpkin pie. Still no pies crossed my path – going on a year and a half until yesterday a gentleman drove out from Casmalia on the morning after Thanksgiving to give us pumpkin pie "because we were humans." I ate my share at lunch and discovered that things have changed inside. After one instant of old flavor memory, I felt a big surge of distaste for the dark yin sweetness that would surely bring clouds to cover my mind in the afternoon. It tasted like ice cream, pop, candy, cookies, and chocolate – like a big unwelcome weight in my system. And it tasted like Christopher. Clearly the value of the pies was the strokes to the ego I received when I ate them, it had little to do with the pies themselves.

---

Heng Chau • November 25, 1977
Afraid you won't get your fill

A car pulls up on this quiet, empty road. A man walks up, a little hesitant but sincere and kind. He makes an offering of food and water and says, "I don't know any thing about you, but I am human and you are human and I can see!"

"His constant wish: to help others and make them happy."

Avatamsaka Sutra
Chapter 12, Part 1

Six kids and their dog hike across the tall wheat colored grassy oil fields and sit on the roadside fence for an hour watching us approach. A few hop down now and then and try out bowing themselves. When we reach them it went like this:

"Hi!"

"Hi."

"We really hope you make it all the way."

"Thanks."

"Bye."

"Bye."

And as the sun sets they hike back home to dinner and we keep bowing.

Called the Abbot about the broken tooth. The Master didn't mince words or let this disciple wallow in self pity. "Your tooth hurts because of false thoughts about food… afraid you won't get your fill. If it's not better by tonight go get it fixed tomorrow. Be patient, endure what others cannot endure."

I wasn't expecting to hear it so straight. I just stood there in the phone booth holding the phone, not knowing what to say. The Master called this one like it was too, "Why aren't you talking? Talk to me!"

"Ah, ah… I don't know." I finally blurted to cover.

"This is long distance. It costs money. Why are you not talking… You called to say 'I don't know'?" I quickly handed the phone to Heng Sure and stepped out of the booth. I was sweating and it wasn't even warm outside. It was just the bitter medicine I needed to strike up my spirits. The Master bolted me out of a nose dive.

"He vows that all living beings forever escape their sick bodies and obtain the Tathagata's body."

Avatamsaka
Ten Transferences Chapter

**Heng Sure** • November, 1977
The fullmoon-crazed mind

I have abandoned my life as an astrologer but full moons bring inner conclusions and truths are revealed. Outside, they bring all kinds of people, situations, and crises. We should run fully awake during those four days.

I have a new capacity for active fantasy that has a life of its own. Yesterday it was a way to calm down and subdue my fullmoon-crazed mind and to round up all the scattered flying parts of my nature.

It was a conversation among the personalities in a herd of horses. The leader, in samadhi, expediently rationally cut through the doubts, fears, and off-center states of the less-concentrated horses. Later they all met in a forum and he spoke from the front row urging them all to recognize the necessity of leaving the world. The horses quietly, slowly saw his light and united their wills to cultivate. A real populist victory for the Dharma.

**Heng Chau** • November 26, 1977
Just checking to see if anyone was sick

Had tooth pulled in Santa Maria. I felt the Master's presence throughout the entire ordeal guiding and protecting.

We went back out to an abandoned field out of view of the highway. Heng Sure bowed in place while I recovered in the back of the car.

A kindly old man in a beat-up camper pulls up and peeks in the door. "Oh, you're ok, huh? Just checking to see if anyone was sick, but you look fine to me," he said cheerfully and in a way very familiar to me. I didn't know what to say or do. He completely surprised me. I was still half dosed-up from the anesthetic

"You're the praying monks, right? Well just you keep on praying and try your best" and he tipped his hat and left.

I felt better immediately and sat up straight to meditate. Then I thought, "Hey, who was he? And how did he find us here? We're completely hidden in this thicket. And 'try your best'?" That's the Master's own words. I turned to see if I could find him but he was gone. Heng Sure made a Poultice of Comfrey and Golden Seal. I stuffed it in the cavity, recited Great Compassion Mantras and sat in Ch'an waiting for my bowing legs to return. Heng Sure translated this passage from the Avatamsaka to give me some Dharma medicine:

> Realize the self does not exist.
> This body is falsely set up.
> Its dwelling place has no fixed position.
> When one truly understands this body,
> then within it there is nothing at all to attach to.
>
> Avatamsaka
> Bodhisattva Enquiries

How much the less attach to a tooth: Good medicine, the Buddhadharma.

Break Through.

I have very little patience. In cultivation there's a tendency to want to smash, break through all obstacles and cut off and put down all attachments in a single swoop. Slash, slam, bang! Enlightenment. It doesn't work that way and can often turn into a demon-state. "I've put down food, I've put down sex, I've this and I've that..." Suddenly the ego is in charge and one is attached to putting it down. "I'm bored. I need something to put down," follows.

Sound cultivation is a question of habits – attrition not revolution. Steady, gradual change and maintaining solid daily practice breaks the coverings. Instant attainment is just another kind of attachment. Underneath it is just laziness. Who wants to work hard?

False thoughts and attachments accumulate to the size of a mountain slowly, over a long period of time. Suddenly recognizing these as false and bringing forth the mind for Bodhi can be sudden – a break through. *But* actually changing faults and ignorance into virtue and wisdom takes time, hard work, and patience. Returning to the self-nature takes minute-to-minute, thought-to-thought vigor and effort. Break throughs and sudden awakenings are tools to increase faith and resolve. They are sudden or gradual only in contrast to how confused we were. But if you think you've made "it" you're ripe for a fall and a setback.

Not force, not laziness, not winning, not losing, just "try your best" and get a little better every day. Attaching to anything is false. When there is no "it" sought or attained, then there is real effort and real results. You are your own "good knowing advisor" but it takes a little skill to learn how to teach yourself.

---

**Heng Chau** • November 27, 1977
What a sacrifice!

Dream: Shih fu shows me all the different methods (dharmas) and "tricks" used to try to "cross over" living beings. He then sends me to a burning house. It's my house! Inside are all the people I know waiting for firemen to rescue them. I go to the back porch and climb up and start helping them down to safety.

When I return the Master is waiting in a large hall alone. He asks, "Do you understand now?"

"A little, Shih fu," I answer.

The Master is warm and personal. "Do you understand how people's Dharma names are chosen, what they mean?"

"Not completely."

Shih fu answers, "It's to wake them up. The name points to the quality or obstacle that stands between them and crossing over."

"You mean kind of like the last little bit of glue or falseness?" I ask.

"Yes." says the Master, smiling. "Then they all go out and find more to 'trick' into leaving suffering and the burning house."

Right then the doors of the hall open and scores of new disciples stream in – wary, uptight, but looking. Shih fu becomes quiet and grave. I feel, "Wow! What a burden to keep taking on new disciples! What a sacrifice!" But there is something quiet and peaceful about the Master's role – like it never began and never would end. Shih fu was a person without a self. He was an infinite source of compassion and light crossing over living beings without a thought, without limit. It made my little hang-ups and thoughts and troubles seem really small.

Some lay people drive out and offer food, water and supplies. and join in bowing every three steps for an hour or so.

Windy and wide open spaces inside and out.

---

**Heng Sure** • November, 1977
Having touched a young baby

The Abbot is soft outside and totally in control inside. His will and inner strength surpass understanding, while his nearly-seven-decades-old body remains as supple and as vigorous as a young boy's.

Few people have the occasion to touch him. Riding in a car on the freeway once, I was sitting next to the Master. We made a sudden stop. He was sitting in full lotus and the momentum pitched him forward. Before he could strike the front seat, I did the natural thing and grabbed his shoulder and arm and stopped his plunge. We continued on and my hands carried a vivid sense impression of having touched a young baby – there was no tension at all in the Master's body – he was fully relaxed even as his head sped towards the hard seat back. Yet in this soft shoulder and arm there was a tangible electric vibrancy that made my hands tingle for minutes afterwards. What a wonderful state must be the purity and calm of one who has "returned to the root and gone back to the source"!

**Heng Chau** • November 28, 1977
You're blessing this highway, aren't you?

We should connect with Highway 1 again in a day or two; past the next valley. We are coming out of a high hilly plateau into a dusty dry flat valley. We can see the lights of Santa Maria at night from where we camp.

Motorcyclist: "I feel a lot better driving this road everyday now."
"Oh?"

"Yes, you're blessing this highway, aren't you?"

**Heng Chau** • November 29, 1977
There's nothing left to burn

A rancher stopped. Very friendly. "Yes I had a friend who became a Buddhist monk… often think about him. You're vegetarians! Oh well, you aren't helping promote my business. I'm a cattleman. But my son will be happy. He's a vegetable farmer – no meat for him."

As he drives away he says, "Don't worry about accidentally starting a fire. The drought hit us so bad there's nothing left to burn."

As he left I thought of how everything in our lives speaks the Dharma. Like this rancher: a son who doesn't eat meat, a friend who's a Buddhist monk, a drought that's ruining his cattle business. And yet they don't all connect and make sense to him. They speak but aren't heard clearly.

I thought of how everyday people and things tell me how it really is – who I am and what it's all about. All around nature and my daily experiences speak of cause and effect, the impermanence of everything, and the importance of going toward the good. But how much do I hear?

I was feeling bummed out and full of faults – dejected and low in spirit. The Avatamsaka Sutra turned it right around and recharged me. What a friend! It said the Bodhisattva "never grows weary. He is unattached and obtains a mind of faith which does not retreat." I stopped feeling sorry for myself and was reminded of why we're out here:

> "If one can leave arrogance and laxness behind, then one can aid all that lives; if one can aid all that lives, then one can reside in birth and death without tiring of it…"
>
> Avatamsaka Sutra
> Chapter 12, Part 1

Pick up the pieces and hit the road! We are back on Highway 1 and heading for Guadalupe, Ca.

---

**Heng Sure** • November, 1977
Water does not work that way

Refueling at Gold Wheel.

We practice for a month fueled by the Master's instructions. His advice feels prophetic, "time capsuled," unfolding as the situations arise outside, timed to our readiness to understand inside.

After a month we return to his presence for more instructions, more fuel and then back out to work.

Each time the last week rolls up, either Heng Chau or I am on the brink of exhaustion. It comes from pushing the ego to the edge and from having not enough skill to balance on the Middle Way without toppling over on the side of force. This is a better situation than falling off the side of laxness, but only because the Master is there to catch us at the end of the month. Otherwise we would regularly push ourselves right off the road into accidents, injuries, and distaste for cultivation. This is a major area of learning that we have only recently glimpsed: much less cultivated. It's called "solid, sincere, and constant": solid faith, sincere vows, and constant practice.

Believe your teacher, know what you want and put your heart into it, and keep up the pressure – everyday. No sudden charges, no spectacular gains, no heroic victories, just steady everyday work and step by step walking forward without retreat.

Here's another way of saying it. A major fault Heng Chau and I share is trying to force the Way. We grit our teeth, tighten our bodies, and plunge ahead as if we could break through our coverings, and views, and desires in one blow. The Middle Way of the Buddha is like water and water does not work that way. Water absorbs all things and does not change. It bears all force used against it and returns to stillness. It produces all life.

When we push past the center in our struggles to "break through," we are at that time in the grip of the Self, the Ego. Fast, hard "cultivation" is not real cultivation. It does not come from the heart. It is just another form of laziness. The motivation for force is to get the job done and over with and then go back to sleep. This is the "vacation syndrome" that traps many cultivators.

Real cultivation is a constant daily pressure that bit by bit makes solid, actual changes in old habits and views.

---

Heng Chau • November 30, 1977
Waiting out the fire pressure

The Avatamsaka Sutra talks about and describes what is experienced and known apart from the intellect. It is the language and wisdom of the true mind in all living beings. No wonder it feels like home.

Getting a little better at "waiting out" the fire pressure that comes with concentration and no sex. If you can bear it, it turns into light and burns up afflictions. If you can't, it turns into fight (anger) and greed. Still full of food false thoughts. Really hard to put that one down.

\* \* \* \* \* \* \* \*
## December 1977

---

### Heng Chau • December 1, 1977
### Business is bad

George, the tortilla maker from Santa Barbara stopped. "Business is bad. I have a medal for good luck my parents gave, here" he said, pulling a chain out from under his shirt. "I don't let no one else touch it. I always carry it with me. But business is still bad. So my wife said, 'Why don't you ask those two monks, maybe they can help us.'" We talked a little. George made an offering and then left to try to drum up some business. I told him "luck" came from what we did and thought. If we did good things we'd have good luck, if we did bad things we'd meet with bad luck. It's hard to run a business and always do good, but in the long run, it's harder not to.

---

### Heng Sure • December 2, 1977
### Welcome back to the world

Note to Heng Chau:

After a long month of forcing the Way. Three days of down-at-heart struggle – emotional turning and hard labor.

Strange, near the end of lunch I felt as if I had finally emerged from a dark cave or found a safe island in my drifting boat or discovered that the war is over. My body and mind relaxed.

Part of me said, "Welcome back to the world. It's nice that you're still intact and able to cultivate."

Part of me said, "Too bad, if you could have held on to your edge you might have taken a big step forward. As it is you haven't lost anything but you stopped just before a turning point. You delayed the resolution of a spiritual crisis same as you always do. You didn't make it off the high-dive tower."

Is this second voice reliable or is it attachment to states?

It did feel as if a long pendulum swing of several weeks or more stopped just short of the extreme. I saw the end of a long tunnel that I had been crawling towards. At lunch, I stood up and said, "Come on, that's enough for now," and walked out. Strange.

> "In the place of turning, if you keep no emotion, then you will always and forever dwell in Naga concentration."

> "Simply let your mind be like empty space without clinging to the view of emptiness and the responding function will be unobstructed. In motion and in stillness do not have thought. Forget feelings of holy or common, put an end to both subject and object. The nature and the mark will then be 'thus, thus,' and at no time will you not be in a state of concentration."

> The Sixth Patriarch

---

**Heng Chau** • December 2, 1977
It was like turning off the power switch

We bow to return all beings to their original, enlightened self-nature. We bow to get rid of false thoughts and attachments. We bow to end disasters and suffering from all living beings.

A cowboy slows his pickup truck alongside and three tough cattle dogs bound out the back and surround us, barking and yelping. They don't know quite what to make of us... neither does the cowboy. We keep bowing and they keep circling and barking. Finally the cowboy slaps the side of the truck with his hand and the dogs turn and leap back into the truck. They slowly drive away and we slowly bow the other way.

The Buddhadharma is new to the West. Really it's not new or strange at all. We all just got a little lost and forgot what the real thing looks like. We are all a little rusty at taming the frontier inside. But it will come back to us.

A false thought is looking forward for something – anticipating and living for the future. Today I found myself uncontrollably looking out for the Gold Mountain van. Someone had told us it would be coming. It was a lack of concentration but I didn't try hard enough to turn it. I kept watching and expecting.

That night I had a dream where I was playing with a little child. I set the child on my lap and it turned into a nasty demon that started to squeeze the very life out of me. I couldn't get out of its vice-like grip. Finally, I grabbed it with both hands and put its ear next to my mouth and recited a line from the Shurangama Mantra five times. It was like turning off the power switch for an electromagnet. The demon immediately went limp and dropped to the floor.

---

**Heng Chau** • December 3, 1977
Bodhisattvas are what people can become

Some quotes from the Master:

"Mantras are the names of the Dharma protectors, the Bodhisattva spirit protectors. You should recite as if they were coming closer and protecting you. The more you recite, the closer they come.

"In reciting Sutras, you take across the soul. A ghost is just a person transformed. A Buddha is just a person who cultivated. Bodhisattvas are what people can become."

**Heng Sure** • December, 1977
When I feel close to death

The warning signals of being at rope's end; at the juncture of ego break up:

1) Fuzzy mind, no concentration.

2) Constant food thoughts.

3) Looking and listening for offerings.

4) Thoughts of lay people, home, family past histories, careers, etc.

5) Sexual fantasies.

When the ego fears a loss of control, when I feel close to death, these images fill my head. This is the top of the 100-foot pole. Time to take another step, shake down the energy and relax. Continue working – all states are false.

Check your posture: head up!

**Heng Chau** • December 4, 1977
Big doubt produces big enlightenment

Why do we shave our heads? So we won't spend so much time looking at our false face. Hair is a big ego identity blanket. What you want to do is look into your original face – the face without a self. To do that you've got to get rid of the covers. Hair is one of them.

Shaving the head symbolizes renunciation of the world i.e. the self as an independent entity. Without hair to hide behind and fuss over, it is easier to find the heart.

The Master on doubt: "Small doubt brings small enlightenment. Big doubt produces big enlightenment. No doubt at all, no enlightenment."

During a pause in the Dharma talks at Gold Wheel a layperson comes up and says to Dharma Master Heng Shun who is sitting next to me: "Do you want some new shoes?"

Heng Shun: "No, these are fine."

Layperson: "How about a scarf and knitted hood?"

Heng Shun: "No, really, I have all I need."

Layperson: "Boy you don't want nothing, do you?" and with a smile returns to her seat.

I turned to Heng Shun and said, "That's it! Don't have any desire – don't want nothing."

Heng Shun, without a thought: "Not to even want 'wanting nothing' is even better."

---

**Heng Sure** • December, 1977

The Ego is really scared and fighting back hard

I am no longer able to pin my problems on external dharmas. I now can only face my mind's projections and own the thought that chase out of my inner gate.

When ever cultivation is stepped up, the mental noise increases and concentration melts away. It comes down to fear, of death. The teachings are full of principles to cope with this fear, but what I am experiencing is not a head trip. Somewhere inside the Ego is really scared and fighting back hard to keep me from going the direction I'm going. This requires relaxation, patience, sincerity, solidity, and constancy.

The other voice, the true cultivator, is impatient with the long hours of unclear headwork. He wants a still mind and right now. He wants the system to obey and he will take no nonsense. As he gets stronger, so does the resistance. Faith in the Middle Way helps the situation. Light eating really helps douse the fire, and reviewing basic instructions helps. What remains is the work of constant mindful maintenance and working out solutions with the Ego as I bow. Gradually it is subsiding. Conscious relaxation of the body helps too. Using the Great Compassion Mantra as an inner exercise and *tai ji* basic movements release the tension of the work. The tension shows up in tight muscles, shallow breathing, uncertain steps, and stooped posture.

Tell myself: Death is just change. It's the end of a round. It's false and there is nothing to fear. What do you hold onto and who holds on? All dharmas are alike; they have one flavor: bitter. Give them up and go home. What is there to hang onto? All feelings that come in through your senses are suffering. Give them up.

---

**Heng Chau** • December 5, 1977
It is the face of the Master

The City of Ten Thousand Buddhas is our own original face and pure nature. It is the face of the Master, the pulse of the Patriarchs and sages and the thread of light we follow inside each of us. The City is a tool for Buddhahood. Ultimately it's all within your own mind.

> "If one wants to understand and know all Buddhas of the past, present, and future, he should contemplate the nature of the Dharmarealm, it's all made from the mind alone."
>
> Avatamsaka Sutra
> Chapter 20

---

**Heng Sure** • December, 1977
I have already surpassed chemical or dope highs

Common people seek to return to ignorance through the Five Desires. They seek a place of total security, all needs filled. They seek the foetal position, all curled up and dark.

Cultivators of the Way are the opposite. They seek to return to their original source before birth and death. There is nothing to cling to, nothing to get that gives security. They seek the lotus posture all straightened out and full of light, like the Buddha.

"Return the light" is an inner practice. You pull back the energy that leaves you through the gates of the sense organs. Thoughts in the mind are a major energy leak. Cultivation is a process of pulling the energy in thoughts back to the energy center in the middle of the body.

When you use the wisdom sword or a hua t'ou (meditation topic) to cut off thoughts as they arise to consciousness it is most effective if you first pull from the energy center, then cut off any thoughts that remain above. By analogy it's like trying to block off the light from a lamp by using your hands and a piece of cardboard. How much better to simply turn off the lamp at the source, than to scramble to catch all the light/thoughts that leave out the top.

I am not bowing for food!
I am not bowing for pleasure!
I am not bowing to survive!

Whatever hard or fearful or unpleasant states arise, you should recognize them as an aid to your practice of patience and equality of all dharmas. Respect all states as equally illusory and don't move. Say thank you with your true heart. They put you on your center.

Say: neither grasp nor reject. Unpleasant states I do not avoid. Pleasant states I do not welcome. I am leaving this triple world through my Buddha porthole. I will be happy on my way out.

We ignore states and comparisons are false but anyway I noticed that I have already surpassed the very "finest" experiences I ever had on chemical or dope highs. In the bowing and the sitting there is peace and stillness.

You never do understand the Way in a dry intellectual way. Only through hard patient practice of a Dharma door, through physical work and mental concentration do you change enough in your electrical and chemical systems in your cells to allow the understanding to come forth in the body/mind/heart. You have to want it enough to follow instructions perfectly. Just go out and work. Try your best to keep all emotion out of your method, keep on purifying the mind without cease. Let the changes happen without choosing or rejecting. Maintain good cheer and good faith as you walk the Sagely Way.

---

**Heng Chau** • December 6–7, 1977
The wordless, silent bowing state

Riding back to the bowing site in an overpacked, top heavy old VW bus stuffed full of offerings for the City of Ten Thousand Buddhas, Heng Shun was wedged between two boxes in the back translating Sutras. Heng Ju, Heng Sure and I quietly sitting in front looking out at the rolling hills and long valleys. Each of us bowing inside and remembering the wordless, silent bowing state. Sharing without talking, bowing without moving.

Thinking less, being more
Talking less, giving more
Eating less, bowing more
With one heart, bowing more and more
To the City of Ten Thousand Buddhas.

---

**Heng Sure** • December, 1977
If you sit more, you see more

There is not a single dharma in the world that carries the label "good for Kuo Chen" or "bad for Heng Sure." All dharmas have one bittersweet flavor. By hard work for a long time you slowly change among them. Even though you grew from the mud, with practice, you leave the mud behind.

If you notice a state and then suddenly there exists a noticer and something to notice, both are not true. In order to notice you have to stop the work which produced the state. States are small. They are tests of your resolve to cut through self and dharmas. On the other side of states is the realization of the all-inclusive Mahayana.

"Working hard is true. Be without fear or joy and don't attach to anything. Then you can reach a state of real accomplishment."

Master Hua – Ch'an Talks

Using the sword feels like combing the mind. You get all the kinks and snarls of thoughts to run straight so that you let light and air in through and through. Don't throw out thoughts, straighten them out.

Sitting in meditation today below Titan Gate at Vandenberg AFB felt better than eating lunch despite the aches and pressures on knees, back, and mind. If you sit more, you see more. If you eat more, your vision dims.

---

Heng Chau • December 8, 1977

Nabbing and shooting the false thought

Strong winds and cold fog hamper bowing. We had to bow in a low ditch as the force of the wind kept ripping our sashes off.

We are camped in a makeshift dump full of old mattresses and wine bottles next to the train tracks south of Guadalupe.

Small discovery: When a false thought arises it can be caught, arrested on the spot, and put to rest. If I just watch my own body, mouth, and mind, I can nab the false before it shoots out and drags me through the dust.

It's like a game. False thoughts sooner or later run out the eyes, ears, nose, tongue, body, and mind (six gates). Using energy to "return the light" and watch the gates, you can turn back the flow. What a fine difference this makes! I no longer feel like what happens to me is out of my control – fated or luck. I never knew how or where to look before. Funny the "secret" was right under my nose all the time.

**Heng Sure** • December, 1977
Staring at the television screen

As a child I spent at least two hours a day and often up to five staring at the television screen. Where did I learn my social values? From my daily lessons in situation-comedy family behavior. Here's a partial list: My Three Sons, Leave It to Beaver, Father Knows Best, Ozzie and Harriet, Dick Van Dyke, Donna Reed, Gale Storm, Andy Griffith, Patty Duke, Lassie, I Love Lucy, Dobie Gillis, The Honeymooners. Add to this countless hours of westerns, crime shows, sports events, cartoons, mysteries, variety shows, Ed Sullivan, Walt Disney, the 20th Century, Camera Three, specials, news, Star Trek, adventure series, military serials, comedy hours, movies by the hundreds, and all those commercials and you have a child whose mind was larded with deviant knowledge and deviant views.

Perhaps five percent of what I saw was beneficial to me in any way. I retain none of it now save a score of commercial jingles and theme songs. Mine is the first generation in history to be mesmerized by a flickering beam of light in the name of entertainment. All those thousands of hours I could have been moving my body, playing, learning, working, exploring, relating to people, reading good books. Instead I sat, crouched or slumped on the living room floor and stared and absorbed false thoughts and poisons.

**Heng Chau** • December 9, 1977
Where will Heng Sure be?

Where is Heng Sure? Heng Sure is basically skinny. When the sun came out and warmed the air he started to peel off his warm clothes. Before my eyes he started to get smaller and smaller with each discarded piece of clothing. In a very short time impermanence will take his eyes, ears, hair, and healthy body and then where will Heng Sure be? We are all wearing borrowed elements and living on borrowed time. Hurry up and cultivate! Where is Heng Sure?

**Heng Sure • December, 1977**
The expression of resolve

Resolve is "bringing forth the heart" literally. You must want to cultivate to enlightenment for the sake of all living beings before the Bodhisattva path responds. Resolve is knowing/feeling in your head/heart what you want and then doing what is necessary to get it. If you do not bring forth a true sincere heart and get behind it, then every move will be a false one and you will go sideways.

What is the expression of the resolve? Vows and practice based on faith. Cultivation is saying no to yourself and yes to others. With each no in the mind, the self dies a little bit more. At a certain point you can see through it to its empty nature.

**Heng Chau • December 10, 1977**
Small town of Guadalupe

Bow through small town of Guadalupe. Inside there is an energy building with no immediate place to go. It builds and throbs creating hot and cold flashes. Feeling a lot of impatience – like ocean tides swelling inside and cramped in a stuffy box.

**Heng Sure • December, 1977**
A trap – a one-way door to a maze

> "The Buddha is the only being on the planet to appear in inedible form."
>
> Poet Gary Snyder

At heart, who isn't afraid of being eaten? Even if in your entire lifetime you never bump into a hungry animal or bird big enough to devour you, in the end, you are eaten by the earth. Who isn't afraid of death? The Buddha isn't, all those who have cultivated to end birth and resolve death aren't either. Most people go about quelling this fear in the wrong way, however. They feel that death is inevitable so the best answer is to work one's way back to ignorance, back to a place where there is no pain or fear. Then when death comes, you've done all you could, you've grabbed all your senses and you can "rage against the dying of the light" all you please. On the way to death most of us grab at five desires hoping to forget more quickly our coming end. We feel that freedom, happiness, peace and security can be clutched and grasped in wealth or sex or fame or food or sleep.

In fact the Buddha tells us that this is a trap – a one-way door to a maze – a no-exit labyrinth that will always bring you to a dead end.

With the Buddha's teachings in the world, however, there is a door out, an exit from the maze, a porthole into inedibility. Where is it? It's not outside of you and it can't be thought about, it can't be bought. But it can be cultivated and opened by anyone who studies the Buddhadharma contained in Buddhist Sutras, who draws near to a wise advisor – one who has already resolved his own birth and death, and by making offerings in faith to the Buddha through the "field of blessings" of the Sangha – Buddhist monks and nuns. This is the final and highest road to peace, freedom, happiness, and security and it's right here among the "dog eat dog" world. Look for it with an open heart and you will surely find it.

---

**Heng Chau** • December 11, 1977
Our boys told us what you are doing

Guadalupe.

We bowed past a cemetery accompanied by six or seven lay people who drove four hours from Los Angeles and got no sleep to join in the pilgrimage.

We ate lunch under a lone palm tree on the main drag. The janitor of the building came out laden with towels, water, and an offer of full use of the manufacturing firm while we were there.

Lots of cars and people gathered and stared. Tense vibrations, lots of cars full of drinking gangs of young men. Suddenly a family walked up and said, "Our boys told us what you are doing. We want to help out." They broke the ice. After that the crowd dispersed and lots of offerings and good wishes came our way.

The police: "You have any problems just give us a call. We'll be glad to help out." they said, looking down the street to where two blocks of solid bars, pool halls, and cheap hotels begin. "It's a pretty rough section ahead – lots of drunks and hecklers – so if you need help, just call. We'll be close by."

"We never expect trouble. We get back what we put out. If we keep cool and don't put out bad vibrations, then that's what we get back."

"Well all the same... (skeptical)... have a pleasant stay in Guadalupe. It's going to be getting dark soon – just about when you reach the bars. Call if you need help or anything." (worried).

"Thanks. We'll be fine." We bowed into the heart of the bars and night clubs. Groups of men and young toughs gathered around to comment and jeer. They were all wound up and waiting for something to pop. Then suddenly a "mom figure" strident waitress swung open the door of her cafe and yelled, "God bless, good luck to you, boys." The tension broke.

One by one the men turned and went home. We transferred the merit outside a boarded up x-rated movie theatre while the police quietly watched in their squad car parked on a side street. "All made from the mind alone."

---

**Heng Sure** • December, 1977
I learned it all by my self

I spent all those years as a student cheating myself, thinking I was smart to be lazy. Life was "getting away with it" and preparing to pass tests any way possible. No one taught me to behave that way, I learned it by my self. Playing was important and hiding my true heart. How selfish and in the end, how poor. What did I learn? The ways of people: how to manipulate them, how to cheat and how to hide.

Now I have found what I want to do. I want to join the assembly of pure Bodhisattvas. To succeed requires the opposite of everything I know to do.

There is no cheating, no charm, no hiding the heart. I have to start over and unlearn then learn the way human beings really behave and then study and practice the way Bodhisattvas live. It's a long road, coming from the muddy rut I began in. That's where it is.

What I want is to help people end their pain and I want to work to accomplish Shih Fu's vows. My heart really wants it to be this way.

-----

Heng Chau • December 12, 1977
Leaving earth like a three-stage rocket

"…small worlds, just these are large worlds; large worlds are nothing but small worlds."

Avatamsaka Sutra – Merit and Virtue of the
Initial Resolve for Bodhi Chapter

Guadalupe is a small world. Bowing down its main street at sunrise we watch it grow and come alive. Guadalupe is different from Los Angeles – the same kinds of thoughts made both the large and the small. Store owners unlock their doors and cash registers. A white side-burned well-dressed man carrying a newspaper under his arm opens the small brick bank on the corner. Flags go up and window awnings come down. People fill their bodies with caffeine and sugar and their cars with gas and hurry to work. No different, big and small worlds are equal.

It's the same all over the world: "small worlds are just large worlds and large worlds are nothing but small worlds." Coming and going, day after day, change without difference. And yet behind it all, behind all the large and small worlds, is something real and true that transcends the mundane. It's so hard to find or even remember in the mad shuffle that all of this "business" of running around isn't real, isn't truly who we are. There are other worlds to discover and always more beyond them without exhaustion.

We crossed into San Luis Obispo County, crossing over the Santa Maria river bridge which is 190 bows wide. The river is a road of sand because of the drought. Artichokes, celery, and broccoli are being harvested.

False thoughts slowly fade and settle like the valley winds and traffic at the close of day. No particular thoughts. Happy to be quiet. Wanting nothing. Going nowhere and coming from the same.

The more we bow, the more simple our lives get. Each day chips away at the fancy embroidery and phoniness. I have been thinking lately of the men I've known who are straight, simple, and unpretentious. My father, my grandfather, and my teacher are such men. They embody an unadorned and honest heart. They don't waste words or "put on a style."

> "When the Bodhisattva, Mahasattva contemplates his good roots in this way his mind of faith is purified."
>
> Avatamsaka Sutra
> Chapter 25

State: "Emptiness." Suddenly there was nothing to do. All my things I do every day turned flat and hollow. Bowing, sitting, eating, reading, writing, *tai ji*, etc. were as flat as dead balloons. A rush of fear and impatience welled up. "Now what!? What's going to happen if there is *nothing* to do? How come everything just went empty!?"

Everything inside and outside for as far and as deep as I could see was empty, without meaning. Everywhere I checked there was nothing to hook onto to chase away this big void that was staring me straight in the heart. My panic itself was empty – I couldn't even find security in fear!

I sat in Ch'an meditation. After a while I had a vision of my body leaving the earth like a three-stage rocket. As I shot out deeper into empty space, I could see my home and the earth get smaller and fade. Then my clothes fell off. Finally I remember seeing my body, an empty shell, floating below. Soon there was just empty space and an awareness.

I made some hot tea, took a walk under the stars, and returned to sit. Time passed quickly. I was chilled but not afraid or panicky. Just nothing at all and all ok.

---

**Heng Sure** • December, 1977
The urges, and cures

Making Practice a Full-time Job.

No vacations allowed day or night. These are moments of unconscious old habits when thoughts or impulses rise and dwell unchecked:

1) The urge to talk becomes a written comment.

2) The urge to eat a bit more; I nibble when full.

3) Tendency to hold the breath when moving from pose to pose.

4) Tendency to close off from people – to put on a mask or hide.

5) The urge to go into a pose or sketch when public speaking.

6) Tendency to smile and shine at acceptable people.

Cures:

1) Cultivate silence. If must write, make it very brief. Consider reader. Be sensitive, expedient. Use Proper Dharma.

2) Stop. No treats. Don't stuff. No desire.

3) Relax. Return light. Use method. Drop energy down.

4) Use method. Expand and drop energy down. Find your heart. Be patient. All beings are level and equal. Help out.

5) Find the actor-kid. Still him. Talk from heart.

6) The jewel is within. Use method. Return light. Close mouth. Open eyes. Expand. Drop the energy down. Allow silence. Be patient.

No strokes! No more returning to ignorance with five desires. Straighten up and get soft.

------

**Heng Chau** • December 13, 1977
Anybody can become nobody

All of the bowing and each "state" of mind we experience points to one thing: the emptiness of self. All of our problems and difficulties on the pilgrimage and in our lives we can trace back to our selfishness. Seeing through the illusory "me" is what it's all about.

Anybody can end suffering and be happy, deeply happy. Anybody can become nobody. One who is greatly enlightened is called a Buddha. The Buddha must be nobody. How could one be greatly enlightened and still have a self?

Praising someone else's cultivation or virtue is not recognizing your own Buddhanature. What is really being praised is the Way. "Hey! I can do it too! I can put down the false and be happy, too!" Evil and good both return to the doer. Praise the Buddha's name and you will be liberated.

> If there are living beings
> Who have not yet resolved on enlightenment
> Once they hear the Buddha's name
> They will certainly accomplish Bodhi

> Avatamsaka Sutra
> Chapter 24

---

**Heng Sure** • December 1977
Boy, you guys got guts

A young man stands silently as two monks bow towards him. His eyes are as large as tea cups. Finally he says, "You two are the ones going to San Francisco?"

Heng Chau: "One hundred and ten miles north of there to the City of Ten Thousand Buddhas."

"And where did you start?"

"L.A."

"Boy, you guys got guts."

Heng Sure (to himself): "Don't know about that but we do have a teacher, precepts, vows, faith, and real work to do. Does that spell guts?"

---

**Heng Chau** • December 14, 1977
We better take less or we'll never make it

Broccoli Test.

A rancher pulling a wagon train of fresh broccoli stopped and offered us more than we could eat in a month. I took a portion and explained we eat only vegetables and one meal a day. "So you better take more or you'll never make it," he said with a laugh.

I thought to myself, "No, we better take less or we'll never make it." This is hard to do: to take just a little and not be greedy for good things. It says in the Sutra in Forty-two Sections "To see something good and not want it is difficult." Make it to where? To no greed, anger, or ignorance. If we get to the City of Ten Thousand Buddhas and are still full of wanting good things then we haven't made it to the City. If we bow all the way to the City and still lose our tempers and do upside-down things we will have bowed 700 miles without advancing an inch. This is the "broccoli test." It is not measured in miles, it's measured in the mind.

Heng Sure • December, 1977
None other than Manjushri Bodhisattva himself

"Great Universal Buddha's Flower Adornment Sutra, Worthy Leader Chapter."

The Chinese title of this chapter could be translated several ways. The character for "worthy" can also mean quality, value, excellence. The word for "leader" can also mean head, foremost, superior. So other ways of rendering the title might be Top Value, Foremost Worthy, Chief Among the Worthy Ones, or Top Quality.

We all look for value in life, both in material things and in experiences. We often hear people say, "Did it cost a lot?"

"Yes, but it was worth it."

We all want the very best for ourselves: quality goods and high times. But how many of us look for quality and value in ourselves? Who do you know who "tries his best" all the time? How do we judge quality in people?

That's what this chapter of the Avatamsaka Sutra is all about. It explains how an ordinary person can transform into a person of superior quality. One can become a Bodhisattva., an enlightened being, a Worthy Leader by studying and practicing the principles in this text. Here is a book of Real Value, worth reading again and again.

> "At that time, Manjushri Bodhisattva, having just spoken the merit and virtue of pure practice which is neither turbid nor confused, wished to reveal the merit and virtue of the Bodhi-mind, so he composed verses and asked Worthy Leader Bodhisattva thusly."

Manjushri Bodhisattva possesses great wisdom and tremendous power. Where did he get it? He got it from the work he did in his mind; from the rules he practiced with his body, and from the words he chose not to say with his mouth. Once upon a time Manjushri Bodhisattva was a human being just like you and me. One day it occurred to him that everyone he met was trying to find lasting peace, freedom, and real happiness. He applied his intelligence and his effort to the search for a path to liberation because he was sincere and unselfish and diligent, before long he met the Buddhadharma and started to practice its true principles. It was then only a matter of time before Manjushri Bodhisattva transformed his greed, hatred, and stupidity into morality, concentration, and wisdom. Gradually his skill and his power grew into the awesome spiritual gung fu of a Son of the Dharma King. The present Manjushri Bodhisattva wields the vajra sword of prajna wisdom and rides a magnificent lion through empty space. If Manjushri Bodhisattva were to appear in America today, and some say that he is always here, he would probably look very ordinary on the outside. Perhaps he would drive a pick up camper and have a big, friendly dog or two with him. His gaze would be quite direct and his manner would be open, kind, and wise.

Bhikshu Heng Ju met a man just like this in 1974 after a ten-month bowing pilgrimage. Heng Ju didn't recognize the man at the time. He described the encounter in his book Three Steps, One Bow. The Venerable Abbot of Gold Mountain Monastery later told Bhikshu Heng Ju that he should have bowed to this man on the spot, because it was none other than Manjushri Bodhisattva himself, manifesting in the world to speak the Dharma for the monk.

In the Worthy Leader Chapter, the topic is merit and virtue, two qualities that all Buddhas have in perfect, full measure. The words merit and virtue don't mean much to most of us because we so rarely meet these qualities in the flesh. For instance, Buddhas can appear in a golden body, complete with 31 other distinguishing marks and 80 more subtle characteristics. This sets them apart as supermen. Buddhas have 42 teeth and their hands reach down below their knees. Buddhas have purple eyes and perfect, excellent features. When people look at a Buddha their hearts feel washed with happy light.

Where do merit and virtue come from? They come from "pure practice which is neither turbid nor confused." Pure practice means cultivating the Buddhadharma. There are 84,000 ways to practice and any one of them, when practiced purely, will result in merit and virtue and will ultimately help one become a Buddha.

The key is purity in practice. On the bowing pilgrimage we have learned that the difference between clarity and confusion depends on one thing: concentrating the mind.

As the Sixth Patriarch's verse says:

> The mind called wisdom,
> The Buddha is then concentration.
> Concentration and wisdom equal,
> The intellect is pure.

In other words, when you practice purifying your mind then you are practicing being a Buddha because all Buddhas come from the mind. The Venerable Abbot of Gold Mountain in his Ten Dharma Realms Are Not Beyond a Single Thought expressed this principle:

> If there are people who wish to understand
> All Buddhas of the three periods of time,
> They should contemplate the nature
>    of the Dharmarealm:
> The Tathagatas are made from mind alone.

Buddhism stresses the importance of the mind. All of the Buddha's dharmas instruct us how to purify it. Originally our minds were not impure but as we grew beyond our childhood's innocence we learned how to think. Just in this thinking we forgot our original purity. We grew turbid and confused.

Buddhists practice the Dharma in order to turn our thoughts around, to counter our bad habits and to return to our natural purity. On a cold November morning the turbidity of thought came home to me clearly. We were bowing along an isolated road through

Vandenberg AFB. Traffic was sparse, the sun was slowly warming the misted valleys. Everything was calm and tranquil. The peace and silence were conducive to concentrated bowing and I felt no afflictions and no obstacles. Then on the ridge to the left a noise broke out. The noise continued without cease. After two hours it crawled in under my skin and completely turned my solid concentration. The noise was a barking dog. He made it his job that morning to protect that square mile of wilderness from bowing monks. His bark was an irritating two pitched yelp followed by a "ruff, ruff" bass counterpoint. He said, "Whee ooroop! Ruff, ruff, ruff..." which translated must have meant, "Go away! Yeah, that's right..." It was a rough-edged bark, in the stillness of the mountain pass. The barking went on and on. Suddenly I realized that when my false thoughts rattle around in my head they are just as useless and just as raucous as the barking dog. Like a radio in a place of worship, the blare and mutter of thought turns the pure silence of the mind into noisy confusion. When we can turn off the radio, quiet the dog, and still the mad mind, all of nature returns to its original perfection and silence. That's pure practice. It is the "causal ground" for creating the Buddha's merit and virtue.

As we took a break to meditate and eat some fuel for more bowing, the poor sad dog was still barking, still unhappy over us. Try as I might, I could not incorporate his noise into the whole of the environment. It was my own dislike of the dog's bark that caused me irritation. It was not the dog's fault. As the Buddha told Ananda, "All feelings are suffering," and by being attached to my own feelings of like and dislike, I made myself uncomfortable that morning. Basically there was no problem – no difference in nature between a bark and silence, but my false-thinking discriminated the two into what Heng Sure likes and what he does not like and my displeasure arose at that point.

I realized at that point that dharmas have no self. Where in all of creation is there a single dharma that has my name on it? All dharmas come together because of temporary circumstances. Being loosely bound and constantly moving, things all fall apart before long. Everything returns to its original, unmoving substance.

Perhaps the dog didn't know that he was barking profound Buddhadharma. Perhaps he did. Truly "everything speaks the Dharma" and how clearly this trip reveals the truth that heaven and hell are both made from the mind alone.

Heng Chau informs me that this was a coyote, not a domestic dog. I was hearing "the sound of the wild."

Manjushri Bodhisattva wants to share "the wisdom that understands merit and virtue" so he asks Worthy Leader to explain the Bodhi-mind. This can be translated as "Bodhi-heart" or the "thought of enlightenment." It means that a living being has seen through the illusion of his mind, his body, and his self. We have resolved to get free of everything that binds us to suffering, no matter what. The Bodhi resolve, the thought for enlightenment, is the first turning point in the career of a Bodhisattva. In a following chapter, Dharma Wisdom Bodhisattva explains that a genuine thought for Bodhi makes one equal to the Buddha in wisdom, in merit, and in virtue, right then and there. This is not an event to be taken lightly.

---

**Heng Chau** • December 15, 1977
Dead ends – pleasant or unpleasant

Rain. The fine dust has turned to silty mud. Bow in rain gear at foot of Nipoma Mesa. A sure multiple collision and death was miraculously prevented somehow when a car spun out of control at high speed and headed for us. One could feel a force like a huge hand divert and steer the car away from us and Barry, a man standing with us who had come to make an offering.

Everyone was speechless, especially the two men in the car. Six cars were involved on a narrow slick road and not one injury or collision occurred. Really incredible!

A man named George made an offering and cryptically said, "I've seen your signs all over the place and although I don't understand completely I hope to someday be able to follow and walk the path you walk." He was an American Indian and he left as he came.

Reporters from Santa Maria and San Luis Obispo stopped for an interview.

Lots of fire. Hard to cool down even after meditation. "Who is this so nervous?" I ask myself. While sitting, vivid and detailed memories from childhood in Wisconsin came to me. I remembered scratch marks on the old Studebaker and nooks and crannies in the neighborhood I grew up in that I never would have thought possible to remember. Then smells from the past came as if they were right in the car with Heng Sure and me: smells of cooking food, the fruit cellar in the basement, smells of summer cut grass, etc. Then came sounds – I heard the sounds of doors closing (doors in the family home), the sounds of voices from upstairs, the furnace igniting. How can this be!? (They were all so real I wanted to uncross my legs and go outside and find them. But these are just states – distractions and games of the mind. Keep sitting, don't be moved!)

Even the feelings and attitudes I had when I was 4 and 5 years old returned. It would be real easy to attach and get lost in these states if I hadn't been warned in advance by a good and wise teacher. They are dead ends – pleasant or unpleasant – they are all illusions. "Don't attach to anything."

> Inside and outside, all worlds
> The Bodhisattva is attached to none of them…
> In all countries and in every direction,
> He relies on nothing and dwells nowhere.

> Avatamsaka Sutra
> Ten Transferences Chapter

Heng Sure • December, 1977
Red and yellow precept-pizza

> "For the sake of all Bodhisattvas I have spoken of the
> pure practices maintained by the Buddha in the past. Now
> here in this assembly will the Kind One explain the
> cultivation of victorious merit and virtue?"
>
> Avatamsaka

Pure practices are done with a pure mind. Cultivation of them
leads to the elimination of greed, hatred, and stupidity – the three
poisons. They encourage the natural growth of morality, concentration, and wisdom, known as the three non-outflow studies. You can
cultivate pure practices anywhere – while driving a car along a dusty,
country road, or roaming the miles of aisles in your supermarket, or
sitting quietly with a group of good spiritual friends and in each place
you can be using your very best efforts in cultivation. The work is in
the mind. It's called the mind-ground because the mind is like a field.
When it is weeded, planted, watered, and tended, up grow sprouts of
Bodhi-enlightenment heading for a big bountiful Buddha harvest.
When we let the mind go its own way, before long it is choked with
weeds and dust. Poison oak and trashy, berry vines will keep you off
the path. Hawks will rule it from the sky and coyotes will hunt it
from below. Your tranquil, fertile field becomes a battle zone of
suffering and fear. Before long someone will drive by and dump a
truck-load of garbage in your bushes. If the weather is hot, you're
ripe for a grass fire which can leave your mind-ground full of ashes.
In general which do most of us prefer; the productive, cultivated
garden or the snarled trashy field? We can have either one. The only
difference is the resolve to cultivate pure practices. The fruits of this
resolve are victorious merit and virtue. In our cultivation we have
vowed to achieve superior victory, ultimate victory in the biggest
battle of all: the struggle to subdue the Self, the Ego. Why it is such

a tough fight? Because it cannot be won by force. Superior victory is won only through patience and hard work. Strong faith, a sincere desire to do what's right and avoid what's wrong, helps us to superior victory.

We must constantly maintain precepts and vows. When practice is pure, tests arrive. Sometimes the tests are obvious, sometimes subtle.

An example of the obvious: We hold the Bodhisattva precepts. These are the ten heavy and 48 light rules for right living. All Buddhas and Bodhisattvas have held these rules — they are the substance, the material of spiritual progress. In a dark world of a hundred twisted roads, the precepts of Buddhism are a broad, level, and lighted highway to peace and happiness. What person in this day and age would believe that real freedom comes from following the rules and not from running wild like the wind? It's true, but most of us have to try it out for ourselves to believe it. After stumbling and falling down enough times on dark roads, after getting dirty and scared and tired, everyone sooner or later comes out of the long night into the bright dawn of the Dharma. Finally we all become Buddhas. Who says so? The Buddha himself, the world's smartest, kindest, most fearless man. Who doesn't want to be smart, strong, fearless, kind, and free? Precepts are the beginning.

Part of the precepts says you shouldn't eat the Five Pungent Plants: onions, garlic, leeks, shallots, or chives because they increase desire. The spiritual protectors who protect us when we hold the precepts will quit anyplace that stinks of garlic or onions. (How much the more so tobacco smoke!) However, most cuisines include these five. We have to be careful about accepting offerings of cooked food along the road to avoid inadvertently breaking the rules. The precept-protecting spirits can keep us out of lots of situations that would be hard to struggle through on our own. Sitting in a field at lunchtime outside Vandenberg Village, we saw a car pull up and a chubby, cheerful lady pop out. "What can I get you monks to eat? How about a pizza?" We both have been fond of pizza in the past but have cut it out of our diets after taking the precepts. No big loss, there's lots of clean food on this planet, and we would both rather go hungry than say goodbye to our protectors.

Heng Chau's response: "That's really a generous offer but we don't eat garlic or onions and most pizzas are loaded with them."

The lady: "That's no problem, I'll tell them to take out that stuff. Be right back."

Chau: "But the tomato sauce usually has garlic in it and if it does, we can't eat it."

"Okay, I understand. Be right back!" Zoom and off she went. We sat down to a cold lunch, no use cooking with a hot pizza coming. Both of us wordlessly agreed that her chances of finding a garlic-less pizza were pretty slim. Still, you never know. Ten minutes later she returned, "Here you are, good luck. Oh, and by the way, the man says there is a little bit of garlic in the sauce but not very much. Enjoy it!"

Test time. Open the big white box and smell the garlic fuming out of a red and yellow precept-pizza. Nice cheese, nice tomatoes and mushrooms... close the box and set it out on top of the car and go back to peanut butter and raisins. We were washing up after lunch pondering the reason why so few people believe that saying no to old bad habits helps go towards the good and avoid the bad. Suddenly a dark cloud of negative energy walked up – a crazy man in a yellow windbreaker, eyes gone pale and unfocused, talking nonsense to himself in a low and slow voice: "...in Marine Corps, '49... oh yes we know China and India ...uh, huh... you'll see how it hurts..." I could sense Heng Chau's defenses move into high gear; the Great Compassion Mantra clicked on automatically in my mind and recited clearly and evenly, as if by itself. The man stood ten feet away and tried to walk closer but couldn't. Something held him back. His hands searched through his pockets and he rocked back and forth, muttering and staring at us without eyes. This was a sick man! The tension broke after a few minutes and he turned and walked away as if blown by a clean wind. The air cleared. We felt as if the sun had come out again. What stopped him from approaching us? Only those same precept protectors that don't eat garlic or pungent plants. Five minutes later a pair of friendly women strolled by with an offering of fruit and nuts. After hearing about our diet they were pleased to relieve us of our garlic precept pizza. Keep the rules and it all works out the way you want it to. Break the rules and you're on your own.

The principles of patience and detachment are found everywhere in Buddhism. Patience is a paramita, a "crossing over," a "perfection," one of the six major jobs before a Bodhisattva. Detachment from all states of being is fundamental to a Bodhisattva's career.

> In the midst of mundane dharmas
> He attaches himself to none of them;
> He practices all victorious Dharmas
> Yet remains unattached to them.
>
> Avatamsaka

Patience and detachment from dharmas are prime testing areas in cultivation. The ego/self expresses its need for existence at these points. For example: Suppose you are a musical person and you take some small pride in your ability to carry a tune. As a cultivator of the Way, your musical output each day is considerable among the hours of daily ceremonies and recitations. It's a good situation for one with your talents. However, the cultivator who stands next to you in the assembly is not musically talented and in fact has a tin ear and always sings off key and out of time. This person is not aware of any distinction or failing in his style of music but to your finely tuned sensitivities, each wrong note is like a finger nail on a blackboard. What to do? If you are really cultivating to reduce your ego and to replace your discriminating mind with the level equality of the Buddha, you will restrain the impulse to create a problem where basically no problem exists. You will be grateful for the feedback on your attachment, and you will "return the light" and investigate what it is inside. Who is attached to hearing sounds a certain way?

That's how it appears when your mind is clear and concentration is good. Then the test appears. A Buddha-recitation session is going on and the sour-note singer is walking just behind you. Every off-key sound pierces your heart like needles. You recognize the state and you resolve not to be moved by it. Why? Because you are cultivating the Buddha's wisdom and the Buddha teaches that all dharmas are the same: they are equally illusory. As the Venerable Abbot explains it:

> "If you practice seeing all dharmas as being the same, then gradually, bit by bit they will be and you will be free of your attachment to the world. If you see certain dharmas as special then you will forever be attached to the turning wheel."

You are bearing the grating noise of your own discriminating mind night and day. The pressure is building inside. After five days of mindful patience, you find yourself at the tea-stand for a brief cup of tea. Up walk two young people who do not have your resolve. They are gossiping about the session and they mention how awful so-and-so's voice is and how hard it is to concentrate when they hear that off-key voice in the hall. Test time:

Do you let your patience go and join in the gossip? Do you bear it past the extreme and keep the rules? If you do, when you return to the hall you may notice things have changed. No longer do you make discriminations between good and bad sounds. That bit of sense input no longer robs your energy. You are now free to be happy and unmoved in the midst of any kind of noise. Because you were sincere in your desire to reduce your own ego's control of your mind, you got a response. Through hard work and patience, you earned that much liberation from the suffering of the mundane world.

If on the other hand, you were turned by the gossip and you fell back into your old habits, when you returned to the hall you would find the off-key voice that much harder to ignore. During the next hour you would pull the person aside and ask him to recite more softly. This would cause him to strike up false thinking and would obstruct his cultivation for the rest of the session. By doing this bad deed you would create offense-karma that could carry you down to the gates of hell. It's said:

> Better to move the water of a thousand rivers
> Than to disturb the mind of a cultivator of the Way.

All of this trouble was caused by your sad little ego, trying to assert itself over your own better judgement. And it succeeded.

> When the mind moves,
> one hundred matters come into being.
> When the mind is still,
> one hundred affairs do not exist.

The difference lies in the power of your resolve to get enlightened. This is what Manjushri Bodhisattva is asking Worthy Leader Bodhisattva to explain. When you really bring out your heart and say "This is what I want to do. I want to be just like the Buddha, no matter what it takes of me to get to his understanding and vision," then the merit and virtue begins to naturally gather around your every thought, word, and deed. If your resolve is not firm then you will always slip and slide, running back and forth, correcting mistakes, now looking out, now looking in, a foot in each of two boats going opposite ways on the river.

---

Heng Chau • December 16, 1977
Don't get angry, swo pe he

My heart feels clean and unbounded.

Thom Halls, photographer from the San Luis Obispo newspaper, came out to shoot some pictures. As he pulled up an angry motorcyclist started cursing him out for going too slow. The motorcyclist was tailgating him and nearly got wiped out when Thom pulled off the highway.

The biker came over then and yelled at us, "Why don't you find some place better to do... to do... uh to do whatever you're doing!?" He really wanted to fight. But he got no response so he peeled out in a cloud of dust and went back over to Thom and said, "As for you @#$%¢!" and tried to get him to fight. Thom didn't do anything. Afterwards, Thom was a little shaken. He had just driven out to film two peaceful monks. "At first I ignored that biker, but the longer I thought about him, the more I realized I let that guy walk all over me. That burns me up," he said. "How do you handle people like that?"

"Don't take on their vibrations; don't get angry. Some people speed and get angry because others go too slow. Some people go slow and get angry at those who speed. We try to keep to the middle – not too slow, not too fast, not angry, not overjoyed, just right."

"For sure. That's the way to do it. I could see keeping to the middle and not getting bothered, but it's hard."

"Yes, it is, but if someone doesn't do it, the bad vibrations spread until families are fighting with families and countries are fighting with countries..."

"Boy, that's how it works, isn't it? My wife has studied Buddhism and the little I know I really like. Buddhism seems more personal, I mean, it takes things *here*." (He puts his hand to his heart.)

Thom asked for some method to control his anger. "I try hard but then something comes up and I can't hold the lid, I lose my patience." I suggested the Master's "Patience Mantra," which goes:

> Patience,
> Patience,
> Gotta' have patience
> Don't get angry
> Swo pe he.

"Hey I like that!" exclaimed Thom with a smile. "Say it again and I'll write it down – it's got a good beat too."

> He is able to bear all manner of evil,
> And in his mind he is totally level and equal
>     toward all beings without any agitation;
> Just as the earth is able to support all things,
> He is able to purify the perfection of patience.
>
> Avatamsaka Sutra<br>Bright Dharma, Chapter 18

Barry, a local man who has taken it upon himself to be a Dharma protector while we bow through this area, brought out a special county map from the Surveyor's office and a report on local traffic conditions.

Man in a VW: "I don't know what religion you are but when I see you out here suffering... well, I'm for you and I hope you make it." Then he takes all of his money out of his pockets – he is very poor, wearing tattered clothes – and gives us 75¢ of the 85¢ he has. "I need a dime to make a phone call. I'm sorry it's so little." We shake and smile. No more words.

----

**Heng Sure** • December, 1977
Who? Is going to be my dinner?

At that time, Worthy Leader composed verses to answer and said, "Good indeed, O Kind One, now listen well. The merit and virtue cannot be measured. I will now explain a small portion of it as I am able. It is no more than a drop of water in the vast ocean. If a Bodhisattva first brings forth the initial resolution and vows to search for and to realize the enlightenment of the Buddha, the merit and virtue of his action is boundless. It is measureless and without peer. How much more is it thus if for aeons untold, one perfects the merit and virtue of cultivating the Ten Grounds and the Ten Perfections. In this case every Tathagata in all ten directions praises such a one in unison and without cessation. I will now explain just a part of it, like the track of a bird flying through space, like a bit of dust on the earth."

Why can't it be measured? Because real merit and virtue surpasses thought. Despite the best efforts of scientists, we don't know much about the world. Our little measuring systems give us courage and provide a place to stand against the terror of the void. In the end we don't know where we come from, how long we'll stay, and where we are going. Why do we cultivate? It is to find out the answers to these basic questions.

Worthy Leader Bodhisattva can explain a little bit of the whole. His wisdom penetrates shallow differences and understands the root sameness of all people who resolve to realize enlightenment. By hearing of one piece of the pie, we share the whole pie. For instance we are bowing this week past miles of broccoli. North, South, East, and West: carpets of blue-green broccoli. Each fourteen inch plant bears a big stalk. Each stalk holds twelve or more budheads. Each budhead produces hundreds of buds. In all the fields in the Santa Maria Valley, how many broccoli-buds are waiting harvest in the morning fog? A limitless and boundless quantity, uncountable. But looking at any broccoli bud, you can know its color. By tasting it you can know the flavor of all broccoli buds.

> "There are animals in odious and repugnant shapes which all come from their bad karma. They suffer an eternity of affliction."
>
> Avatamsaka Sutra

I popped out of the Plymouth at 4:00 am to get some fresh air. The local airlord, a huge white owl spoke his hua t'ou (meditation topic) "Who? Is going to be my dinner? Who whooo? is speaking Dharma?" Six feet away, moving fast, a frightened coyote dashed past the white-wall tire and away, barking his coyote dharma, a chilling lonely sound. I wanted to speak to them about the Dharmas in the Avatamsaka Sutra, to help them realize their part in things. No

way. I have a vow of silence. Who knows what affinities are set up as
we bow past these ranchlands? We say our mantras in valleys of fog,
under trees, next to roaring passenger trains. We bow on the edge of
America.

---

**Heng Sure** • December 17, 1977
The Buddha's giving is basic to all

Why would Buddhas praise any one? Aren't Buddhas at the top?
Don't they just receive praise? On the contrary, Buddhas know how
to give. They do it all the time. On the way to Buddhahood, each
Buddha perfects giving. Buddhas can give up what is hardest to give:

> "There is not a mote of dust in the world where a Buddha
> in the past has not given up his life for the sake of living
> beings,"

is a well-known fact in Buddhism. In the Flower Garland Sutra
whenever a Bodhisattva prepares to speak, he first gets a gift of light
and energy from the Buddha. In fact, the Buddha's giving is basic to
all that we know and cherish. It is said:

> "If Buddhas did not appear in the work, not a single
> living being would ever attain peace and happiness."

As soon as we begin cultivating the Way, we step into line to receive
a gift of the Buddha's boundless infinite light. How does this work?
The Buddhas want us to be Buddhas too, the sooner the better.
That's the Buddhas' job and their ways and means of bringing us
along are infinite. It's all part of the Dharma. By cultivating, practicing, investigating the Dharma, you keep the Buddhas in work, you
keep them in the world, and you win their praise. And there's
nothing that makes the world a better place for everyone like having
the Buddhas present among us. There is no better, happier place to
be than in a Buddhaland.

Turning point today. Light, flexible, forceless concentration on the method. The Sutra, the Flower Adornment Sutra, and the Flower Adornment Assembly and the Triple Jewel came closer today, allowing me to stand among the Bodhisattva-assembly infinite, infinite clouds of reverent beings listening to the Dharma in all directions, all dimensions. Simple unity. Harmony. Clean and silent worship. The state passed quickly – just another false thought, but briefly – how wonderful!

New unity of bowing, Ch'an sitting, 42 Hands and Eyes, eating, and working times. All based on the wisdom sword, the "who" and returning the light to the center: conscious of holding the head up and standing straight, dropping the energy to the middle. Eating less! Less fuel means slightly cold and hungry at night. Small discomfort compared to clarity and calm during the day. States and non-states pass like the weather. Thoughts like highway traffic – now still and clear, now roaring. Hard work and concentration needed here!

---

**Heng Chau** • December 17, 1977
In the pursuit of happiness, we miss it

Where is happiness? Happiness is nowhere. Happiness is our own original natural resource. It doesn't come or go; it can't be pursued or bought. Happiness appears within when the mind is pure and quiet.

> When the mind is pure,
>     the moon appears in the water.

This kind of happiness is like returning home after a long, hard journey. It never leaves us, we just forget it's there and turn our backs on it in pursuit of happiness. But as it says in the Avatamsaka Sutra,

> Of all the happiness in the world,
>     there is none which is not suffering.

This is the trick: it is just in the pursuing of happiness that we miss it. Thinking peace and security are in things outside, we leave the true and grasp the false. With each move we go further away from it and get all stuck and glued down with attachments. It's like the clown with glue on his hands. Everything he touches, he sticks to. Every move brings more problems. Pursuing happiness is like that. When all seeking and pursuing stops, happiness naturally appears.

Suffering has become bliss; what was bliss is now suffering. Someone offered us a small pastry cake – guaranteed bliss with every bite. We ate half of it. It was just like being drunk. Our minds filled with desire-thoughts and our bodies turned dull and lazy. Bliss turned to suffering.

After bowing out in the wind, rain, and mud we found our spirits again. The longer we bowed and the harder it rained, the happier we became. Why?

"Bitter practice, sweet mind."

What was once suffering is now bliss.

Sex is fear of death. Fear of death is being afraid of losing self. Fear of losing self is just confusion about dharmas (things). It's hard to put down sex. That's why we die.

Ending confusion is easier than ending sexual desire. In the end they are identical. Studying the Buddhadharma clears things up. It makes you so happy and delighted that you forget about sex and then suddenly you become enlightened. No more confusion. No more fear.

**Heng Sure**
Tend their Bodhi-fruit orchards

As water has just one flavor
But is different according to the vessel that contains it,
So it is with the Buddha's field of blessings,
The differences are in the minds of living beings.

Avatamsaka Sutra
The Bodhisattva Inquiries Chapter

On our bowing pilgrimage, the people we meet are looking more and more like family, like kinfolk in one big Dharma-family. What is it in two monks making ritual movements on a country road that causes some people to honk their car horns? What do others see that makes them instantly get angry? Why do some people stop their busy worlds, park their cars, and walk over to find out about these two bowing men? Every day strangers appear who spontaneously support the trip with bags of vegetarian food, with money offerings, with kind words and offers to help? What do these people share in common? I believe it is the core of our work to simply be there on the public road doing Dharma work as sincerely as we can. We are celebrating and exercising our inner Buddha-seed. We bow and pray, making efforts to give it what it needs to bloom and grow a Buddha-fruit. There's something magical in it: other people look at us and feel their own Buddha-seeds stirring. If conditions favor its growth, the response feels positive and we hear "bless you," "good luck," "right on, brothers." If conditions do not permit the expansion of the seed, those people with heavy karmic obstacles feel the turning of their seed and resent being reminded of their burden. We hear "Go home!" "Freaks!" and harsher words from these people.

The Buddha sees all beings as Buddhas. Some, potential; some, actualized. Some, Buddhas of the past returned now to help others tend their Bodhi-fruit orchards. The Venerable Abbot encourages every one of us to uncover our Buddha-capacity. He speaks and our glowing wisdom seeds spark and hum into life no matter what size they are to begin with.

This process in small measure is what goes on when people stop to talk to us on Three Steps, One Bow. The people who make offerings look like family: nearly all wear the same look – a look of happiness with their humming, inner Buddha. When they give to the Triple Jewel, they nurture their own Triple Jewel within. There is real magic here. We don't yet understand but it feels clean and bright.

> "It is also like a skillful magician who can please the crowd. The Buddha's field of blessing works this way in that it causes living beings to be delighted."
>
> Avatamsaka Sutra
> Bodhisattva Inquiries Chapter

---

**Heng Chau** • December 18, 1977
We try to provide an alternative

The rain stopped. Everything is wet, and happy, and celebrating.

> Snow and rain, like the Way,
> Falls on all the same.
> Rain and snow, no home, no name,
> The Sage treats all the same.

Norman and Arleta Hammond and their two children came out with a meal offering. Norman is a rescue fireman and teacher at a local college. Although they didn't know much about Buddhism, they felt a strong affinity with what we were doing. Although they could be very successful and live in affluence, they consciously choose not to. Instead they try to find what's pure and natural – from food to their basic attitude and values. "We don't want our kids to grow up wanting things and full of endless greed. We try to provide an alternative to the false values that they see on T.V."

To do it, they back pack together and try to stay clear of the cities. "They're plastic and too fast," said one of the kids. Their style of hiking is to go slowly and just be quiet, taking time every few steps to watch around them. "Boy, it's a lot like your Three Steps One Bow," said Norman. "I've often wanted to explore a canyon, or just sit at one lake for a week." We noted that Buddhists explore inside and sit quietly (dhyana meditation) and contemplate the "mind ground." "Yeah, that's it!" exclaimed Norman. "It's on the inside, really."

Norman later went on to describe a dream he has and hopes to fulfill some day: "I'd like to go out on a long walk and never come back – you know, just put it all down and keep going. Someone said that was a good definition of monks and nuns (left-home people). Just when I come close to connecting through, kind of losing myself and merging with something, it's time to come back and return to work and all."

> He does not seek what living beings can speak of.
> These are all conditioned, false, empty affairs…
> He gives rise to the supreme thought for enlightenment.
>
> Avatamsaka Sutra
> The Transferences Chapter

The kids really liked the chanted prayers before and after lunch. The Hammonds are typical of a lot of bright, young families who come to offer help and check out the Buddhadharma. They have lots of energy, compassion, and good roots. They are a special breed of people who aren't afraid to question and turn around from false values and empty highs. They want the truth, and they want to benefit the world. Politics and traditional religions have left them cold. They are starting to look within. Yoga, *tai ji*, meditation, natural foods, and alternative life-styles are just scratching the surface of this vast potential. The back-to-nature impulse will lead eventually back to the original self-nature and "supreme enlightenment." It's just a question of time and exploring. "Some day," says Norman, "Some day soon."

All beings have the Buddha nature;
all will become Buddhas.

said the Buddha. Some day soon...

Everything that happens to you
comes from what you do.

Avatamsaka Sutra

A man runs over to us seeking our blessing, "We don't do that. You bless yourself, it's in your own heart."

"Pray for me then?"

"We pray for all beings everywhere, equally. We pray for all like they are our family. But, you've got to go towards the good. *That's* what matters; it's what you do."

"Not even the sign of the cross of something?" he pleaded.

---

## Heng Sure
Happiness is the highest of achievements

Signs posted in our 1956 Plymouth Vihara:

Save Worlds!                    Keep Bowing
Save Worlds!

Working hard is true
Be without fear or joy          Constantly
Don't attach to anything        Real
Then you can reach a            Constantly
state of real accomplishment    Reverent

Lunch is work
No vacation
Concentrate!

"Real affluence is not needing anything."

Gary Snyder

When we really concentrate (an act of will – a pure desire) we fall off the center of the world. We become no more than just a part of it like the road, the flowers, and the sky. No more feeding the self with "the best the world has to offer." Why waste energy chasing such foolish fine discriminations while standing in a blazing house? In our search for the way out of the house we have given up our attachment to fine material things. We eat roadside weeds, coarse grains, and cold water, things no one fights for. We walk in the gutter wearing patched robes while the world flies past. Bearded chins, scruffy heads, an unused, cracked mirror. We prefer silence.

"The force of words is soon lost. Far better to keep what is in the heart."

Tao Te Ching

We have music: diesels, engines, tires, hawks, and crickets.
We have friends: mountains, streams, sun, and moon.
We have a pillow: the palm of the hand.
We have food: fields full of healthful weeds.
We have drink: water falls from the sky.
We have clothing: patched with clean gutter rags.
We have entertainment: we sing praises of the Tripe Jewel
(in our ceremonies day and night.)
We have joy: sitting still.
We have a teacher:
"The stupidest one on earth. Lower than a ghost."
We have maps: in eighty-one garlands of flowers.
We are satisfied: We are wealthy beyond measure.

"When selfish desire is ended forever,
This is true riches and honor.
When false thoughts no longer arise,
This is the true field of blessings."

"They rest peacefully in empty space
Within this ocean of worlds
The variety of Buddhalands is
Difficult to conceive
Each and every one is free and at ease."

To the West, a silent mirror of ocean. To the South, the brooding Mesa. To the East, the Santa Lucia range, now green after the drought-breaking rain. To the North, the skinny coast road, cliffs and waves. Little towns; Oceana, Grover City, Pismo Beach, Shell Beach: wide spots where people cluster to soothe that lonely ache of too much emptiness, too much silence.

Holi-day Holy day. Each day is a holy day when you slow down and look within. The lesson we relearned each year and then forgot each year: Happiness is the highest of achievements, not an easy or a simple state to maintain. No wonder it is the foremost practice of a Bodhisattva's ten practices. You can't hold it, buy it, drive it, or eat it. The more of it you drink or smoke, the less of it you have.

Happiness is a balance between no expectations and no regrets. When you need nothing, this is true freedom. What is more valuable than fullness in the heart, peace and purity of mind? The big basic truth of Buddhism is to understand that when you look outside of your own mind/heart (*syin* 心) for what you need, you're on the road to more pain. The harder you look outside, the more false everything becomes. Everyone loves what is true and rejects the false and when we find the truth, something inside changes for good. What was once valuable, no longer seems so. What we took for granted now holds mystery and infinite wonder.

Heng Chau • December 20, 1977
The Bodhisattva should be like the sun

" All dharmas have no true reality, all dharmas are
empty...

> Avatamsaka Sutra
> Chapter Fifteen

Dick and Bill from Oceana found us camped on a side road in a
grove of trees and offered us a place to stay and to take care of our
needs. "Stay at our place on the beach. There's Gene, a big Indian
with long, black hair and a beard, and Pete, he's got long blonde hair
and a parrot on his shoulder," said Rick.

"We're not the peak of spiritual attainment, but we're an okay
group," added Bill with a grin, "You see lots of chopped-up dead
bodies show up on the Mesa because they're easy to hide in all these
trees, but there's a totally different element on the beach. No worries
there."

Why did Dick and Bill come out? Said Bill, "I gave up my social
life for three years and tried to do for the world what you're doing,
only through politics. I kinda' felt like a priest. Okay, you know? I
thought all that politics needed was some new blood, but all I got
was drained and nothin' changed.

"Besides, I've done some traveling and wandering and I know
what it's like to walk cold into a strange town and not know anybody
or where to go for help."

"That's what it's all about, isn't it?" I said. "One substance with
all beings."

"Yes," said Rick smiling.

"Yes," adds Bill with a grin, "That's all that counts."

"When the Bodhisattva sees this (suffering of living beings) he gives rise to a mind of great compassion and a mind of great benefit. And, he wishes that all beings obtain liberation."

Avatamsaka Sutra<br>Ten Transferences Chapter

\* \* \*

Meditation feels like being a caged tiger floating in empty space.

\* \* \*

Barry, the man who has taken upon himself to watch over us, stopped with some tea and a map.

"People got lots of different opinions about you guys."

"Oh?"

"Yes. Some think it's a gimmick, a come-on. Some think you should be emptying bed pans in old folks homes if you really want to do some good. Some think you're just plain stupid. One guy wants to teach you mortification of the body with a tire iron. Some say you stop for steak and cocktails at the end of the day," related Barry.

"That's interesting."

"The way I figure it is that most of the problems in the world come from people trying to do big things, be heroes. All the wars and killing come from this. What I try to do is not do any harm in my own small way. Nothin' big, you know? I just try not to harm anyone in my own life and figure this is at least a little start."

"If you can do no harm, that in itself is great good."

"I think so," said Barry, checking out a storm rolling in from the ocean. "So, anyway, what you guys are doing may not count two farts in a hurricane, but it's not doing any harm. So, who knows? Well, you all take care. See you."

Barry's point has principle: when you know it's right, no matter what others say, you should do it.

It's just like the sun,
Which appears in the world,
But does not hide or fail to appear,
Because there are blind people who fail to see it.

Avatamsaka Sutra<br>Chapter Twenty-five

The Bodhisattva should be like the sun.

Norman, the fireman from Aroyo Grande, stopped again to ask about the Avatamsaka Sutra and to say he was really moved by the idea of transferring the merit and virtue of one's work to all beings. He copied down the repentance verse from the end of the Avatamsaka, because he felt it was "right on."

"Of all bad karma which I have done, based on beginningless greed, hatred and stupidity, committed with body, mouth, and mind, I now repent and reform."

"I can just recite this on my own, right?"

"The more the better, right."

---

### Heng Sure
Buddhas yield to others in the supermarket checkout line

Happiness is surely the highest state. Buddhas are happy all the time. Buddhas do the work of making others happy. So it's no wonder you never see an unhappy Buddha. Who wouldn't enjoy that job? You never see an angry Buddha, for that matter, or a Buddha who's got the blues. Buddhas never feel depressed or uptight, no matter what situation occurs.

Buddhas don't cheat, and they don't smoke or gossip. They don't insist on their rights when driving; they yield to others in the supermarket checkout line.

Is it good to be a Buddha? You needn't ask others to find out. You can find out for yourself in this life, while you wear this very body that you woke up with this morning. Why wait? How to begin your new life as a Buddha? Be happy all the time. Don't be angry or depressed, don't smoke or gossip, don't do anything that your heart knows is wrong. Do everything that your heart knows is right. Cultivate the Dharma and purify your mind. What else is there to it? All Buddhas, to become Buddhas, did just those things. So get going! As the Venerable Abbot says, "Advance like a wild tiger charging downhill, chewing all karmic obstacles to death." And while you go, don't forget to be happy. It's the highest good. Who has ever seen a frowning Buddha, anyway?

> "Those beings who see him, hear him, listen to him, receive him, and make offerings to him – all such beings will be caused to get peace and happiness."

Avatamsaka Sutra
Worthy Leader Chapter

------

**Heng Chau** • December 21, 1977
But for some reason, we've been blessed here

The County Sheriff stopped, "What you are doing is really commendable," he said, and advised us against continuing on Highway 1 ahead. Heavy rains are expected, and it's already been raining for a week. The roads are slick and dangerous. The shoulders are oozing mud and ankle-deep puddles. Where to bow?

Barry stopped again. "You are between the West Coast's biggest ICBM strike-force that could destroy the rest of the world and an unsafe nuclear power plant that's built on an earthquake fault-line. Best to take one step at a time, huh? The winds are expected to get up to 100 m.p.h."

Last night we read from the Avatamsaka:

> When the Bodhisattva takes on
>     all this grievous suffering,
> His vigor increases.

He does not cast if off, he does not hide (from it).
He is not scared or startled.
He does not retreat, he is not frightened.
He has no fatigue.

Avatamsaka Sutra<br>Ten Transferences Chapter

It helped somehow – the verses gave us that little extra courage to chin up and keep going.

The rain stopped while we were bowing. In the middle of a black-clouded sky was a clear circle of blue. All afternoon it followed us overhead. As we did our last bows and transferred the merit, two red clouds appeared momentarily in the blue patch, and then it closed completely.

By the time we reached the car, it was pouring rain and blowing cold winds.

Sitting in meditation by oil lamp. The rain and wind continued through the night. It's too dark to tell where we were camped. It doesn't really matter, anyway – wherever we are inside is all that we need to know.

Barry stopped by again. Storms and winds swept across California – winds up to 100 m.p.h. destroyed a couple towns and turned over trailer homes and diesel trucks near here. A big fire just a few miles south of us swept across Vandenberg AFB, killing the Base Commander and others. "But for some reason, we've been blessed here (the Mesa)," said Barry. "Nothin' much happened at all. Kinda' strange, huh?"

"Do you eat clams?" he asked.

"No – nothing that lives."

"Vegetables live, they just don't scream when you kill them – ha, ha, hee, hee," chuckled Barry. "Well, if you need anything, just call."

As he started to get into his truck, he turned, "Oh, by the way, it's a good thing you have that cop keeping an eye on you."

"Oh?"

"Yeah! There's some pretty bad characters on this Mesa. These woods have turned up a lot of bodies."

We could spend a lot of time worrying about what lies ahead and the mistakes we left behind. This is false thinking and cripples you to the present. So it's said:

> When one attends to the here and now,
>     the false returns to the true.

---

**Heng Sure**
A mistake, a fault of vision

"I" is a Lie.

We seek the true heart within. There is no "me" at the center of the world. We have dropped out of the race for the first place. All the time we spent looking out for ourselves, trying to find the real – all the time, the real was waiting to be found right inside the one who was looking out. The "I" who used to fight for the spotlight at center stage is a lie, a phony. "I" is a mistake, a fault of vision, a bad habit.

No more chasing the best of everything. What comes is what's best. Why look at the scenery? What is it but more pictures of empty, self-seeking self?

> Outside is in.
> Inside stays home.
> Watch the gate closely.
> Protect your own.
> No one will miss you.
> No one will care.
> Lost and forgotten,
> Already there.

**Heng Chau** • December 23
Sitting on top of the car

Storm continues and so does "donut hole" clearing overhead. Black clouds for miles, and in the middle a patch of blue. We are reaching the end of the Mesa and can feel a strange kind of energy building.

Some laypeople from Gold Mt. (the Bachs and their baby) stopped with a picture of Guan Yin Bodhisattva and a copy of the Shurangama Sutra. Just yesterday we had been thinking about those two items, and today in the middle of a rainstorm they appear.

At the foot of the Mesa our water jugs blew off the roof of the car and were crushed by a passing truck. This hill coming off the Mesa is steep and fast with no shoulder. It's going to be tricky even walking down it. The alternate road is impassable and was ruled out by the CHP. Neither of us likes the "feel" of this road, but we have no choice but to bow it tomorrow. Christmas traffic is heavy and if it rains – okay, well.

> When one attends to the here and now,
>     the false returns to the true.

The reason the water jugs were run over was because I was thinking about tomorrow's bowing route and drove off with them sitting on top of the car.

**Heng Chau** • December 24, 1977
He was too nice for that

Bowing at the bottom of the hill coming off the Mesa. A car slides out of control and heads straight for us. Suddenly, as if an invisible broom swept it off the road, the car veers away and tail-ends into a deep muddy cauliflower field. The man gets out and sinks up to his knees in oozing, thick mud. We try to help push him out, but the car just keeps sinking deeper. Then the man gets really angry at us. Bad vibes.

A woman drives up with an offering. Quite a scene: happy and full of goodness this woman handing us some home-made food and just across the road the man in the mud cursing and shaking his fists at us.

We decide to move and bow in place half mile up the road.

The new picture of Guan Yin has a kind of magic about it. We could feel a change since its arrival yesterday. The atmosphere in the car is cleaner and enriched, and so are our minds. A new and powerful sense of purpose and mindfulness has been added to our work.

While bowing, I remember back to when I was twelve or thirteen. I remembered wanting to "go it alone" and figure things out until there wasn't anything left to figure. But a fear of facing the ultimate truth of no self came up. I knew the girl-boy business was fed by fear and insecurity – not wanting to give up the mother figure. But choices were few then, or were they?

The Hammonds stopped with a meal offering. Why is Buddhism appealing? Because it doesn't just go along with things in the world. It goes a little deeper and hits a place we all remember and want to explore.

Arleta: "It's like when I was a kid. My father had a gas station. He never got rich. He was too nice for that. He had a lot of friends and a lot of unpaid accounts. We were happy. We had little, but we had much."

Norman: "I'm happy when living close to nature. There's something spiritual at root in all of us, as opposed to having nothing in a sea of nothing."

"He vows that all beings leave behind all worldliness and dwell in all-wisdom... That they dwell in the ultimate path and in places of peace and happiness."

Avatamsaka Sutra
Ten Transferences Chapter

The "place of peace and happiness" we all seek is what the Hammonds are talking about and looking for. It's Christmas Eve. But lots of folks are still looking for the "ultimate path." The mind doesn't rest until it's home.

Christmas Eve: "To Help You on Your Way."

A retired minister: "I served in the pastorate for over forty years... What if you don't find the peace you seek when you are done?" he asked.

"There's no end or beginning. We find it everyday in a sincere single mind – in the right here and now."

"Hmmm. Well, yes, I guess that's right, but I would never find it in the rain and mud," he said laughing.

"Even more so in the rain we find it. The harder the better."

A big powerful man in a cowboy work clothes: "You guys have a merry Christmas and thanks for prayin' for us." He made an offering and left with a big smile.

A family with four teen-age children: "We've been looking for you for two days. We think what you're doing is marvelous, really for the good."

A bag of food appeared on the car with a note: "To help you on your way."

A big blue Cadillac stopped and a gentle, well-dressed man in his early fifties came over and quietly watched us bow. Suddenly he became very happy and excited. He ran over to me extending his hands to shake. He gestured that he was deaf and dumb. I hesitated, showing him I was covered with mud and rain. A big smile came up right from his heart and spread all over his face. "Oh, what's a little mud at a time like this," he seemed to say. So we shook – muddy monk and he in a blue suit with a flower in his label.

He knew Heng Sure didn't talk and I think felt an affinity that went beyond words. He came right up to my face like a little child and extended his hand. There wasn't the slightest trace of fear or phoniness about him. As we shook, he pointed with his other hand in the direction we were bowing (City of Ten Thousand Buddhas) as if to say, "I'm with you all the way, keep going."

I felt humbled and deeply happy that anyone could be so real and open without a second thought. He made an offering and then gave a look that went straight to the real and true place inside of me. When he knew we had touched in that place, he smiled as if to say, "Wonderful!" And then he left. Not a word was spoken.

"The Buddhadharma is subtle, wonderful and difficult to measure. All words and phrases cannot come up to it."

Avatamsaka Sutra

Mesa Vision:

Who are we? In the morning I have been waking up and feeling I am not alone. I am in the midst of a new and bright understanding, but as I reach for it or try to look at it closely – Poof! – it's gone. Was it real or just a dream? Why did it feel so liberating and peaceful? Where did it go?

This morning it stayed awhile and I got to see it and feel it. A big relaxing deep smile almost a laugh filled me. I saw: All of us and all the things in the universe are made up of billions upon billions of countless infinitesimal particles, each with a consciousness and awareness of all things in the past, present, and future without beginning or end. These little particles, identical in size, are so small they could never be seen by the human eye. And because they are so small, they are actually one substance that fills up the universe and pervades throughout all directions of space. Everything that ever was, is, or will be is already known and contained with each and all of these tiny dust-motes.

There really is no me or Heng Sure, no car or blankets, no wind, trees, town, or ocean. All is one and the same within an infinite variety and differentiation. These little atoms contain all without containing anything. Everything is made up of these equal and omniscient little "things," without anything being made or existing whatsoever. No words could fully describe or capture this vision.

> "My body further manifests bodies as many as dust motes in a Buddhaland. Each of which simultaneously bows to Buddhas as many as dust motes in a Buddhaland. In each dust mote are Buddhas as many as dust motes. Everyone of which dwells in an assembly of Bodhisattvas. Inexhaustibly throughout the Dharmarealm in every mote of dust it is this way. I deeply believe they are all filled with Buddhas."
>
> Avatamsaka Sutra
> Chapter Forty

I had the feeling of stumbling into a secret world that is always right here but we can't see it even while immersed in it. I knew it was my boxed-in rational mind with all its attachments and discriminations that blinded me to the wonderful mystery of this always-so truth. It was like a rare animal of the forest that takes flight before anyone gets close enough to even know of its existence. Maybe only the sun and moon and fog ever get to see it.

I feel full of mistakes yet happy beyond words. I am sitting with a good Dharma friend reading the Flower Garland Sutra under a new Guan Yin picture in our four-wheel Bodhimanda. We are camped on the edge of the Mesa in a dripping eucalyptus grove outside Oceana, California. It's Christmas Eve and a full moon. A lonely dog howls and in the little town below a scratchy record keeps playing "O, Come All Ye Faithful."

**Heng Sure** • December 25, 1977
The old Christmas stocking

Santa Claus Bodhisattva Cultivates the Perfection of Giving.

In 1975 I took a big step and moved into the monastery. I held a job, working as a file clerk and joined the Gold Mountain's assembly's activities the rest of the day. My resolve was firm but my habits hadn't yet fully made the transition to a Buddhist way of life.

Christmas came and with it, the annual winter Amitabha meditation session which celebrates the birth of the Buddha of limitless light. Buddhist holidays are wonderful occasions, full of light and peace, but this was to be my first non-Christmas in twenty-four years. In my head I was prepared to miss the music, the trimmings and the spirit of the Noel season. I felt pretty lonely being new in the monastery. Even though my neighboring laymen down the hall were an open and supportive group and the monks were kind and patient, I saw the world through narrow eyes. I was uptight and full of doubts, but determined to carry my decision out. There was truth in Buddhism and I was going to endure this rough time of emotion and change at the beginning and make my new home in the Dharma.

The session began on December 23rd and the Buddhahall was filled night and day with the happy sound of voices praising wisdom and compassion. Adults' voices, children's voices, men and women's voices chanting the holy name Ami To Fwo, Namo Ami To Fwo. Each evening when the work was done we gave the merit of our work to all beings everywhere. Turning over the fruits of the work is true Buddhist giving. On Christmas Eve during a break in the ceremonies I was unpacking a trunk of clothes and found my old Christmas stocking. I had hung it on the mantelpiece every Christmas since I was five. It was red velvet with white trim and decorated with Christmas trees and wreaths made of green felt. I couldn't resist the urge to hang it on my door. It was Christmas Eve and this was a Buddhist Monastery. I thought, "Here's the best way to break my old attachment to this stocking. You can't just drop it in the garbage. Hang it up. When the other laymen see it they'll take it down – they might even rip it up and throw it away for you. It's hard to part with it that way, but it's now or never." The Transference of Merit was done for the evening and I prepared for hoots of laughter as I tacked the old stocking onto the door of my room, on the monastery's third floor. I lay awake feeling the pain of doubt: "Would I be ostracized from the new group? Shouldn't I just quietly store the thing? Why obstruct everyone else with your attachments? You're just going to cause more false thoughts this way."

Sleep took me and visions of sugar plums filled my head, each plum gracefully walking and chanting Namo Ami To Fo.

Four A.M. Time for morning recitation. Fearing the worst: would my stocking cover the hallway torn to tiny bits? I opened the door and what to my wondering eyes should appear but the red velvet sock stuffed full of gifts. There were little Buddha images, tiny Sutra editions, new rolls of 35mm film, a tin of tiger balm, packs of hot chocolate, a toothbrush, a pocket-sized mantra and a string of recitation beads. Someone had put effort into filling my Christmas stocking with wonderful treasures. I was stunned speechless. Far from ridiculing me, these men that I lived with had accepted me, attachment to Christmas and all. I was the one with narrow eyes and a narrow heart. My neighbors knew how to give. They welcome me without conditions. I felt humbled, subdued. My defenses and fears were so useless! Buddhism is big and open and inclusive. My views were tight and stingy and dark. As the session began on Christmas day the words Na Mo A Mi To Fo filled my heart with light and I could not hold back the tears. It was still dark in the Buddhahall and no one could see my streaming eyes, but I had no reason to hide my heart. Kuo Kuei, Kuo Fa, Dharma Master Kuan and the others cracked open my fearful state. Their compassion and kindness to this new disciple of the Buddha taught me more about the true spirit of Buddhist giving in one night than my four years of studying academic Buddhism in the university had done. How far I had to go, how much to learn! And how good it feels to open the heart to the Buddha. Na Mo A Mi To Fo.

On San Bu Yi Bai everyday is like Christmas. We give our work to everyone when we transfer merit and offerings to the Triple Jewel coming from people in all walks of life. When our work gets sincere, we will disappear: offerings will pass right through two transparent monks and plant good roots in the field of blessings. Our work will generate itself without defilement or error and everyone will join together in the Flower Garland Ocean-Wide Assembly of Buddhas and Bodhisattvas.

---

**Heng Chau** • December 26, 1977
Anything's possible if you put your mind to it

Sutra is a Sanskrit word which means "a tally." A sutra tells it like it really is. It matches up with the true principles of all Buddhas above and tallies with the hearts of people below. Squeeze the sutras with a skeptical mind and test them against your deepest experiences and you won't find them wanting or phony anyplace. Sutras are permanent and unchanging. They were true in the past, are true in the present, and will be true in the future.

No one actually knows how old the Avatamsaka Sutra is. Properly speaking it has no age, no beginning or end. The principles of a sutra are within the minds of living beings. And each of us in our lives naturally probes and tests by trial and error until we get back to the root and tally with the source. So Heng Sure and I don't mind being asked a lot of questions by children. It's natural.

Yesterday a little boy, Jackie, said, "Anything's possible if you put your mind to it." Although Jackie had never read a sutra or even "seen anything like *this* before," as he said from his bike, still he spoke true principle. His observation was a clear statement about Buddhism and the bowing pilgrimage. If one can concentrate and bring the mad mind to a stop, there is no place you won't penetrate and nothing you can't accomplish.

"Sure!" concluded Jackie. "It's all in your mind." Jackie was speaking Dharma. The Sutra was in his heart. Buddhas are made from people's pure minds.

> "If one wishes to know all Buddhas of the past, the present, and future, contemplate the nature of the Dharma-realm — Everything is made from our minds."
>
> Avatamsaka

---

**Heng Chau** • December 27, 1977
They were exactly what we needed!

A vicious guard dog charged us as we bowed past a farmhouse. We kept bowing and before long the dog just lay down and quietly watched us pass by.

Heavy rains continue. Creeks are flowing and gurgling. The hills and fields have come back to life in a burst of green.

We needed a special kind of rubber gloves to bow in the rain. The water pours down our sleeves. All our clothes are soaked. Since we vowed to camp outside, it's important to keep as dry as possible. We can't hop into a hot shower and throw our clothes in the dryer at night. We debated buying some gloves but decided to bow instead and let things happen naturally. It doesn't feel right to go into a store and buy things for ourselves.

As we bowed past a liquor store, the owner came out and handed us two pairs of long-sleeved yellow rubber gloves. They were exactly what we needed!

"Hope they help. Bless you!" he said.

Clear Circle of Sky.

When we stop to eat and sleep it pours rain. When we go out to bow the rain lets up. For the last three days there's been a hole of blue sky above us in the midst of black rain clouds. At the end of today's bowing a storm hit – one of the heaviest I've ever seen. Within minutes the streets turned into rivers, flooding stores and houses. The road is starting to cave in and erode from underneath.

We made it to an empty Laundromat and did *tai ji* between the washing machines while our clothes dried. "It's funny," I thought as I looked out at the flooded streets. "The world looks so solid and permanent, but in a snap of a finger it can all melt and float away right before your eyes." So it says:

> All dharmas have no dwelling.
> No fixed location can be obtained.

> Avatamsaka Sutra – Verses in Praise on
> the Peak of Mount Sumeru Chapter

---

**Heng Sure**
Every one a priceless treasure

How come I'm so happy? Look what this trip has brought me: I'm now

blind: no glasses.

mute: no talking.

helpless: the Dharma Protector cooks, drives, protects, decides.

dull: no relating, no emoting, a dead bird.

stupid: thoughts subdued, personal history forgotten.

ashamed: constant review of bad deeds and faults.

hopeless: desires squelched. Future unplanned.

powerless: all conveniences unplugged and abandoned.

sore: new plumbing and wiring, calluses, aches.

– every one a priceless treasure. Earned with hard work. Getting deeper. Wouldn't trade any of it for gold.

Heng Sure • December 27, 1977
We are what we eat; we are what we do

> Living beings' bodies are all different
> They come from adhering to distinctions in thoughts.
> So, too, are the many kinds of Buddhalands.
> None do not come from karma.
>
> Flower Store World Chapter<br>Avatamsaka Sutra

We are what we do. When you slow down the input in your life, you can discover that you're full already! We all have within our minds complete memory tapes of everything we've done. We also carry the seeds of all actions from past lives. It's all there: the events and the views that created this choice and lead to that road. Our identity is not fixed. We are a random collection of names and guises, all coming from the same causes: what we do, what we say, and what we think.

Clearly we are what we eat. Meat-eating types are fierce. Plant-eating species are gentle. But who recognizes that we are what we do?

> Good deeds make you rise, offenses make you fall.
> It has nothing to do with anyone else at all!
>
> Ten Dharma Realms Poems<br>By Master Hua

As we bow we slow down our mental-input. We don't read newspapers or magazines; don't look at T.V., movies, or billboards; don't hear radio or phonograph records. No matter where we are the quiet in our minds depends on how we handle the tides of thoughts, desires, memories, dreams, and reflections that come and go inside. The Buddhadharma is all about controlling the mind this way. The bowing calms the body. Stillness calms the mind. A quiet mind calms down the world.

When "personal history" comes to mind it seems less important now than it once did. I had a share of good and bad times as a child, just like everyone. I traded identities and kept looking for the truth. I learned habits that now appear as "bad habits." They were bad because they wasted energy on selfish ends; they helped no one. But there are ways to grow out of bad habits.

If you cultivate the Buddha's Dharmas you turn into a Buddha. If you use effort in your mind all the time to clear away the noise from your inner memory tapes, then before long your mind will settle into a wonderful, clear tranquility.

The Buddhas praise you, the world goes your way and everywhere is peaceful, even in a rush-hour traffic snarl, or a crowded supermarket line. If you behave like a Bodhisattva, you turn yourself into a Bodhisattva. If you give when there is a need and you don't think of your own benefit, this is a Bodhisattva's practice. If you refuse to go along with the gang when they are heading for drinks, drugs, and improper deeds, you are keeping the Bodhisattva's Dharma alive in the world and you are planting the seed of great happiness and freedom. Who are you? Nobody special? Take your identity from your practices – we are what we do.

---

**Heng Chau** • December 28, 1977
We would have never made it this far

The clear circle of sky was above this A.M. again, surrounded by dark thunder-clouds.

Barry stopped. "You're lucky you're not on the Mesa," he said.

"Why?" I asked.

"It's all flooded. Everything is under water!"

The Mesa was the only place not hit by the typhoon when we were bowing on it last week. Now the very same Mesa is flooded after we are two miles safely past. Heng Sure and I really feel protected, like someone is compassionately watching over us every step of the way, shielding us from harm and dangers. We would have never made it this far without help.

Rainbows and Birth and Death.

The sky fills with a full double rainbow. The colors are striking against the deep purple storm clouds. My eyes drift and fix on the beautiful rainbow, almost unknowingly. Instantly my mind is flooded with defiled thoughts and images. "What's going on?" I say to myself. "Just a minute ago your mind was clear and pure and now it's running wild in the garbage. Why?"

Then it came to me: looking at the rainbow was running outside after forms. All desire is one desire; one desire is the same as all desire. Gazing at the rainbow was desire for forms. It set off all the upside-down circuits in my mind as surely as if I had gone to an x-rated movie.

"If you can really put down the desire for forms, then everything is finished. No matter who it is – heroes, great people, and cultivators too – they all fall to beautiful forms. All of the problems of the world, all of the troubles and afflictions begin right here.

"If you want to end afflictions once and for all, then end your desire. If you want to follow your afflictions, then just let your desire run free… We are born out of desire for form and we die out of desire for form."

Master Hua – en route instructions
Marshall, California May 18, 1977

An older woman walks one block in a heavy downpour without shoes or a raincoat just to offer a big smile and a dollar.

In the early damp foggy morning, another elderly woman stopped her car in the rush-hour traffic. She shuffled across the highway in her slippers to offer a few dollars. "To help you, bless you!" she said full of pep and kindness.

**Heng Sure**
From 3:50 a.m. to 11:00 p.m. daily

What goes on inside that 1956 Plymouth 2-Tone Vihara.

3:50 Alarm clock — brrrrrrring! From a heap of blankets a hand appears to reach for matches on seat-back altar. Uncover kerosene lantern from near food-box. Light it and trim wick. Stretch; take off blanket poncho. Praise Guan Shi Yin Bodhisattva; begin Da Bei Jou. Unwrap lower blankets. Say mantra against harming insects. Step out of car, relieve nature, check the sky, and do *tai ji* waist circles. Four Da Bei Jou's.

4:00 In full lotus, don seven-piece sash. Light incense; begin morning recitation. Trade off *wei no* (conductor of ceremonies) duties each week. Instruments: small, red, wooden fish, brass bell and a Sierra Club cup struck with a wooden clothes-pin.

5:00 Bow to teachers and elders and parents. Sutra reading by Heng Chau. Currently: Sutra in Forty-two Sections.

5:15 Write in journals. Drink tea, if thermos water is hot. Drink warm water if not.

6:00 Roll out for *tai ji quan* basic exercises and set of movements. Fifteen to twenty Da Bei Jou's under the stars (recently under the rain clouds!) Always cold at first. *Tai ji* starts engines turning, like pulling rip-cord on a chain-saw. Rrrrrmmm! Basic warm-ups done. Heng Chau practices Shao Lin Quan or T'ai Kwan Do movements, then we begin the *tai ji* set.

6:45 Fold blankets, store gear in stuff sacks, take water jugs off car roof. Start car. Drink juice or tea when we have it. Don gray monk's robes, precept sashes. Heng Sure takes blue Sutra pack, Heng Chau prepares yellow carry-all monk's bag. Five to ten Da Bei Jou's.

7:00 Drive out to bowing site. Heng Sure begins prayers and bowing. Heng Chau drives ahead one-half mile, arranges gear, locks car, walks back, joins bowing. Sun appears.

7:00-10:30 Single-minded bowing to the City of Ten Thousand Buddhas.

10:30 Heng Chau checks watch, signals recess. Return to car; sit in full lotus – five to ten Da Bei Jou's. If weather permits, Heng Chau sits on tailgate. Otherwise both sit inside car. Forty-two Hands and Eyes.

11:00 Heng Chau starts Svea stove, opens cans, washes vegetables, heats water for thermos. Heng Sure studies sutras or writes in journal.

11:25 Heng Sure offers food to Buddhas, feeds peng bird and spirits.

11:30 Recite Meal Offering Praise. Lunch: three bites of Ritz crackers to accompany Three Recollections. Begin Five Contemplations. Lunch rules: no talking, reading, writing notes. Pass only food. Stop eating when 80% full. Typical menu: crackers, nut-raisin mix, apple and orange, cheese, bread, peanut butter and jelly, granola. Alternative: hot vegetable stew over cooked whole grain brown rice, bulgur wheat, beans, soy sauce, miso, sesame salt, pickles – menu varies according to offerings.

12:15 End meal. Heng Sure translates from Ven. Abbot's writings: poetry, talks, and essays.

12:30 Clean-up, brush teeth, repack car – ten to fifteen Da Bei Jou's. Return to bowing site.

1:00-5:00 Single-minded bowing to the City of Ten Thousand Buddhas.

5:30 Triple Refuge, Transference of Merit, bows to the Master. Return to the car. Wash hands and face, stow bowing gear. Heng Chau finds campsite along the road. Ten to fifteen Da Bei Jou's.

6:00 Ch'an meditation. Forty-two Hands and Eyes.

7:00 Evening Recitation. Sutra reading / translation from Avatamsaka Sutra.

8:15 Sutra study, journal writing. Ch'an meditation. Finish Da Bei Jou's.

9:30 Shurangama Mantras, Triple Refuge, bows to Patriarchs.

10:15 Standing meditation. Finish Da Bei Jou's. Put on sweater, vest, jacket, down parka, hat, hood, sweat pants, blanket poncho. Blow out lamp.

11:00 Fall asleep sitting up. Exhausted, free, and happy.

> Like the ocean beats the rugged shore,
> Day and night, without a moment's pause.
> Big rocks wear smooth, small rocks wear out.
> Bowing breaks thought-covers in this way.
>
> Heng Sure

Inner changes resulting from hard work. Long bowing – four hours, no break. Long sitting – three hours, full lotus. New energy rubs old blocks, leaves, and debris. New eyes see old habits. Tests and trials.

Shih Fu: "Now that you know false thinking is not okay, you can't do it anymore, can you?"

Riding a yin-yang see-saw. Great Compassion Mantra great equalizer. Too tense? Recite to relax. Too scattered? Recite to concentrate. Feel old and dirty? Recite and feel new and clean.

Slowly closing gaps in mindfulness. Less time wasted not cultivating every day. Pay a price for this quality work: Ego fights back. Smoke screens, afflictions, twisting, turning, schemes to sabotage:

> The Way grows by a foot,
>     and the demon's already on top.

No vacations. Got to watch at all the time. Who watches? Heng Sure. Watches who? Heng Sure. All states of the mind working back to simple harmony in the Original Middle. What counts? The bowing, breaking thought-covers like the sea smoothes rock.

Heng Chau • December 29, 1977
If you want to know why there are wars

We are bowing in heavy traffic. Chen Lee and his family from Los Angeles stopped yesterday on their way back from the City of Ten Thousand Buddhas. They brought some clothes and food. They had attended the winter meditation session. Although they themselves weren't aware of it, they were full of light and peace. Everyone looked so good and calm.

Meat and Disasters.

Barry stopped to report the road conditions and keep us up on local point of interest. He checks on us every day. There's always a little Dharma that gets exchanged too. Today it was on killing and vegetarianism.

"You eat fish?" asks Barry.

"No." I answer.

"How about clams and oysters?" he wonders.

"Nothing with blood and breath. It's the first of our precepts: no killing. I heard a wise old monk say that the cause of cancer was from eating too much meat. The hateful energy an animal feels just before being killed is held in its body and absorbed by the one who eats it. As the monk put it, 'The slaughtered cow says, "All right, you killed me so I'm going to give you cancer."' The old cultivator observed that animals and people fill up with revenge for killing and hatred. They keep looking for ways to vent it. Soon it fills up the world until war breaks out. So there's the saying:

If you want to know why there are wars,
Listen to the cries at the slaughter house at midnight.

The value of holding the precepts is right here: to eradicate disasters and make the world a better place. Not eating meat reduces calamities and disasters."

"Oh, so that's it," replied Barry looking down at a package of fish he just brought. "Well, plants scream too when you eat them," he said as he left, "maybe not as loud, though..."

---

**Heng Sure**
Exhausting your blessings, ending your sufferings

The Buddhist and the Cynic:
A Conversation About Fun.

Cynic: I still don't understand this business about bitter practices. What kind of perverse high do you get from cutting out everything that's fun?

Buddhist: If you had to label the biggest difference in my life since I became a Buddhist, it would be something like this: I act on the faith in true principles. Okay?

C: Yeah, okay, so? Answer my question.

B: Right. What I used to call fun I now call blind self-suffering, delayed pain. What I used to consider perverse self-denial I now recognize as true happiness. Are you with me?

C: I'm listening.

B: The principle behind it is this: "To enjoy your blessings exhausts your blessings; to endure suffering ends suffering."

C: What's a "blessing?"

B: It's what we used to call fun. If you go live your life totally in your senses grabbing for pleasure and running from pain, you wasted energy, you hurt people through selfish behavior and in general, you waste your share of light. Did you ever find any fun that lasted?

C: No, that's true. It always goes flat.

B: And the constant search for more and new fun is exactly what is meant by "exhausting your blessings." At a certain point, I just stopped beating the dead horse called "having a good time." The desires I was scrambling to satisfy have pushed me around long enough. Pushing for fun turns on you and makes you less free that if you just sat still, content to be right where you are. What do you get when the thrill is done? Heat, hassle, pain, and dust – over and over again. Boy! I've had enough of that for this lifetime!

C: I hear you, I hear you. For a Buddhist you still can get pretty riled up!

B: When you see the truth, how can you ever again be satisfied with the false?

C: Well suppose I gave up good times, what do you do with yourself, stare at your navel? It won't ever be more popular than color T.V., you know.

B: Remember what I said, "Act on faith in true principles." Action is what Buddhism stresses. Not a milk-toast belief, but do it yourself trial and error practice.

C: You practice having no fun?

B: You practice saying no to desire because the principle points you to something a little more solid and fun, and on lot less selfish. When the urge to run outside and buy a little fun rises up, the "bitter practice" cultivator chooses not to satisfy the urge. He has patience instead. His faith in the truth holds his energy in. He's cool and calm in the beginning, in the middle, and in the end. When the thrill seeker comes dragging home miserable and deflated after another flat round of being pushed by his desires, the cultivator of virtue is just as happy as when he began. Maybe he's a bit wiser than before. He certainly hasn't lost any of his juice and spark.

C: Cultivator of virtue?

B: Yeah, virtue.

C: Like little Mary Sunshine?

B: No, like the Buddha, the smartest, most fearless individual who ever walked the planet. One of his names is "adorned with the perfection of ten thousand virtues."

C: Oh, that's virtue, huh?

B: You could call it by other names: happiness, freedom, and power. It comes from enduring suffering and not cashing in blessings.

C: Kind of makes thrill-seeking seem pale and shallow by comparison.

B: That's the point. Once you know that there's more to life then being trapped in the cage of your desires then this whole new world of real happiness and pure freedom opens up for you. Sages with virtue have what is called "the power that cuts without harming."

C: Say, what do you call this true principle you study?

B: We call it the Proper Buddhadharma.

C: Sorry about this edge on my words but it's hard not to be cynical these days. I've been taught not to trust in anything. It's the sickness of the scientific age.

B: Don't I know it! That makes the discovery of true principle even sweeter.

C: Even the bitter ones?

B: Here's another one to start you out on: "Bitter practice, Sweet mind."

C: By the way, what are bitter practices?

B: They are doing whatever you don't want to do. That is the bitterest. Say no to your ego. If you can do that all the time, everywhere, that's a bitter practice. The Buddha taught twelve beneficial "bitter" practices for cultivators of asceticism on the way to Buddhahood. Does that describe you? A future Buddha?

C: Maybe I am, but just don't know it?

B: Right. Happy cultivation to you.

C: You sure I won't have a good time?

B: Try your best!

**Heng Chau** • December 30, 1977
Don't try to do what nature does by itself

> See all things howsoever they flourish,
> Return to the root from which they grew.
>
> Tao Te Ching

Back to Nature: Return to the Source, Go Back to the Root.

A young family, who is really into the back-to-nature movement stopped out with a meal offering. They spend a lot of time back-packing together and we ate mountain-style: nuts, dried fruit, wayfarers' bread, sprouts, cheese, and yerba buena tea they gathered themselves from nearby hills.

The parents, who are local school teachers, saw a story about the pilgrimage and said, "We all wanted to come out, we felt as if we had a lot in common even though we've never met and none of us know much about Buddhism." After the meal they told us of a plan called "benevolent neglect" that would allow the National Parks to return to their original state simply by not messing with the environment. "The idea is a sound one," said Jack. "Don't try to do what nature does by itself."

We talked about how we people cover over our true self-nature with false thoughts and attachments just like Yellowstone Park got covered over with camper villages, tourist traps, and electric mobile home hook-ups.

> "The nature of people is basically pure. It is because of false thinking and attachments that the True Suchness is obscured. Simply have no false thoughts and the nature will be pure of itself."
>
> The Sixth Patriarch – Great Master Hui Neng

"Boy, that's just the way it is, isn't it?" reflected Jack. "Life after life we keep turning on a wheel, never getting free."

So many people we meet on the road share a sense of having lost something real and simple. They are looking to fill a hole with a natural freedom and innocence to regain a spark and child-like wonder. They know it begins inside, in a pure state of mind, not in the superficial of politics, health foods, and earth shoes. Buddhism is the ultimate and original "back to nature." When you cultivate, you borrow a path and go back home. The self-nature doesn't come or go. We just cover it over much like the parks get covered over temporarily. The nature of all living beings is the same, originally pure and complete. It cannot be added to or depleted. Following the self-nature is the same as following the Middle Way. It is always in perfect harmony, neither too much nor too little. This is the root from which we grew.

When Great Master Hui Neng experienced enlightenment he said:

How unexpected! The self-nature
is originally pure in itself.
How unexpected! The self-nature
is originally neither produced nor destroyed.
How unexpected! The self-nature
is originally complete in itself.
How unexpected! The self-nature
is originally unmoving.
How unexpected! The self-nature
can produce the ten thousand dharmas.

**Heng Sure**
The blood was only make-believe

The Buddha said to the Four Heavenly Kings, "Kings, to killers, Earth Store Bodhisattva speaks of a retribution of a short lifespan…"

Earth Store Bodhisattva Sutra

Beneath my nose as I bowed to the blacktop I found a killer. Lying prone, one eye squinted, the other eye aiming down a long, deadly rifle barrel: a plastic toy soldier. I used to have a boxful. My brother and I would set up battles and execute the slaughter of each other's troops, day after day. Each tiny cavalry man, each gunner, cowboy, pirate, and marine must have died thousands of times. Who killed them? Not the other toy figures. We killed them. We knocked them over with a finger or a marble, killing them in our minds. Entire generations of good men perished on the carpet of our bedroom. What seeds did we plant?

Of course, we were only children playing games. We did not make the connection between the horror and suffering of war and killing. The toy guns were silent, the blood was only make-believe. It was just like the violence and death we watched on television – when the program was done, we went to eat dinner – unharmed and intact. But how about all those bodies left dying and maimed in our minds? Who consoled the families of the dead? Who swept up the mess, who washed away the blood? Don't be silly; it's only a T.V. show. What attitudes did we absorb?

My brother and I were lucky. He went to war and came back, without dying and without directly killing anyone. I met the Buddhadharma and received the precepts against taking life. But how about the thousands of young men who weren't so lucky? Men went to war like toy soldiers or T.V. phantoms, only to discover that when metal cuts flesh the pain and fear and grief are unspeakably awful. Each death echoes through families, bringing sorrow to many people. It makes you sick with pain. It makes you resolve to kill no more and to be careful planting seeds of killing in children.

**Heng Chau** • December 31, 1977
It made me feel real proud

Pismo Beach...

A woman called Janie stopped with her aging mother. "We are really moved by what you are doing. We read about it in the papers. It's so rare to find someone who really believes in these things anymore these days. My mother and I want to help out," she said.

Two older women in a car: "We just came from the doctor. Are you doing this for health?" asked one.

A man stopped and offered to share some prayers "with a 2-by-4."

A young man named Roger: "I read about your trip. I feel one with you. Is there anything I can do for you... I really feel a oneness with what you are trying to do."

Barry stopped with his wife and children. They brought out a carved wood bookstand for our Sutra volumes. They were all really happy and clear-eyed. The bookstand fitted perfectly on top of the car seat.

Arthur, a local gas station owner walked up to say, "It made me feel real proud that you prayed at my station... it was a real honor."

Natural Foods Store owner: "Can I give you something to help you on your way?"

It was positive and good energy like this all day. Some people stopped in the early morning to warn us, "We are worried for you. Pismo Beach is a mean little town." We found it just the opposite, though. Basically everything is the same: it's our false thinking that creates differences.

> "Within all Buddhadharmas there is no defilement or purity. There is no darkness and no light. There is neither difference nor unity. There's no truth or falseness, neither security nor danger."
>
> Avatamsaka Sutra – Ten Practices Chapter

\* \* \* \* \* \* \* \* \*
## January 1978

**Heng Sure • January, 1978**
It doesn't come easy!

If I ever make progress in Ch'an meditation, it will be the first thing in my life I've earned through real, physical sacrifice. It doesn't come easy! The fruits are wonderful! I have to sit through what feels like aeons of discomfort before I settle into stillness. Attached here and stuck there, it takes all I've got, every trick and tool, to keep patiently going. Sometimes it feels like a tug-of-war between a dump truck and a rhino, with me as the rope between. And then, when the ultimate limit is reached – suddenly it is all worth it, every bit. More! More patience!

**Heng Chau • January 1, 1978**
The pulse of the Patriarchs hangs by a thread

We spent New Year's Eve sitting in Ch'an on a muddy road next to a cauliflower field. I had this thought: a new year, a new mind. There is no time; there is no measure. Whether sitting in meditation or spinning in the busy affairs of the world, all discriminations are false coverings. Everything returning to "0," (zero).

Right now it's perfectly all right to completely let go and put it all down. Why don't I resolve today to be "right on" in every thought, word, and deed, and not be the least bit pretentious. Whatever is holding me down is an illusion. My attachments can melt like snow in hot water with a single thought for the Way. I can truly be free and happy and make it my job personally to deliver all beings from suffering so we all get perfect enlightenment together. Yippee! Happy New Year!

"Disciples of the Buddha, the Bodhisattva, Mahasattva, gives away everything in the land, up to and including the position of king. He can forsake all of these. Amid all worldly matters his mind attains independence. He is not bound, tied, or attached to any of them. He leaves behind all evil deeds and benefits living beings."

Avatamsaka<br>
Ten Transferences Chapter

This morning we read The Buddha Speaks the Sutra of the Ultimate Extinction of the Dharma. It is a detailed account of the conditions and changes that will appear just before the Proper Dharma disappears from the world.[1]

I had a strong response. Every word felt like it came from my own heart. I recognized the Sutra and felt totally familiar with it. I knew I had heard it before, long ago. Tears began to come to my eyes as I remembered dreams and visions of the very things the Sutra describes that will come about.

Somehow it became as clear as the sound of hammer hitting steel that this bowing pilgrimage, the entire Sangha, and the Master were all woven inextricably together in a deep and vital vow to protect and uphold the Orthodox Dharma. Our job was to prevent this Sutra from coming true. Truly the "pulse of the Patriarchs hangs by a thread."

Without regard to time or place or self, we come together life after life riding a vast and deep promise to cultivate to Buddhahood together and not allow the Dharma Ending Age to happen. Worlds and personalities come and go like the changing seasons but these vows never end. In my heart past all words I know this is how it truly is – throughout all numbers of kalpas, without cease.

---

[1.] See Dharma Master Sure's translation of this Sutra in the prefatory pages of the Shurangama Sutra

"He further makes great vows, vowing to receive all Buddhas' Dharma wheel, vowing to gather in all Buddhas' Bodhi, vowing to protect all Buddhas' teachings, vowing to maintain all Buddhas' Dharmas – vast and great as the Dharmarealm, ultimate as empty space, exhausting the boundaries of the future, throughout all numbers of kalpas, without cease."

Avatamsaka Sutra<br>Ten Grounds Chapter (Ground of Happiness)

Impermanence.

> Things aren't always what they seem
> Bubbles, shadows, echoes, dreams.
> Quickly come, they're gone as fast,
> Drops of dew, a lightning flash.
>
> No one stays and nothing lasts –
> Reflections in a looking-glass.
> Nothing lasts and no one stays,
> As in the burning house we play.
>
> Take heed, my friends, for who can tell?
> Don't wait for thirst to dig your well.
> The lonely graves are for the young
> In the vain my foolish song is sung.

Kuo Gao, Kuo Te and her children stopped on the way back to Los Angeles. They attended the winter session at the City of Ten Thousand Buddhas. They bowed in the morning with us and made a meal offering. Kuo Gao just took the Bodhisattva precepts and was like a little kid, excited and happy.

**Heng Chau** • January 2, 1978
A hundred-year-old letter

> "If there is a living being who has a thought of hostility toward the Bodhisattva, the Bodhisattva views him with kind eyes as well. To the very end he has not the slightest anger."
>
> Avatamsaka Sutra
> Ten Transferences Chapter

Two motorcyclists drove up and stopped next to us. They were drunk and hostile.

"Hey! What are you guys, anyway?" yelled one.

"You Moslems, Hindus, Krishnas, or what?!" demanded the other.

"We're Buddhist monks."

There was a pause as they checked us over. "Oh, Buddhists, huh? I don't have anything against them." says one as he digs into the pocket of his black leather jacket. He pulls out a handful of money and stuffs it in my yellow monk's bag. "Good luck, man," he says, and pats me on the shoulder.

No matter how people treat us, we try to be good to them. If we are good to people, they will be good to us. Ray, an older man, who has watched us for weeks as he drove back and forth in an old Ford, finally stopped to ask about our journey.

"What do your parents think?" asked Ray.

"It's because of my good family that I got into Buddhism."

"Yes, you're lucky," he said. "You know, my boy is in San Quentin Prison," he said sadly.

"Do you visit him?"

"Yes! Every two weeks," said Ray proudly.

"That's great!"

"Can't let him down, no matter what. He's in for life… Well, good luck and thanks," said Ray, shaking hands. "See you later, I hope."

We stopped to write under a tree by the road in Sheel Beach. "Can I get you some tea?" asks a kindly old woman bending over us. She has a heavy German accent. "We are closed for the day, but I can do it specially for you," she offers pointing to a quaint Bavarian restaurant/lodge next to us.

"All right, we accept."

"You can't come inside?" she says after hearing of our vow. "Well, I can tell you sleep out… look at your eyes! Tsk! Tsk! They are all red! Not enough sleep last night!"

We sit on the back porch stairs sipping tea. "Will you have some cookies? Special home-made German," she whispers.

"We eat once a day, but we'll take a few with us, if you like."

"Once a day only!" she exclaims. "No wonder you're so skinny! Tsk! Tsk!"

She and her husband are accustomed to wandering mendicants from the "old days" in Europe. They are happy to see this tradition still alive in America and host us with pride and special etiquette reserved for pilgrims.

Even though those wandering monks dressed in rags and had renounced the world, they were traditionally well educated and devoted their lives to serving humankind. The woman is delighted when Heng Sure consents to translate a hundred-year-old letter written in Chinese they had in an antique wooden box.

"Isn't that something, after all these years!" she exclaims. "Do you really think he can do it?"

He did. They were happy. It was just the right thing to do. "Just like it used to be" was written all over their faces.

> "He upholds all the Bodhisattvas' vast, great vows and practices, and he constantly takes delight in being of service to all his good friends."
>
> Avatamsaka Sutra
> Ten Transferences Chapter

**Heng Chau** • January 3, 1978
Don't fear anything except laziness

Quiet, overcast winter day. Rain clears in the morning, just before bowing. Windy and solitary. Sometimes nothing at all happens. In a way, every day is that way.

> "All in the mundane world is quiescent and still... the substance and nature of the Dharma Realm is level and uniform."
>
> Avatamsaka Sutra
> Ten Practices Chapter

Words of encouragement: Don't fear anything except laziness. If you make a mistake, don't repeat it. If you do good, don't notice. To doubt or be afraid is worse than anything you could actually do. Doubt cripples the spirit; fear paralyzes the mind. Just be happy and try your best. Everything's is OK. Be pure, peaceful, and happy.

**Heng Sure**
Fame is selfish and greedy

> The Bodhisattva thought, "The five desires and dharmas that obstruct the path can even prevent one from gaining supreme and perfect enlightenment. I will not, therefore, have even the smallest thought of desire."
>
> Avatamsaka Sutra
> Ten Practices Chapter

Of the five desires, fame counts big. The desire for fame in a cultivator is deadly. It must be purged in the seed stage or there will be no harvest of enlightenment-fruit. Do not compromise. When the thoughts of "big me" rise up, cut them down.

Why would this Bhikshu seek fame? At the root of it, because he fears death. Does this sound familiar: "Fame. Big self. Everyone knows me. I'm important. My name is big. My power is respected. Birth is a laugh. Sickness and old age belong to others. In me, all faults are glamorous because I'm famous. My life is not dull, not common, not average, and not ugly. My life is special, exciting, beautiful."

What is wrong with this monologue? Surely we have all had these thoughts before. The problem is this: fame is based on a lie. The self does not exist. You can't find it anywhere, not in your body, not in your family, not in your possessions. When death stops your movement and takes away your warmth and breath, where is the self? Is it still reading the paper over breakfast? Does the self still drive the car to work? Can you find the self at the movies sitting with popcorn after you die? If the self is true, where does it go after death? It never existed in the first place. What is fame based on? A lie.

Fame has no heart. Fame is selfish, greedy. But when it comes our turn in the spotlight who can stand aside and yield it to others? It's not an easy desire to subdue.

Greed for merit is still greed.
Good done in secret is truly good.

If you do lots of good deeds what could be better? Good deeds make you rise. An old laywoman saw a broken down temple and made it her job to repair it. The Buddha-images were exposed to the wind and rain because the roof leaked. The laywoman had no wealth but she has spirit. She got thirty-two of her friends excited about the project. She made them feel, as she did, that the work of protecting the Dharma was their own work – it couldn't wait for others. In no time at all the roof was made sound, the images restored, and everything was set to rights. The thirty-three friends, because of the merit of their deed was so great, were reborn in the heavens. The old laywoman was their leader.

If she had gone around in her village bragging about her excellent virtue, she could not have succeeded in fulfilling her vow.

But she had wisdom and understood the fruits of good deeds can be blown out of the mouth before they ripen. Good done in secret can mean simply: "Don't talk about yourself." If others don't know what you've done then they can't get afflicted or jealous. By guarding the tongue you not only don't lose your merit by bragging but you also avoid all sorts of offenses that come from afflicting other people. Good indeed!

The Buddhas and Bodhisattvas know the workings of your mind better than you do yourself. Your every good deed and your every offense is clearly seen and clearly known to the sages. In terms of cultivation, they are the ones whose opinion of you counts the most.

> "The Tathagata completely knows and sees the thoughts
> of all living beings of the three periods of time."
>
> The Vajra Sutra

It is all right to be famous among sages for your excellent virtue. But you don't win that kind of fame by bragging or by posing or self-seeking among people.

---

**Heng Chau • January 4, 1978**
I began bowing to my parents

Ray stopped again with an offering. "I wanted to give you something the other day but I was broke. This isn't much but it's from here (he points to his heart) not from here (he points to his wallets)."

"Then it's a lot."

He and his wife wanted to invite us to dinner but I explained our vow. Ray understood. He asked for one of our papers to send to his son in prison. They write often and visit every two weeks.

"I don't go to church. But ever since I was this big I got 'the man' in the corner every night... Last night I said a prayer for you," said Ray. "I pray every night. Stopped drinking four years ago when I got a stroke. Now I smoke cigarettes instead. I pray. I get the man in the corner and try to get the hate out of my heart. Even when I was so drunk I couldn't stand, I'd pray."

People sometimes ask us for "your prayer." Our prayer is simple:

> "Of all the bad things I've done with my body, mouth, and mind from beginningless greed, hatred, and stupidity, I repent of them all."

And then bow. This feels really natural to me.

Who do you bow to?

> "When I was twelve years old I began bowing to my parents. Later, not only did I bow to my parents, I bowed to heaven and earth, officials, parents, and teacher. Then I started bowing to the world's great good people because the good they do can influence others to do good, so I should thank them. I also bowed to the great immortal beings and the great sages of the world, the great filial ones and eventually I started bowing on behalf of the great evil people of the world, repenting on their behalf, hoping that they would change their evil and go towards the good. So every time I bowed I did more than 500 prostrations.

> "Where did I bow? In the morning before others had awakened, I went outside to bow. If it was raining, I bowed. If it was snowing, I bowed. In Manchuria, it snows a lot and I would put my hands down in the snow and make a full prostration just the same. Why was I so stupid as that? I felt that if everyone in the world were smart, the smarter the world got, the worse it would get. So I did this stupid thing hoping that the world would not get so bad so fast."

(Venerable Abbot relating his practice done in his early teens when he still lived with his parents)

"Bow to your parents. Bow to the good people in the world. Bow for the bad people. Bow to be the best person you can be. Bow away the bad things in your heart. Bow yourself smaller and smaller, and your Bodhi mind will get bigger and bigger. Offer your prayers to end suffering in the world, for peace. Bow for everyone."

Disciples of the Buddha, the Bodhisattva, Mahasattva, sees living beings creating bad karma and suffering heavily as a result. Because of their obstacles they do not see the Buddha, they do not hear the Dharma, they do not recognize the Sangha. Then he thinks, "I should stand in for living beings, amid all evil paths, taking on their sufferings and causing them to be liberated from them."

Avatamsaka Sutra
The Transferences Chapter

"Got to move that car, Mister." Ray's car was blocking the road and a police stopped to tell him over the loudspeaker to move on.

"Well, I better go," says Ray. "Take care and keep me and the boy in your prayers, if you remember... If you ever get up to San Quentin, go see my boy, huh? He's a good boy – but liquor and drugs and bad friends and other things – well, he's not really a boy anymore. He's thirty-eight and serving life. He's repented now, but you still have to pay your debts, don't you?"

---

**Heng Chau** • January 5, 1978
We forgot the stamp

Little Good Lucks.

We mailed an important letter to the Abbot on New Year's Day at the local Post Office. However, we forgot the stamp. What to do? It's a big holiday and everything is closed. We recited Namo Guan Shi Yin Bodhisattva. Out comes a postal woman who just happens to have a key to the box we dropped the letter in. She gladly helps us out. What are the chances for that happening – especially on a holiday?

Someone left an offering hanging on a road sign with a sketch of two bowing monks and an encouraging note. We found it today still intact and undisturbed. It had been hung up over a week ago. (part of sketch shown below):

Our wet clothes need a dryer. There is a chance to meet with the Master in Los Angeles this weekend if we can find a place to store the car. We meditate on it and wait. In the morning we find a laundromat. As we pull up, a local supporter drives up.

"What a coincidence!" he says. "I've been thinking about a Sutra for the last few days and here we all are. You've got the Sutra I want to read. I've got a pocketful of quarters for your laundry and… gee, strange, huh?"

He borrows the Sutra and as he starts to drive away he shout, "Oh, if you ever need a place to store your car I can keep an eye on it at my house."

Like it says,

> "The Way and the response intertwine and are hard to conceive of…"

This month: Lots of miracles, lots of mistakes. Up and down the hundred-foot pole, but never jumping off. Getting rid of bad habits is hard. Going astray is easy. Cultivation is wonderful. One of these days we will all take that "one step further" and fly away.

> "Cultivating the Way is like climbing a hundred-foot pole. Coming down is easy; going up is hard. On the top of the pole if you can go one step further, then you are fee to come and go anywhere in the universe."
>
> Venerable Master Hua

---

**Heng Sure**
San this and Santa that

Note from Heng Chau: Purpose of San Bu Yi Bai Journals.

San Bu Yi Bai is an "internal" pilgrimage, leaving one world: comfortable and familiar but impermanent and full of suffering, for another world: almost completely unknown. Think in terms of two pioneers traveling an old, forgotten road, a trail to City of Ten Thousand Buddhas (self-nature's wisdom storehouse).

We have guides (teacher and Sutras) and a little thread inside that glows and pulses when we are on the Way and doesn't when we leave it. At first we rely almost exclusively on teacher and Sutras, but gradually learn how to weave and work our own thread and "mesh with the source, merge with the substance."

We write a map and journal to those friends and family who will follow and add to the maps and markers of those who we follow – maintain the trails, build cairns, and build bridges. The Avatamsaka is the large thread, and as we follow it on the mind-ground, we make fewer gross mistakes. It is our touchstone until we join the Assembly and reach "home."

We bring the guides to bear on the territory we cross. Still, we are all going to the City. Although it's a long and sometimes painful journey, we all must follow the thread. We all want to get there, but we follow dark trails outside. We all get lost in greed when we look for the City outside. From the City of the (Fallen) Angeles, past all the Saints' cities, San this and Santa that, all holy in name only. All testify to the truth that material dharmas don't meet our needs. But, the thread is still there, the path back home. Our job is to keep weaving the threads, keep shining them back. We journey down into dark places, go deeper than Western minds have been. Our family is all coming along, too. We must leave clear trail-markers, and leave a trail of light.

Finally, we leave this truth: it never gets any bigger than one person doing the work alone, just using energy alone, turning the wheel. Hard work, practice, patience.

Woman: "Thank you for what you are doing for everyone. It must be really hard."

Monk: "Not doing it is even harder."

---

**Heng Chau** • January 6, 1978
Hard to keep dry

We just left Shell and Pismo Beach, bowing towards Avita Hot Spring. Rain continues. Hard to keep dry. Constant state of sogginess. Flooding is a common sight.

A young man stopped with a food offering and a detailed county map to guide us on these back roads. "I'll scout out the unknown areas ahead for you tomorrow," he offered.

**Heng Sure**
My reflected face faded and disappeared

> "Just like seeing a Guiding Master in his many forms and distinctions, according to what beings practice in their minds, their visions of Buddhalands are similar."
>
> Avatamsaka Sutra

The gear was all ready, stuff-sacks were all stuffed, stacked, and covered with the poncho. The water jugs had come down from their storage spot on the car roof. Dew drops shivered on their plastic sides as the engine warmed up. I swallowed the last drops of water from the chilly thermos bottle. Counting mantras on my beads, I sat in the car in full lotus waiting to drive out to the bowing site and begin the morning's journey. Heng Chau shut the door and released the hand brake. The first rays of sun crossed my face and reflected on framed glass of the Guan Shi Yin Bodhisattva image that adorns the car. Still reciting the Great Compassion Mantra, I turned to contemplate the image. Because the sun struck the glass in that way, at first all I could see was my own reflection mirror back at me: lean, unshaven Bhikshu in a blue knit skullcap. Then the car began to roll and the image of Guan Shi Yin Bodhisattva emerged from the sun's glare. Serene, powerful, totally free and comfortable, the Greatly Compassionate One who Hears the Sounds of Living Beings was right there beside in the car. My reflected face faded and disappeared to a shadowy silhouette and Guan Shi Yin Bodhisattva's image filled the space where I had seen myself. I thought, "Right on, brother. If you do your work well, you can really disappear just like that. Don't be selfish, don't seek fame or any greedy desire and you can face out of your old ego. Guan Shi Yin Bodhisattva can fill you up and use your body and life to save people from pain. That's where it's really at. Namo Greatly Compassionate Guan Shi Yin Bodhisattva. Na mwo he la da nwo dwo la ye ye."

**Heng Chau** • January 7, 1978
You still haven't transcended the wind and rain

Gold Wheel Temple. We tell our stories about the storms and the rubber gloves and raincoat and all the magic happenings of the last weeks. We probably thought we were pretty hot stuff and real cultivators. After we finished, the Master spoke and set the record straight and put us back on solid ground. This is part of the Abbot's speech:

"We feel like the world is a big place, but when we see the Avata-msaka, we see the world is all contained within a hair pore of the Buddha. And yet we don't think we are small. Big and small mutually interpenetrate and are totally unobstructed. This state is inconceivable...

"To make humanity happy, you are doing Three Steps, One Bow. At all times concentrate your minds and unify your will. Then you can turn what is in-auspicious into the auspicious; and what is unlucky will become lucky.

"But, cultivators of the Way should be patient. Everything is in practicing the Paramita of Patience.

> If you are off by a hair in the beginning,
> Then you will be off a thousand miles in the end.

"This is like having false thoughts. What kind of false thoughts? False thoughts are like stealing rubber gloves. You should endure the cold, heat, wind, and rain. Use patience to cover all states. But you felt you need the gloves, so you had false thoughts and they appeared. If you had no false thoughts, the gloves would have come and been a real response. Instead, they were a product of your false thinking. So it is said,

With one thought unproduced
The entire substance manifests.
When the six sense organs move,
You are covered by clouds.

"You still haven't transcended the wind and rain. Do you understand? If you understand, then your function is unfathomable."

---

**Heng Sure**
Body and mind is a garden plot

Wisdom Garden: Easy Do-it-yourself Instructions.

Body/mind = garden plot

Wisdom seeds = Buddha-nature

Buddha = sun

Dharma = water, tools

Sangha = fence, stakes

Cultivation = plowing, planting, weeding, watering

Patience = allow for natural growth

Good, Wise Advisor = source of know-how; expert

Laziness = no crops, no nothing, weeds

False-thoughts = birds and insects eat seeds and sprouts; no growth; plague of pests

Desire = over-watering; seeds rot; no harvest

Love = harvest before crop is ripe; no yield

Jealousy = watching neighbor's field, not tending your own; weeds, brambles, pets invade

Arrogance = too much sun; drought

Doubt = not enough sun; weak crops

**Heng Chau** • January 9, 1978.
What kind of samadhi have you entered?

Los Angeles.

The Gold Wheel Temple people loaded us with new shoes, food, clothes, supplies, and a wealth of encouragement and good energy.

We bowed goodbye to the Master.

Shih Fu: "Any more questions?"

Heng Sure: "No, Master. The ones we have we must answer ourselves."

Shih Fu: "Okay, see you later."

Weekend bits and pieces:

I told the Master my discovery that staring at the rainbow was just like being turned by a woman. He replied, "Cultivation is right at this point: You can't run out looking even just a little bit." I felt ashamed at being so inexperienced and inept. The Master kindly said, "But even though you take a fall, you don't lose your gung fu. It's not like before you started to cultivate."

We are sitting together on the floor of the Master's room. He invited us in very casually and like little kids we got on our hands and knees to examine a big hunk or rock sitting in the corner. "See this rock? It's jade. See how ugly it is? Before it's cared and polished, it's useless. Cultivation is the same way. When the rock is carved into a Buddha image or an incense burner, then it's beautiful and useful." The Abbot paused and then went on. "You know why it's just an ugly rock?" We shake our heads. "Because in the past it ran outside after forms too much," he says with amusement. "Looking outside just that little bit is where you must cultivate."

Leonara, a disciple, comes in smiling. "It's a miracle!" she says. "My leg is better." She had fallen yesterday and couldn't walk. This morning she asked the Master to help. Now, this afternoon, she's back proudly walking about. "I can walk on it," she says, giggling.

The Matser continues, "Treat your bowing like a Ch'an session. Don't write so many notes back and forth. That's the same as rapping in the kitchen during a meditation session. You want to give bright light to the world and further Buddhism... really help people. Do you understand?"

The teacher is like a fisherman. The disciples are the fish. What kind of fish? Self-fish. A weekend with the Master is one test after another. He skillfully and effortlessly baits an un-barbed hook with whatever we can't put down: food, fame, wealth, sleep, and dangles it in front of our greedy eyes. Or maybe it's "Oh, who would like to talk? Who has wisdom and eloquence?" The Abbot beckons during a lecture. Or "Now you tell everyone about your states... Say whatever you please, I, myself, can't speak well..." With no self, there's no hooks.

I'm a real sucker. I'm always looking for something for myself. Hook, line, and sinker, I swallow the bait. "Snap!" The Master reels you in out of your illusion-pond. As he gently lifts you off his harmless hook he says,

> Everything is a test
>   to see what you will do.
> Mistaking what is right before your eyes
>   you will have to start anew.

He tosses you back in the water with a "Try your best!" King Yama's hook is sharp and deadly. The Master is trying to teach us how to end birth and death, how to gather back our energy and swim upstream to Buddhahood. When we stop taking the bait, we're free. With no self, there are no problems.

We drive the Master to the airport. En route we get some last minute instructions in the back seat. Helen Woo (Kuo Hsiang) and another lay disciple are talking in the front seat.

"You know, it's really strange," says Helen, "Every time the Abbot comes the weather changes."

"Oh? How's that?"

"Well, if it's cold and rainy before he arrives, then it changes to just like spring – warm and sunny. Not too hot, not too cold. Then as soon as he leaves it's cold and rainy again."

"Hmmm." says the other person.

"Then sometimes if we really need rain, it starts to rain when the Abbot arrives and stops when he leaves. Really funny, huh?"

"Uh huh."

I've decided I'm just too scattered. I resolve to concentrate at all times: walking, standing, sitting, and lying. I enter a studied trance-like state reciting on my beads. We arrive at the departure gate pressed for time. Tickets and baggage need to be arranged, but I sit like a lump of cement in "stillness." The Master looks at me and shouts, "Wake up. What kind of samadhi have you entered?" I recall our earlier instructions:

"You're the Dharma Protector. Don't enter samadhi. There will be lots of traffic. It's for sure the cars won't enter samadhi. If you don't stay alert, they'll smash you to bits."

In the terminal the Master suddenly hands me a wad of singles. "Here, you buy the tickets." There's a flurry of activity-crowded lines, baggage confusion, backup due to fog – the Master puts the heat on me. "Hurry up, don't just stand there, we'll miss our flight." I'm trying still to recite silently and hold on to my "samadhi," while counting the money and squeezing in line. I hand the money to the clerk. "It's $40.00 You're short," he says.

"Shih Fu, I need more money," I turn and say.

"I gave you enough. You miscounted," replies the Abbot. I thought I counted it right but I was sloppy, not concentrating. They were all one-dollar bills and now I wasn't sure what had happened. Hooked again.

The Master smiles and hands me the balance but doesn't let me off the hook. "You were careless. You took a loss because you weren't according with conditions." I wanted to insist that I had counted it correctly but it was useless. The money wasn't important. It was the principle.

"When you asked for more, you already had enough. You counted wrong. It's right there that you have to be careful. You 'entered samadhi.'" Finally the Master drove home the lesson with a verse:

> Seek movement in stillness,
> Seek stillness in movement.
> Movement does not obstruct stillness,
> Stillness does not obstruct movement.
> When you concentrate
> Movement and stillness are one.

Then we were in the crowded pre-boarding room writing down instructions, kneeling at the Master's side. Curious businessmen peek over their Wall Street Journals and listen as the Master goes on. "This is just the same principle:

> The eyes see forms
>     but inside there is nothing.
> The ears hear the mundane sounds
>     but the mind does not know of them.
> With one thought unproduced
>     the entire substance manifests.
> When the six sense organs move
>     suddenly you are covered by clouds.

"Do you understand?" asks the Master. "They're all interconnected. When you master one, then the rest are easy." The fog lifts and the flight is cleared for boarding.

"Okay, you're almost half-way there. Be careful. See you later."

A lot of valuable instructions to keep in mind from a good advisor.

> "He vows that all living beings constantly keep in mind the instructions of good knowing advisors; that they concentrate on them and vigorously protect them; that they do not forget them."
>
> Avatamsaka Sutra
> Ten Transferences Chapter

Another storm hits. We decide to eat lunch at Gold Wheel. Leave about 1:30 packed tight in an old 1956 yellow school bus destined for the City of Ten Thousand Buddhas with furniture and offerings. Heng Ju starts driving. We rotate until San Luis Obispo.

The Hammonds are waiting up for us even though we arrive late at night. Norman has worked on the car and everyone is excited and happy. Arleta warned us about another big storm and heavy winds expected for sure tonight and tomorrow. "The area you are bowing in by the Hot Springs and bridge is subject to heavy flooding. Be careful, please," she says.

We camp on high ground to avoid the floods. Lightning and thick dark clouds gather and fill the sky. We do our mantras (Shurangama) and crash – really tired.

On Weather: The Master says:

"All weather – the winds, rain, storms – are caused by gods and spirits. Weathermen call it high and low pressure systems and sunspots, etc... but they haven't opened their eyes."

**Heng Sure**

The Buddha started off as a common person

> "The Bodhisattva sets his will on the search for Bodhi. This is not without a cause, nor does it lack conditions. He brings out true faith in the Buddha, in the Dharma and in the Sangha. From this faith comes a vast resolve."

Avatamsaka Sutra
Worthy Leader Chapter

The Bodhisattva chooses. He sees an ultimate aim: enlightenment. This is the beginning of action. Once he sets his will with deliberate purpose, the world becomes a different place, nothing is ever again the same. Where does he draw his strength from? What is the source of his will? It comes from true faith. Do you have true faith? We all have a thread of the Buddha-nature within us. When we do good deeds, it hums and glows.

When we see it and feel it growing as we do more good and less evil, we begin to rely on it, to seek it more and more. One day we meet the worlds, Buddha, Dharma, or Sangha, and the inner thread radiates a light in the heart. It is unmistakable; all disciples of the Buddha have had this experience. This is the awakening of faith. It is true because it actually exists. The golden thread of the Buddha-nature is not made up or just a name. It's like a vibrating seed, like a little running stream. You can trust, rely on it. This is true faith.

When we first meet the Buddha and look upon his earthly form and hear of his power and goodness he seems awfully big. He is big and very pure. We seem small and dirty in the Buddha's pure mirror. But, because of the seed, the thread of Buddhahood within is within us, we feel drawn to the Buddha and encouraged by his size and wonderful purity. By the power of pure virtue, the Buddha causes us all to want to be like him. How wonderful to discover that we can do it! There is a way to walk and the Buddha walked it. He resolved to get enlightened because of his faith. To paraphrase the Venerable Abbot: "You should understand that the Buddha became a Buddha from the stage of a common person... (he) did not descend from the heavens or ascend from the earth. As a person (the Buddha) cultivated the Dharma and now (he is) a sage, a person who has realized the result... When a human being becomes enlightened, he's a Buddha, too."

The Way of Enlightenment is the Proper Dharma, and it's in the Sutras spoken by the Buddha. It's also right in our hearts.

---

**Heng Chau** • January 10, 1978
You've got to treat the primary causes

Rained all night. Clears during morning ceremony. A circle of sun and blue sky and rainbows return in the middle of black, rolling clouds. It hovers above us as we bow.

Neil, a disciple from Los Angeles, stops to bow and make a meal offering.

"It's really something," he remarks. "It was raining and blowing all the way up from Los Angeles but up here it's beautiful. Blue and sunny."

> "He vows that all living beings forever escape their sick bodies and obtain the Tathagata's body."
>
> Avatamsaka Sutra
> Ten Transferences Chapter

Neil is a chiropractor. He just passed the difficult board examinations and was admitted into the profession. "I recited Guan Yin's name through the whole thing," says Neil with a smile. He sees a deep connection between Buddhism and all of the healing sciences and arts.

"We are all coming to see that all illness is chronic. That is, it comes from long-standing habits and patterns that ultimately are made from the mind," observes Neil after lunch. "Those who are really interested in healing and not just making a buck – and there *are* some in every profession and field of medicine – are beginning to make these connections and links. If you care about relieving suffering, then you've got to treat the primary causes. It's not all right to just run patients in and out of your offices, taking their money with one hand and slapping a band aid on their problem with the other."

> "He vows that all living beings become great kings of medicine who always remove the many sicknesses and do not allow them to reoccur."
>
> Avatamsaka Sutra
> Ten Transference Chapter

Neil is talking straight about something he feels strongly about. "If that's all you do, they are sure to never get well. They will keep coming back and you'll keep taking their money, and... That's not for me!"

Neil saw similarities between the bowing and true healing. "It's just like a good medical treatment: don't try to suppress or cover over, rather, root out the disease once and for all. Often you get worse before you get better because you're really breaking up and getting rid of long-standing disorders and blocks. It's just like Buddhism – you work from the inside out," observed Neil.

In cultivation one goes to the root and the source. You change faults and bad habits right at the place they start: the mind. After that everything else heals itself.

Neil was on his way to the City of Ten Thousand Buddhas. He bowed with us for two hours before heading north. "There's a lot of exciting things happening along these lines... other doctors and therapists who are really committed to healing are discovering the same principles hold true." He pointed out that the best minds in medicine are just beginning to make breakthroughs into understanding the pivoted function of the mind to all matters of health and disease.

"When you get right down to it, the body is just a body – very limited and temporary. But as healers and scientists make these new discoveries about the mind, they are stretching as far as their limited knowledge can stretch. Looked at from the study of Buddhism, they haven't even scratched the surface. For over 3000 years Buddhism has deeply penetrated what modern science is only now getting a glimpse of."

"That everything is made from the mind alone, huh?" I asked.

"Exactly!" said Neil.

Neil told an interesting story about his discovery of Buddhism. He just stopped by one day to visit a Buddhist temple and when he heard the Chinese chanting and instruments, it "rang a bell" deep inside. "I liked the lecture. It was very familiar somehow. I decided to stay and follow the bells."

That's what it's all about: "following the bells" that ring in your true heart. We all have these bells. It's just a question of learning to listen and of faith. You have to trust. Accomplishment in cultivation is the fruit of having faith.

> Faith is the source of the Way,
> The mother of merit and virtue.
> It nourishes all good Dharmas.
>
> Avatamsaka Sutra
> Chapter Twelve, Part I

Afternoon: The police stop and politely ask us to remove our drying clothes from the freeway fence because it's a "traffic obstacle."

A local teacher stopped to borrow a Sutra and Buddha Root Farm.

A car pulls up behind the unmistakable rumble of an oversized Chrysler Magnum engine of a California Highway Patrol car. I figure we were in for a citation as I park on a narrow shoulder for lack of any other space. The door slams and footsteps come up behind while I'm down in a bow.

"Excuse me," says a strong but respectful voice, "May I contribute." The police officer quietly hands me some money and leaves.

I pick up a rock to mark our last bow for the day. From the underside of the rock a black widow spider scurries between my fingers. I shake it out of my sleeve and remember the Master's words, "Be careful. Don't enter samadhi. Stay alert."

---

**Heng Sure**
Come on world! Make more like this one

"To realize Bodhi, therefore becomes his resolve."

A young man drove by and talked to Heng Chau and is now hot on the trail to the home of the Sino-American Buddhist Association. It's hard to know for certain until you have eyes to see – but it looks to me like this man has given rise to the resolve for enlightenment. That is the rarest, most valuable moment in a human life. He's living in a van, the front seat is covered with Buddhist books. He's escaped from Orange County where he's "really starved for the Dharma." He's looking for an enlightened teacher who can give him the precepts and ways to practice the Dharma. He says he's "tired of dragging this carcass of a body around." Do we know about the Four Noble Truths and the Eightfold Path? Do we practice meditation and looking into the emptiness of states? Do we? Wheeoo! This person is halfway home! And he has never even looked at a Buddhist Sutra. From what I gather (second-hand) this person is bound to find the Proper Dharma. Best thing we can do is give him the phone number at the City of Ten Thousand Buddhas, stand aside, and let him go. Zoom! And off he went to a very happy future of cultivation, or I miss my guess. What a lucky thing that he happened to see two monks bowing on a soggy highway frontage road south of San Luis Obispo and that he had the will to stop and talk. Heng Chau says the man was so excited his questions all tumbled out at once. Come on world! Make more like this one.

Wait until the Buddhist Text Translation Society's work becomes known to seekers like him. Buddhism, the Proper Dharma, will flourish on all sides of us like "mushrooms after a spring rain," as the Chinese phrase goes.

There's such an infinitely rich treasury of good values and human wisdom in the Proper Dharma. Everyone who tastes it grows stronger, wiser, and more human. Doctors, ploughmen, Indian chiefs, all can find a place to stand in the Great Vehicle. The Buddha's ground is a fertile field for planting deep flourishing roots.

---

**Heng Chau** • January 11, 1978
But shouldn't you go East?

Young man on street corner: "So, what's in it for you? What do you get out of this work? What's your payoff?"

Monk: "When you give your parents a present or take care of them when they are sick and getting old, what do you get out of it? What's your payoff? How do you feel?"

Young man: "Well, nothing. I mean, you just feel happy and peaceful inside because they're… well, uh, you know…"

Monk: "It's the same way with the Buddha's work – the same way."

Young man: "Hmmm. I think I get it now. You just like to do giving."

"Toward all living beings he attains indestructible faith and therefore with kind eyes he regards them all equally. And he transfers his good roots for their benefits. He gathers together blessings and virtuous conduct and practices great giving."

Avatamsaka Sutra
Ten Transferences Chapter

We drove into San Luis Obispo to contact local authorities. County Sheriff Captain Wood came out of his office, recognized us and invited me in.

"My kids saw you and I read the story in the paper. You'll have no problems. You got a clear road from us." he said stamping our papers and shaking hands.

He was very frazzled and harried with two and three phones ringing all at once – he was in the middle of cracking a big dope-smuggling ring. Looking up he said, "All I can say is you have to be really dedicated."

"Aren't you?" I asked.

"I suppose so," he answers, shrugging his shoulders as if to say, "I don't know, though... sometimes I wonder..."

He walked me to the front door and let his phones ring. We often get the feeling that a lot of the people we meet are old, old friends and would like to just put it all down and come along.

> "He vows that all living beings get their good wish come
> true and that they follow good friends and never leave them."
>
> The Avatamsaka Sutra
> Ten Transferences Chapter

Got cleared and a new map detailing bicycle routes and alternative roads from the California Highway Patrol. "Good luck. Once you hit Highway 1 it's clear sailing all the way to Monterey. But shouldn't you go East to Mecca?" said the officer with tongue in cheek.

"No. We're Buddhists. We're going to the City of Ten Thousand Buddhas."

"Well, good luck. Really thoughtful of you to contact us. Thanks."

Bound for Bodhi.

An excited young man named Steve stopped as we bowed on the freeway frontage road. "I know you are busy, but could you spare just a few minutes? I mean, I know what you are doing... I just know... and, well, I've been looking for this and I think I've found it!" he said, half out of breath.

Steve left everything behind in Orange County – his job, family, girl friend, and house. He was living in his van while looking for a place and a method where, "I can get beyond this carcass body of mine and 'astral souls' and all the rest and get to the ultimate, the oneness with all things," as he put it. "I am really seriously looking for a spiritual community to go to the ultimate and also help others. I don't want to just do my own thing and withdraw." This was a Bodhisattva-talk Steve was voicing.

"He concentrates and seeks only proper enlightenment to take across all living beings. This thought he does not forsake for an instant. The Bodhisattva in this way reverently contemplates and thoroughly practices all kinds of vast and great deeds."

Avatamsaka Sutra
Ten Grounds Chapter

Steve was interested in the City of Ten Thousand Buddhas. "Do you practice the Four Noble Truths and the Eightfold Path? Can a layman study there and work in the community too? Are there enlightened Masters there to teach the real thing?" he asked.

"I want to learn how to hold precepts and read a sutra first-hand. All I've ever seen is the superficial stuff that's not very deep – you know, the paperback books on Buddhism. I want to really get into it. Can I do that there?"

"Yes. It's all there. Everybody holds the precepts. It's a very pure Way-place. Everyone there is devoted to getting enlightened and ending suffering of all kinds for all beings. That's the City of Ten Thousand Buddhas in essence." I said.

Steve took a map, grinned a big "Thanks," and drove off for Ukiah in his van. Bound for Bodhi and living on deep faith.

With deep faith in the Buddhas and all Bodhisattvas,
As well as faith in the path
    traveled by all Buddhas's disciples,
He believes too, in unsurpassed enlightenment.
Thus the Bodhisattva first produces the resolve.

Avatamsaka Sutra

**Heng Sure**
I'll not make them again

Offense and Reform.

My shame grows deeper for my past
As I remember more.
Selfish greed and arrogance
Was all I knew before.
I met the Buddhadharma,
And now although I've erred,
I'm sorry for my past mistakes,
I'll not make them again.

**Heng Chau** • January 12, 1978
The oldest rules for moral conduct on the planet

The people who own the Avila Hot Springs came out in a cold
pouring rain to welcome us and invite us to take a hot bath. We
politely declined both the bath and an offer to "help yourselves to
our snack bar." We could see a big lit up red Coca-Cola sign and the
Master's words came to mind:

"Drinking Coke? If you don't drink coke, you won't fight
with each other. Then you can have some accomplishment."

May 1977

I made a promise not to be late for the bowing anymore. But this morning I broke it and started out over 30 minutes behind. As I drove, the water jug spilled over and soaked my gear and then I cramped up with stomach pains. As I pulled off the road the brakes failed. When I got out to bow it began to rain. It's called karma.

"Everything that happens to you comes from what you do."

Avatamsaka<br>Bodhisattvas' Inquiries Chapter

As soon I began bowing my stomach pains disappeared and the sun came out.

During lunch, Norman Hammond, the fireman and college teacher from Arrayo Grande stopped with some fresh-pickled greens. He showed us how to identify and prepare them. "I don't know why exactly, but I always say a little prayer to the plants before I cut them. It feels right. And I never pull them out of their roots. That way they can grow back," he adds.

As we ate together in the car on the side of the road, Norman talked. "You'll find these plants along the coast and upland. They're beautiful and nutritious. You know, I get a lot from you guys, even though you don't talk much. It's a non-verbal kind of communication. I've started thinking again about a fantasy I have to put on a pack and just take off. I know enough about herbs and plants and the likes, I think I could do all right. There are just too many *things* in life. We've all kind of lost our hinge, you know? I could put down work just like that," says Norman, snapping his fingers. "I read in a Sutra once that 'everything is impermanent.' Most people freak out when they hear that. But there's a beauty in impermanence. It's natural. Some people stockpile for security, but security is like the sweat left on the plate after the last piece of toast has been taken."

When Norman saw our brakes were out, he offered to have them repaired. Heng Sure went to bow alone in a small woods while I took the car with Norman to a local garage. As we drove, Norman talked about some thoughts he's had since starting to read the Wonderful

Dharma Lotus Flower Sutra. "We come face to face with impermanence and the emptiness of our self and freak out and go chasing things trying to fill the hole. Desire piled on top of a desire until we can't move," reflected Norman. "Day after day I pull people out of auto wrecks and burning houses – bloody and spewing their insides out – without letting up. People keep messing up their lives and doing it. But I like my work. I like helping people."

> Then the Bodhisattva thinks, "All living beings flow and turn following their karma into the bitter and difficult places of birth, sickness, old age, and death. They possess deviant views. They have no wisdom. They destroy their wholesome dharmas. I should save them and cause them to escape."
>
> Avatamsaka Sutra
> Ten Transference Chapter

"I've pulled people out of burning houses and they turn around and run back to get their possessions and die trying to carry them out. We are all in a burning house, just like the Sutra says. I really like that part about the Buddha trying to get the kids to leave the burning house. I'm happiest when I've got all my possession in a pack on my back," said Norman with a big smile as we pull into the garage.

Norman was referring to the famous parable of the burning house in the Lotus Sutra. In short, the little children enter a decaying old house to play. It catches fires but they are young and foolish. "They take delight in play and cling to their amusements."

The father returns home and seeing the extreme danger, tries to save the children. But the children, even though they hear their father's warnings, "still cling to their amusements and sport without cease." So the father cleverly devises an expedient.

> "He said to the children, 'I have all kinds of precious playthings: Fine carriages wonderfully bejeweled – sheep carts, and deer carts, and great ox carts, now, right outside the door. So come out, all of you. I had these carts made, and just as you wish, you can play with them.'"

The children raced out in a scramble and were saved. The elder father is the Buddha, the children are all living beings the Buddha vows to save. The burning house is the Triple Realm, that is the world of desire, form and formlessness.

I ask the mechanic please not to smoke cigarettes when he works inside the car. "It's our temple on wheels. We have all our holy books in there."

"Huh?" he says as he looks over his shoulder. He sees our altar and the sutras shelved below Guan Yin Bodhisattva's picture, next to the Abbot's photo. "Yeah, sure, ok," he says and puts out his smoke.

The Dharma-protecting spirits and Bodhisattvas do not like smoke. They leave when people smoke. It breaks the precepts. And when they leave, the demons come. Some people find it hard to believe. We may have been a bit skeptical ourselves at the start, but now we are very careful of our daily behavior. Holding precepts protect us.

As case in point: The mechanic took the car for a test run. The Plymouth's got new brakes! After, as I drove back to the freeway, the car sputtered to a halt. Out of gas?! "How could you be out of gas!? I just filled you a few days ago and we haven't gone more than a few miles!" I got out to grab the spare gas can. When I opened the back door, water gushed out! The water jugs spilled over and would have ruined the Sutras and mantra books. Apparently the whole altar came down and the jugs spilled during a stop-start brake test by the mechanic. If the car had not stopped to "tell me" we would have lost our Dharma jewels. Only one page of text got wet. Another minute and all the books would have been ruined. I couldn't say for sure, but I feel that in asking the mechanic not to smoke, our wheeled Way-place was protected and a tragedy avoided.

A California Highway Patrol officer stopped, "Everything okay?"

"Yes, Sir!" I said with a big smile. "Everything's okay!" We got a little help from our invisible friends. When one holds the precepts purely, all the Buddhas protect him.

> "The Buddhas of the ten directions take pity and constantly guard and protect him."
>
> Brahma Net Sutra

A policeman stopped to see if everything was going smoothly. With the police it's not what we say, it's what we do that counts. This officer had been watching us for a week. After we had passed through his beat without any incidents he stopped to talk. His tone was respectful. "We all want to know down at the station how you make it out here on the road without fighting."

The answer is simple. Precepts. We follow the oldest rules for moral conduct on the planet. The Buddha spoke the precepts and out of kindness and compassion. They are all rooted in filiality. In holding the precepts, one naturally comes to see all beings as his parents and family. And when you treat people with kindness and compassion, even without speaking a word, they return it. That's how we go from town to town without fighting. Instead, we make new friends. (Actually we are just renewing old friendships.)

> "At that time, when Shakyamuni Buddha first sat beneath the Bodhi Tree, after realizing the supreme enlightenment, he set forth the Bodhisattva precepts out of filial compliance towards his parents, his masters among the Sangha, and the Triple Jewel... A Bodhisattva's thoughts should always embody the most ultimate degree of kindness, compassion, and filial piety."
>
> Brahma Net Sutra

Heng Sure's rubber boots got dragged off by some unfriendly farm dogs. We went toward the farm house to retrieve them. The dogs barked and growled and got ready to attack.

"Don't come any closer," shouted someone from the house. "Stay where you are. They bite!"

We finally got the boots back – chewed and ventilated. That was our "facing the mountain of knives" for the day.

**Heng Sure**
Overcome pain and desire

> "Smashing completely all existence, the wheel of birth
> and death, turning the pure, wonderful Dharma-wheel,
> unattached in all the world, he teaches this to all Bodhisat-
> tvas."
>
> Avatamsaka Sutra
> Ten Dwellings Chapter

Sages say that the self is false, illusory. When you see through it, the false mind appears no bigger than a bubble on the vast ocean. Before you see through it, the self appears as real as the bars of a cage, as real as the pain of worry and fear. The will to survive as a separate ego is strong. The glue of habits keeps us stuck to our frail identities until we cultivate the Way and transcend the views of "me and mine." It's a long, slow road.

The Venerable Abbot recently said that cultivators of the Way have to overcome two big obstacles if they are to succeed: pain and desire. The pain is the pain of re-building a solid body from our decaying bags of flesh. The pain that arises in meditation is hard to take if you haven't really resolved to leave the world. Once the resolve is made to sit still and be "thus, thus, unmoving," even unto death, then no pain can turn you. The pain becomes fuel for concentration and before long it stops hurting. This process develops gung-fu, spiritual skill. "Enduring suffering ends suffering," so the saying goes.

Cultivators still must overcome desire, defined by the Venerable Abbot as, "I'm feeling lonely! I want to find a boyfriend (or girl-friend)." This urge is not a joke. Many cultivators have set out on the path and fallen back because of loneliness. We talk glibly of ascetics who live in the wilds all alone, eating pine nuts and drinking stream water, but this requires a great deal of determination and stamina. It's hard to be alone. The ego/self feels threatened by solitude.

Alone most of the time, Heng Chau and I have worked to a place where cities and countryside feel pretty much the same. We have cycled through the changes that come with facing loneliness. We have emerged on the other side with the realization that all dharmas, North, South, East and West are the same – it's your views of them that creates an illusion of difference.

Above Malibu, Ventura, Santa Barbara, we made nervous inner preparations for the wide-open spaces, only to discover that the boondocks are fine, just like town. What on the map looks empty fills in as we bow through. When the house and people fall behind, what does the struggling ego do? It seeks support for its life in nature. The wind becomes a close friend – after a week you can read it like a newspaper. The Big Dipper guides our steps North at night as it has for millions of travelers. Even plants take on a cheering aspect. Malibu's purple, wavy pound-grass is unique to the South Coast and it grows entirely without water – we liked that. As a prop for loneliness a clump of pound-grass brought a bit of life to the dying self.

As confidence grows with experience, the need to confirm existence dwindles, bit by bit. Like climbing a mountain: from below it looks so tall, but the first step is the last step. Start walking and mind your toes, just be where you are all the time. Make a halt. Look around. "Hey! Way up in the air! I guess I didn't need to carry all this gear up here did I? I could have left it behind at the bottom, along with all my fears and false thoughts. The walking would have been much easier." It takes a little time to adjust to cities and back to country but the bowing levels them all into one seamless inner landscape.

Two highway hermits in a cave on wheels, we have felt alone at times but we have always received what we needed. It seems that by not seeking, everything comes, right on time. By Lompoc we became wise to the games the mind plays with imaginary needs.

Yesterday as we left San Luis Obispo it came as a surprise when I felt the old need to clutch at material life-support. Our local

Dharma Protectors all signed off, wished us luck, and said farewell. I felt a twinge of excitement and anticipation. I looked with fresh eyes at Heng Chau and the dragon-car. This is the jump-off. There's one more small city ahead – Morro Bay – and then it's goodbye pavement. We're heading into the land of disappearing ego. Nothing shows on the map at all. It should be just what we need to finally end the self-deception, to lift the mask and see who has been inside all this time. As Heng Chau put it, "With constant pressure on the ego, before long you can bring it gasping into stillness;" and let the true heart emerge. We are very lucky!

---

**Heng Chau** • January 13, 1978
Close down, gather in, and focus

We take Higuera St. into San Luis Obispo, the last major city for the miles of coastline ahead. We decide to bow through town. The alternative routes are too dangerous – no shoulder, high-speed traffic, and rain.

Focus! Cut the Fat!

> To accomplish pure white dharmas
> To perfect merit and virtue –
> These are within all-wisdom
> And not apart from the concentrated mind.

> Avatamsaka Sutra
> Verses in Praise in the Tushita Heaven Palace

Concentration is everything. Heng Sure and I today made a decision to close down, gather in, and focus. It's called,

> Block the passages, shut the doors
> And till the end your strength shall not fail;
> Open up the passages, increase your doings
> And till your last day no help shall come to you.

> Lao Tzu

1) Limit the writing to a few hundred words per day.

2) Stop talking in notes back and forth.

3) Concentrate on the Avatamsaka exclusively. It is said, "Enlighten yourself to the original substance, in one penetration, penetrate all." We have been studying three and four sutras at a time. After reading the Shurangama Sutra this morning, I was late for bowing. The Sutra is wonderful, but too much is the same as not enough. It felt like overeating. One can be greedy with Dharma, too. There has to be a proper balance of study and practice otherwise nothing connects.

4) Simplify diet: eat more "road greens" and rice. Avoid "good food." Most canned foods have rich oils and sugar in them. They fog the mind and increase desire.

5) Keep ch'an meditation steady and regular. Increase in winter with less daylight bowing time.

6) Start to memorize sections of the Avatamsaka Sutra.

We picked some wild edible plants from a nearby field and prepared them for lunch. What an experience! We both felt clean and charged with light energy after lunch, not dull and sluggish. It was a small breakthrough. Natural food is so good and clean that no one remembers. We get lost in the race for fast food and big flavor. This simple diet of rice and greens and tea is real "left-home" food. It keeps you light and clear and on the non-dwelling Way.

> With vegetarian food and clear tea
> The mind errs not
> Enjoying Dharma day and night.
>
> Venerable Master Hsu Yun<br>"Song of the Skin Bag"

Some Self-Reflections.

When I have felt anger and began fault-finding in the past, I just let it blow-up and shoot out. This is wrong. All it does is create a lot of bad karma and oppress others. Bowing is giving me a handle on my emotions. I can begin to see that behind my anger and criticism of others is a big self. The fault is always mine, not the other person's. Learning to really give and be compassionate comes through shrinking the self. I've got a big self to shrink. Today I felt deeply ashamed for being so full of greed, anger, and stupidity after 250 miles and 8 months of bowing. I resolved to shut my mouth and really use effort at cultivation. Pure precepts and single-minded focus are hard to maintain. The self looks for outs like a deep sea diver out of air looks for the surface.

Someday my heart will be so pure and uncovered and my samadhi so unwavering and true that it won't be a fight to stay "home." Let it all go and there are no worries. Stop seeking and everywhere is cool and soft.

> He makes no mistake
> His heart is vast, apart from all worry and vexation.
> His mind and will are soft and flexible.
> All his sense organs are clean and cool.
>
> Avatamsaka Sutra

The Irelands from San Luis Obispo stopped and introduced themselves. "We've got a grandson who's a monk at your monastery. He told us you might be coming through. He's a good boy. How can we help you out?" they said.

---

**Heng Sure**
Swinging a vajra ball-bat instead

> The Bodhisattva thinks, "I should penetrate through all states, leave all errors behind, cut off all discriminations and forsake all attachments."
>
> Avatamsaka Sutra – Ten Practices

Rooters for the Detroit Tigers in the early 60's will remember Charley Paw-paw Maxwell who played left field. Paw-paw used to hit a home run every Sunday. When we investigate Ch'an we "strike the seven." We beat at the seventh consciousness, the brain's traffic cop. This is the faculty that directs sense impressions, memories, and thoughts through the mind's highways.

In Ch'an meditation the purpose of striking the seven is to transform the seventh consciousness from an active to a passive role. The job is to take charge of the mind. How? By using a method, either a hua t'ou, a topic of doubt, or a meditation topic selected for you by a wise advisor. The vajra wisdom sword is a good tool for slicing at the seventh. The thoughts that arise quickly fall to the skillful alert swordsman.

Bowing on the road last Sunday I realized in my false-thoughts that I had never used a sword before, not a real one, and I didn't really know how to hold it. What did I know? Baseball! How about swinging a vajra ball-bat instead? That I can do in the mundane world. Can the transcendental dharmas of the Path accommodate a vajra bat? Try it out! Crack! One false thought over the fence. Hey! Charley Maxwell used to strike at the seventh every Sunday. Good old Paw-paw! Crack! Home Run! Keep on swinging! The ball-bat is a good warm-up but the vajra sword is a gem beyond price. I want to learn to use it next. The vajra ball-bat has its use but my head is full of more than vajra baseballs! Get to work! Swish! Slice! Silence!

"I should use clever skill to make my escape, my mind constantly dwelling in peace..."

Avatamsaka Sutra<br>Ten Practices

**Heng Chau** • January 14, 1978.
Hi, there, **yoo hoo**!

San Luis Obispo.

Police give us the okay and "good luck." Rainy and windy. The Santa Lucia Mountains are ahead, between us and the next town, Morro Bay.

Norman and another fireman, Scott, stopped with an offering of hot tea during a rainstorm at lunch. All four of us huddled together in the back of the Plymouth and quietly shared the meal. After they listened as Heng Sure read one of the Master's verses. We try to end each meal with some Dharma.

"Hey, that's *good!*" exclaimed Norman.

"Yes, really good," said Scott. "Could you read it again?"

This was the verse:

> If you can't put down death,
> You can't pick up life;
> If you can't put down what's false,
> You can't pick up what's true.

"Boy I could chew on those words for years!" said Norman. Two people walk out in a pounding rain with hot tea, nuts, and sandwiches.

"We really respect your journey. Hope this helps you make it," they said.

High winds and heavy flooding. Trees are uprooted and power lines down. The long drought is over. Rivers are flowing for the first time in years. So are the streets. I opened the door of the car and set a kettle on the ground outside. The kettle floated away.

A car full of young women flirting and giggling: "Hi, there, yoo hoo!" following us for the last hour of the day. We've learned it's best to mind our own business and not even lift our eyes in some situations. We don't argue with people and try our best to cause no one any trouble, even with a single unsteady glance. This verse from the Avatamsaka Sutra guides us along the highway and through the towns."

> He is quite free from contention
> From troubling and harming, and from hatred.
> He knows shame, respect, and rectitude.
> And well protects and guards his faculties.
>
> Ten Grounds Chapter

**Heng Sure**
Is wonderful beyond words

> "All living beings have the Buddha nature. All will become Buddhas. It is only because of our afflictions and our thoughts that we do not realize it."
>
> Shakyamuni Buddha

There is magic in nature. In nature, things work themselves out in silence and wonderful light. Humankind has tried to control nature's force and magic and we have nearly destroyed the harmony of our earth. Through greed, hatred, and stupidity, all brought about by false thinking and attachments, we have obscured the light of wisdom within us. Our basic instruction on the bowing pilgrimage is still the hardest to carry out: "Don't do any false thinking." More specifically the Master said last week, "Be 'men of the Way without a mind'. No thoughts is just no mind. No mind is dwelling nowhere. Dwelling nowhere, attached to nothing is wonderful beyond words."

Why would one want to be without a mind or thoughts or a dwelling? The Buddha realized his true mind, his natural mind when he attained enlightenment. That is the goal of cultivation, to break through the ceaseless flow of the common, discriminating mind and unite with the "True Suchness" mind. The Buddha compared the common mind to a bubble on the ocean of Truth. When false thoughts stop, the truth appears.

The mind attempts to control Nature with false, common thoughts. When the false mind rolls on unchecked, we feel lonely and we act selfishly. We make karmic mistakes and suffer for them. Such a price to pay for having left the very home we seek so frantically. It is said, "The sea of suffering is boundless; a turn of the head is the other shore."

> The manifestation of spiritual power:
> This is called the Buddha.
> In all the three periods of time you may seek
> But there is nothing at all which exists.
>
> Avatamsaka Sutra – Verses in Praise
> in the Tushita Heaven Palace

---

**Heng Chau** • January 15, 1978
No matter what comes, don't get angry

"Never get angry…"

We were reading from the Sutra in mid-afternoon on a lawn under a tree. A man named Frank stopped cutting his lawn and came over.

"Are you praying for peace?"

I nod.

"Boy we really need some, huh?"

"Mostly we are trying to turn back some of the disasters and suffering in the world. There's too many earthquakes, plane crashes, families fighting and not taking good care of each other," I said. Frank sat down with us on the grass.

"There's a lot of that. You know I almost died two years ago, but I surprised them. I used to be a rough and tumble guy, but now I'm as gentle as a kitten," he says laughing. "I don't worry and *never get angry*. Otherwise it's all over."

Frank made a connection between unrest in the world and unrest in himself. I remembered the Abbot's words to us just recently:

> "You must have patience with every single state. Patience will win. You may not get angry with anything. No matter what comes, don't get angry. This matter of no anger will be of great significance in the future of Buddhism in the United States."

Frank recognized how anger could kill him and mess up the world with bad energy. All disasters in the world come from acts of destruction that begin with anger. In a way that's the heart of this pilgrimage: by getting rid of our own anger we reduce disasters and suffering in the world by a bit.

Frank brought out a food offering. He gave us a lot of easy laughter to loosen up our overly serious faces and brighten our way. When Frank first came we were reading from the Ten Transferences Chapter of the Avatamsaka:

> "He vows that all beings ride the patience vehicles and forever leave behind their hateful, turbid attitudes towards all living beings."

Never getting angry is just "riding the patience vehicle."

Sometimes the Sutra, the people we meet, and our own thoughts mesh and synchronize. Everyone and everything speaks the Dharma. It's as if the whole world is contained within our own minds.

For example, tonight we camped at the end of a dead end street off the main road. A heavy storm made us nearly invisible. We had just finished reading in the Sutra about giving when a car pulls up alongside.

A man knocks on the window. His face and eyes are clear and bright. The air is full of good energy. He holds out a bag of freshly picked organic vegetables. "These are from my father's garden in Merced. I have watched you every day since Guadalupe," he says.

"This is the first time I stopped but in my thoughts I am with you every day. We deeply appreciate your efforts towards peace and hold your journey very close to our hearts," he nods toward his wife and children who smile and wave from their station wagon. "I hope you will accept this token of appreciation and support."

As he left we both wondered how they found us on this obscure street on a dark, rainy night. We had just read from the Sutra:

> "The Bodhisattva is mindful and protective of living beings in this way. He wants to make his own body into the foremost of stupas and universally make everybody happy... He wants to be a pure and cool pool for all beings and to give them every peace and happiness."
>
> Ten Transferences Chapter

**Heng Sure**
Would you pass the secret on?

> As one who is born into the palace of a king
> Yet suffers from hunger and from cold
> When one does not cultivate the Dharma
> Mere study is just like this.
>
> As one who floats in the water
> Fears drowning and yet dies of thirst,
> When one does not cultivate the Dharma
> Mere study is just like this.
>
> Avatamsaka Sutra
> Bodhisattvas' Inquiries Chapter

Suppose you were working in a library and you come across a book that solved all your problems. Would you put it back on the shelf and forget it? Or would you take it out and try its methods in your life?

Suppose you were managing an orchard and you discovered that the fruit of your trees could feed and nourish all the hungry people on earth. Would you pass the secret on? Would you eat the fruits yourself?

These examples illustrate my experience as a graduate student after encountering the Buddhist Sutras. I felt like a drowning man who suddenly discovers an island beneath his feet. I could hardly contain my impulse to shout, "Hey! This is the real thing! Wake up, everybody! This is what we've been looking for!"

My impatience with those who treated the Dharma as a topic of study, as a "field of inquiry," pushed me right out of the university. The principles of Buddhism are true. They are solid and active in the mind. They are wholesome and good for everyone. I felt a moral need to take action, to bring the Dharma out of the books and into the streets. The need for Dharma medicine in an ailing world was too great. Who could leave his family to suffer in a sinking ship when he possesses the plans and the materials for a ship of salvation big enough to seat us all?

> One may be the captain of a steamship
> And still drown in the ocean.
> When one does not cultivate the Dharma
> Mere study is just like this.

Avatamsaka Sutra
Bodhisattva's Inquiries Chapter

---

**Heng Chau** • January 16, 1978
Today's test was anger

San Luis Obispo.

Little things: Someone gave us a fruitcake and said it was "clean." Turns out the cake was loaded with alcohol. A few bites and we were flushed and dizzy. Tough bowing all afternoon. Alcohol brings out the worst in people.

The local Beacon gas station has a washroom with hot water. A rare find! We took turns shaving and bathing, first time in weeks.

We suit up in a rain gear under store overheads like a Quick-stop Store or gas station and bow all day. At night if there's a Laundromat we dry our gear and do *tai ji*. If there's no Laundromat the wet clothes get piled in the front seat until the sun comes out and we hang them out to dry on fences and trees.

For the fifth consecutive day the storms clear while we bow. When we stop to eat or at the end of the day the skies let go with all they've got.

Heng Sure and I have never seen a heavier rainfall than the one that fell today. Within minutes the streets turn to rivers and the cars look like boats ploughing through. We camped by a cemetery on Elks Road. The bridge ahead was blocked and couldn't be crossed. Work crews with a crane worked through the night trying to break up the jam of logs and uprooted trees caught on the bridge piling. There's a large pyramid in the cemetery. We are parked between the stone pyramid and the busy Elks Club nightlife.

Inside it's howling too. The slightest looking outside with the six sense organs or being turned by emotion is felt instantaneously. What does it feel like? Like a sudden storm filling the cloudless sunny sky or a thick covering of fog. It's said,

> With a single thought unproduced,
> The entire substance manifest.
> When the six sense organs move
> One is covered by clouds.

When you cultivate, you gather "steam." It is usually lost chasing worldly dharmas. One suddenly discovers a new source of energy and you feel years younger. If you can hold the steam, it makes a new person out of you and smelts true wisdom. If you can't hold it, you lose it all and have to start all over.

Bowing in rainstorms and high winds makes it that much harder to concentrate. And inside the furnace steam blazes. Right at the point when you can hardly bear the pressure you get a test. Today's test was anger. I flunked.

The steam was screaming to shoot out all day – by rapping, watching people come and go, the urge to sleep, and the desire to overeat. But I held on. Then at the end of the day as we scouted for a Laundromat I let myself get angry at Heng Sure about drying the clothes. I felt something leave me right then.

At night I had bad dreams of evil and heavy violence. Packs of wild dogs and gangs of toughs were running all over killing virtuous people. The forces of evil were out of control. They attacked our car. Shih Fu was there with another religious leader trying to quell the debacle. "They are afraid of Sutras and really upset by their appearance in the West, that's why," said the Master.

When I woke up I realized the dream was all made from my own mind. The dogs and demons were the "living beings" set loose by my anger. I was just seeing another side of my self-nature. So it says in the Avatamsaka,

"As one thinks, so one receives in return."

A concentrated mind is a peaceful mind. A single thought of anger in the mind of a cultivator is worse than an atomic bomb.

---

**Heng Sure**
A better investment than blue-chip stocks

"He constantly purifies his deepest thoughts of faith and understanding, with utmost respect for all Buddhas and with reverence for the Dharma and for the Sangha as well, with ultimate sincerity he makes offerings and his resolve comes forth."

Avatamsaka Sutra
Worthy Leader Chapter

There's one sure way to purify deep thoughts: by cultivating any of the 84,000 Dharma methods that the Buddha left behind for us. One can't go wrong by developing faith and understanding in Buddhism. Utmost respect for the Triple Jewel is a better investment than blue-chip stocks. You get a higher dividend that is paid in wisdom, self-control, happiness, and the goods return for a longer term.

Heng Chau has identified a look he calls "Dharma Protecting Eyes" that is common to all those new Dharma protectors who make offerings to the Triple Jewel through us. The look is wide open, happy, full of light and faith. It's the look of someone who feels the inner Buddha seed pulse and glow as they give themselves away. Next comes a resolve to get enlightened!

---

**Heng Chau** • January 17, 1978.
Sinking beneath the waves of a violent river

San Luis Obispo.

As we bowed outside the Recreation Dept., a well-built heavy-set man walked up and blocked Heng Sure's way. He was hostile and itching to fight.

"I don't see where the Lord said we have to do this… whatever it is," he said, squaring off and flexing his fists. One arm was cocked ready to hit Heng Sure at the slightest excuse.

"You don't talk, eh," he provoked. "Well, there's sure a lot of noise coming out of you." Heng Sure didn't respond and kept bowing.

"You need a shave," he said, trying to egg Heng Sure on. "What's the matter, don't you shave?" He waited. His muscles were tense and bulging. His fists were white. There was more here than met the eye. It felt like a test, almost like the guy was an *agent provocateur*. But even more visible was his pain. People who are full of hatred and anger are really hurting inside. We really feel sorry for them. Seeing the suffering behind the hate and anger, you're no longer afraid for yourself. You only feel pity. He swaggered over and tried the same thing on me and then left. It takes two to fight. We would rather be beaten than hurt anyone or clog our hearts with hate.

> "By nature he is apart from hatred. The Bodhisattva thinks of all living beings with kindness, with thoughts of benefiting, happiness, harmony, and gathering in. He has forever left behind anger, hatred, animosity, and harm."
>
> Avatamsaka Sutra
> Ten Grounds Chapter

Lots of people stopping and offering food, kerosene, and good wishes! A guard from a nearby prison stopped and gave us a bag of oranges. He had some prisoners with him in a caged van.

"We sure need this," he said. "Good luck!"

A man named Sam who is a tax appraiser and Jehova's Witness stopped to tell us he admired our devotion and didn't like his job.

"I'd like to do something creative, like you're doing," he said.

I told him a little about the pilgrimage and said I hoped he found a better job. "Proper Livelihood is one of the Noble Eightfold Path."

"Maybe I will someday… and I'll do it full time like you're doing…" said Sam thoughtfully. "Someday I'll be knocking at your door." Sam works for the State. He may have meant "knocking at our door" as part of his job or to cultivate the Way. I'm not sure which. Since we live in a car and also cultivate non-attachment I said, "We don't have a door."

"How will I find you?" wondered Sam.

In the Avatamsaka Sutra there's a section where the Bodhisattvas come to see the "measureless and boundless great suffering that the Ten Evil Deeds produce for living beings. He then resolves to cause all beings to leave behind all evil and go towards the good." One of his reflections concerns jobs, what people do to make a living.

He further reflects, "All living beings are greedy and grasping without ever getting enough. They only seek wealth and profit. They live by deviant livelihoods. I should cause them to dwell in the pure karma of body, mouth, and mind and the dharmas of right livelihood."

Avatamsaka Sutra<br>
Ten Grounds Chapter

The happiest people we meet are ones engaged in meaningful work, work that benefits others and adds good energy to the world. Seeking wealth and profit seldom makes people happy, and often creates a lot of offenses and bad karma. We are what we do. It was like a fireman said last week, "I like my work. In a small way I help people when they really need it. I can save lives and avert disasters. I'm helping people and get paid enough to live comfortably on. It's clean, you know?"

The Irelands stopped with a cooked meal and some dry clothes. They said another big storm was rolling in tonight. As we cleared the dishes Mrs. Ireland said, "Don't bother washing those dishes, we've got running water at home."

At that point Heng Sure opened our car door, letting out a gush of water that accumulates on the floor and under the seats when it rains – the car is old and has lots of leaks.

"No problem, we've got running water too."

Norman Hammond rove by to offer some fuel oil. He had been reading a Sutra and wanted to know, "What's the root of birth and death for women?"

"Same as for men and all living beings: sexual desire."

"That's what I thought. Boy, one could put down a lot of things, but to put down *that* one is real tough, huh?"

In the Avatamsaka love and desire is likened to sinking beneath the waves of a violent river. We people casually enter the river only to end up in the "whirlpool of birth and death," unable to get out.

"They float and turn on the river of love. They rush over the rapids without stopping to think what they are doing, and how it awakens desire, anger, and harming. And they follow along without forsaking it... and there's no one who can save them and take them across."

Avatamsaka Sutra
Ten Grounds Chapter

In bowing, I've just come to see how much desire and greed I really have. I never imagined I was so defiled and attached. Like Norman said, it's really difficult to put it down. But like the Sutra points out, you'll never be free or have any wisdom until you do. And it's not for sure you will get another chance. Greedy desire can easily cause one to fall into the lower realms of the hells, animals, and hungry ghosts. So there's a saying in Buddhism,

"It is not easy to obtain a human body."

Sutra in 42 Sections

Once you lose it, who can guarantee if and when you will get another? This life is very precious because human beings have the best chance to cultivate and get enlightened.

"All dharmas are like illusions, dreams, shadows, and echoes; like the moon's reflection in water, like images in a mirror, like flames and transformations, and thus level and equal."

Avatamsaka Sutra
Ten Grounds Chapter

While bowing, everything looks empty. Shapes and forms floating and arranging, breaking apart and reforming – like the whole world is a disconnected jigsaw puzzle floating in a pool. On and on, life after life, we people come and go without beginning or end. We are caught up in some kind of turning wheel. We run across each other again and again without remembering or recognizing. "Nothing is new under the sun" as one man put it yesterday.

Last night I dreamed that I was in a previous life remembering this one. I don't know anymore. After a good day of bowing it all seems like a dream. I used to think I knew how things are. I'm not so sure anymore. There are many strange and wonderful things in the world that just can't be known.

The sand bags are still in position on the storefronts to hold the flooding back. Although people try to be "business-as-usual" there's a grim and sober tension in the air. As we bow by, people are looking up at the dark clouds. They are standing next to limp sand bags that didn't quite do the trick in keeping the rising flood waters out of their stores and homes. Nobody wants to think about what another storm could do. But they think about it anyway. They just don't talk about it.

Flood mud is super-fine, silt-soft and minute. It seeps into everything. Folks are using shovels, hoes, rakes, and brooms trying to save their homes and possessions. Down the center of the main street is a trail line of debris (branches, bottles, broken furniture) where the flood water receded this morning. It's a real reminder of impermanence to see a river winding its way into a drug store, and around a bank. Then it buries a mailbox on the main drag of San Luis. This is the nature of all conditioned things.

> "Disciples of the Buddha, the Bodhisattva, Mahasattva dwelling on this ground contemplates all conditioned dharmas as they really are.
>
> "They are: impermanent, suffering, impure, insecure, decaying, short-lived, produced and destroyed in an instant. They don't come from the past or go into the future, nor do they stay in the present."

This is how it really is. I see it right before my eyes and yet can't accept the truth. Instead I cling to the things of the world as if they were eternal and my own body immortal. The Buddha's message is simple: It's only because of these false thoughts and attachments that we living beings suffer and don't attain ultimate wisdom and liberation. We hold on and try to make the world fit our egoistic yearnings and desires. But it doesn't fit. All our problems come from this confusion about the nature of dharmas.

> "He also contemplates that dharmas cannot be preserved or relied on. They are the companions of worry, grief, suffering, and vexation. They are bound up with love and hate. Grief and distress increase and accumulate without stopping. Greed, hatred, and ignorance blaze on without cease. They are conjoined with a host of calamities which grow by day and by night…"

And then the Sutra says that all of this mass of hardship and anxiety we create for ourselves is because we just can't let go and take the world for what it really is. All dharmas are just like dreams. There's nothing at all to attach to. So the closing line of this passage reads:

> "The dharmas are like illusions. They are unreal."
>
> Avatamsaka Sutra
> Ten Grounds Chapter

The flood was speaking Dharma loud and clear.

On an empty street corner next to a park bench, it's quiet. There's no one around for blocks. If anyone approached we could surely hear and see them, even from behind. And yet as I come up from a bow suddenly there's a young woman sitting there, swinging her crossed leg in my face with one arm resting over the back of the bench. It's as if she had been there for hours and yet she wasn't there fifteen seconds ago and there wasn't a sound or a shadow made. Poof! She's seductive and trying to catch my attention.

"Well, when are you going to talk to me, baby, huh?" she says coyly. I don't dare talk or even look at her. I kept bowing and didn't look back.

Everything is a test
To see what you will do.
Mistaking what's right before your eyes
You'll have to start anew.

Police stop at night and inform us there's a "no night camping or sleeping in your vehicle" ordinance. We drive to a dead end road next to the 101 Freeway outside of town. We are always moving, even when we stop.

---

**Heng Sure**
But no one actually does it

"With profound faith in the Buddha and in the Buddha's Dharmas, as well as faith in the path traveled by all Buddha's disciples, he belicves, too, in the unsurpassed great enlighten-ment. Thus the Bodhisattva first produces his resolve."

Avatamsaka Sutra

Vickie, a college student and housewife: "Everyone talks about the spiritual life. I've been looking around and checking it out. Everyone talks about the Path but no one actually does it. When I saw you two bowing, I realized that you were walking the Path. I couldn't wipe the grin off my face all day. You were doing it! Here and now! And that meant that I could do it too."

**Heng Chau** • January 18, 1978
The more I bow, the more I find

San Luis.

Dharma Master Heng Lai and Upasaka Kuo Chou Rounds show up to bow and share a meal offering in a small city park. Kuo Chou sang a praise to Guan Yin Bodhisattva he composed. It was good to hear.

John, a minister from Unity Church made an offering and an expression of solidarity with the pilgrimage. "It's what it's all about, isn't it – just keeping our hearts open?" he said.

Woman: "You're the ones bowing for peace?"

Monk: "Yes. We are trying to stop disasters and calamities in the world."

Woman: "You're not Moonies?" (Hesitant and cautious.)

Monk: "No, we're Buddhists."

Woman: (Relaxed and happy) "Oh, good! Here, and God bless you." She hands me an offering of money.

Hard-hat construction worker wanted to know the details about how we bow in rainstorms and flooding. "We really need the rain, but isn't it bad for you guys?"

"If it's good for everyone, it's good for us."

"That's wonderful. I like that."

"That's Buddhism. When everyone is truly happy, we are too."

"Yes. Well good luck to you. It's really something."

Local radio station and Cal Poly newspaper stop for interviews.

Sometimes, when least expected, you get a clear picture of your true "self." I saw mine today. It was towards the end of the day as we bowed past a hamburger stand. I came up from a bow and saw how impure and phony I am. So much greed, anger, and stupidity after 250 miles of bowing! The more I bow, the more I find. I wanted to cry. I felt so unworthy to be a monk.

Just then, an old silver-haired lady with a deep, warm smile and tears in her eyes walked up. She put a large offering of money in my hand. She never said a word. Neither did I. But somehow, I feel, she knew and was silently saying, "Everything is okay. It's just part of a long journey home. Everything's ok. Raise your spirits!"

Inside I promised to try harder and really do it well. We have been well received in San Luis. Offerings and good wishes abound.

Thom Halls, a photographer from the San Luis Telegram-Tribune stopped to shoot some pictures. I remembered him from back near the Mesa. (He was the one who had the run-in with the motorcyclist and almost lost his temper.)

"How are you?"

"Pretty good – in fact, real good!" said Thom.

"No more getting angry?"

"Hey!" says Thom with a smile. "That little saying... I mean mantra... works. It really does!"

"Oh?"

"Yes. It's really amazing. I blew it once last week, but I have been able to stop my anger. Sometimes I only need to recite part of it, like 'Patience, Patience...'* and something inside clicks and says, 'Wait a minute. This isn't right,' and presto! No more anger. I just crack up and laugh at it all. No kidding, it really works. Tell your teacher thanks."

[* Thom copied down a mantra in English by the Venerable Abbot to control anger when he first interviewed us. The entire mantra is:

Patience, patience
Got to have patience
Don't get angry
Swo Pe He

]

## Heng Sure
On faith alone can you enter in

> "Faith is the source of the Path and the mother of merit and virtue. It nurtures and raises all wholesome Dharmas. It cuts through the net of doubts and leaves the flow of love. It opens up the highest road to Nirvana."
>
> Avatamsaka Sutra

After you've seen a healthy person, you won't tolerate being sick again. We think we're on the winning team, until the big illness, death, comes to end the game. What to do? Run from the truth? Face it and "rage, rage, against the dying of the light?" Neither answer solves the problem.

Before we meet the Buddhadharma, "death and taxes" as the saying goes, seem inevitable. When we hear the good news, that the Buddha appeared in the world to answer the basic question of birth and death, it's like a lamp in the gloom. Faith is born. We want to investigate further.

It's said, "The Buddhadharma is a great ocean. On faith alone can you enter in." With so much darkness and sickness in the world, who needs to be told twice? Who would turn down a lifeline when sinking in quicksand? Where does faith come from? It comes from needing the truth. Those who need to know where they came from and where they are going will find out sooner or later. The character for faith is 信 (*hsin*), which breaks down into 人 man's 言 words. You hear about the Buddha then go investigate for yourself. Faith is born. Have no fear. Cut your doubts. Your Buddha-seed is ready to grow.

Heng Chau • January 19, 1978
A field of blessings

Bill Ireland stopped by with a meal offering. "Do you enjoy the food? I mean, are you happy with it?" he asks.

"Buddhist monks and nuns – the Sangha – are called 'a field of blessings.' That just means we accept offerings in order to give people a chance to do good. They plant blessings by giving. They give through us, not to us. So if you like to make offerings through us, that's all that counts. Besides, if we let ourselves enjoy it when it's good, then we will be unhappy when it's gone. We try to be impartial and work hard to be a pure field of blessings that people can believe in."

"Well, I don't care. We really like it and want to do it. It makes us happy," said Bill.

"That's it. If you are happy, then we are happy."

"He vows that all living beings become foremost fields of blessings that the world can believe in, and fulfill the unsurpassed perfection of giving."

Avatamsaka Sutra<br>Ten Transference Chapter

"Oh, yes," added Bill, "if you run into any problem with people giving you a hard time – police or anyone – no matter how far North you go, you just tell them to call us, Bill and Pat Ireland in San Luis. We'll explain everything, by gosh, you bet we will."

Norman Hammond came by to borrow another sutra (The Vajra Sutra) and offered a book on wild edible plants for the journey up the coast.

"Those sutras really make sense. The commentary by the Abbot says exactly what I was thinking and feeling... like the words came right out of my mouth and mind! I really like reading them."

"I vow that all living beings will obtain the benefit from the extremely profound proper Dharma and completely destroy all afflictions without exception."

Avatamsaka Sutra

The Sutras are the Proper Dharma. If you study them, you become happier. Norman related his experience of feeling that the Sutra's principles were just the same as his own ideas. It reminded me of something the Master said once.

"To listen to Sutras and hear the Dharma is to study our originally existent wisdom. Although it is called studying our originally existent wisdom, this is not how we acquire it. We already have it. We already have this kind of wisdom but we have forgotten. For a long time we have not used our extremely profound prajna wisdom. We have forgotten it. Now hearing the Sutras and listening to the Dharma brings back our originally existent wisdom."

From lecture on the Avatamsaka Sutra

That's what is meant by people's minds are just the Buddha. It's all within. We just forget and get rusty.

So many people we meet share two things: one, a feeling of futility and emptiness with seeking peace and happiness in material things, and two, a deep spiritual longing and quest – a kind of rootlessness that keeps them moving and unsettled. Norman said it like this: "San Luis is getting polluted. I always thought this would be the last time I'd move, but I guess I'll forever be picking up and putting down my roots."

It's so clear the West is ripe for the Buddhadharma. I think in the future there will be a great flourishing of Buddhism in the West comparable to or maybe surpassing its flowering in Asia. The roots are thirsty for the sweet dew. We are all the roots. The Dharma is the water.

As one thirsty thinks of icy water,
As one hungry dreams of good food,
As one sick reflects on wholesome medicine
As a bee is greedy for good honey
So too, do we in just that way
Wish to hear the Dharmas of sweet dew.

> Avatamsaka Sutra
> Ten Grounds Chapter

I talked too long and it started to rain. It felt like a lesson. I realized what a gaping outflow my mouth is. I repented and vowed to try harder not to rap on in a casual and frivolous way. It just obstructs everyone, myself included. For example the karmic retribution for irresponsible speech is of two kinds if one is born as a human:

The first is, no one accepts what you say.
The second is, what you say is not clearly understood.

> Avatamsaka Sutra
> Ten Grounds Chapter

After I repented, the rain stopped and a rainbow came out as if to say, "That's right. Clean up your act. Now that you know, don't do it again."

We camped on a frontage road next to the Sheriff's Department and County Jail facility. We have found that camping right in plain view or in the center of things, we can often pass the night undetected and undisturbed.

A very confused woman driving a Cadillac without a reverse gear ploughed into a ditch at the end of the dead-end road we are camping on. She knocked on our window and asked for help. She was all dressed up in a white pelt fur coat. She didn't know where she was or where she was going or how she found herself driving this car alone in the middle of the night. We maneuvered the car around. It was a very strange encounter. We pointed her to the highway and went back to our meditation.

When I saw the white fur coat I remembered a dream I had where a white animal, like a mink or seal, attacked us while bowing. So as we helped move the car I recited the Great Compassion Mantra. Heng Sure indicated that he had been too because he felt danger.

Patience Wins.

Most dreams are about false thoughts and attachments. Most states and experiences are just dreams. The key to success in cultivating the Way is patience – patience to the extreme. The Chinese character for "patience" is 忍 (jen). It is a picture of a sword suspended above a heart or the mind. There's no secret to cultivation, you just overcome all states with patience. And it always feels like there's a sword dangling above your heart.

> "Cultivation is all about patience. You just have to be able to bear pain. Also you must be able to be alone and not go seeking a partner to release your desire... If you can be patient with both of these and be happy, then you can succeed. Of course you're uncomfortable most of the time, but that's just how it is. Patience wins!"
>
> Master Hua
> Instructions en route
> December 1977

**Heng Sure**
Doubting is a heavy habit

> "Faith has no turbidity, no stain. It purifies the mind. It eradicates arrogance and forms the basis of respect. It is also the primary asset of the Dharma-treasury. It purifies the hands. One can then begin to practice."
>
> Avatamsaka Sutra

Faith was a word I heard on Sundays. It was a cause for sleep in the pews. Faith meant the opposite of vibrant life-experience, so I thought. Losers and old ladies clung go their faith. It was blind. Faith meant that this life was a failure, a bummer, and all that's left is to aim at future happiness in the hereafter.

Faith in the Buddha-dharma is alive, dynamic. Faith in the Way is wide-open eyes and here-and-now. It is practical; it is joyous and magical.

"The Way and the response intertwined are hard to conceive of," as it says in the Great Compassion Repentance. A day of effort yields a day of response. The best part is Buddhism's focus on the individual. Faith is your own business. Your resolve and your own efforts in practice will realize your faith. It has nothing to do with external forces. As pure as your faith becomes, so do your mind and your body grow in purity.

If we truly believed in the teachings of the sages, we could become sages ourselves on the spot. But doubting is a heavy habit. Doubts grow like a forest, like a net. Long-term hard work is the way to success.

> "Like drilling wood to make a fire, if one rests before the sparks appear, the fire, like the effort, will disappear. The lazy person is also thus."
>
> Avatamsaka Sutra<br>Bodhisattvas' Inquiries Chapter

**Heng Chau** • January 20, 1978
He just doesn't use his vocal cords

Salvador, a young apprentice to a Sioux medicine man, stopped by. We don't eat meat or fish and Salvador gladly offered to take some tuna fish sandwiches someone left on our car. He said he felt "directed" to us.

"You know I seldom go jogging and never come this way. This morning I had a strong feeling to jog and take this particular road... And bam! Here you are!" He was very excited about the purposes of the pilgrimage and felt an affinity with Buddhism even though he couldn't get a handle on it. "It would be hard to put into words. I just feel we have a lot in common and are on the same path somehow," he said.

Salvador also commented that Heng Sure's silence "spoke" as loud as words.

"Oh, he talks, he just doesn't use his vocal cords," he said with a knowing smile.

**Heng Sure**
All take and no give

"With faith, one can give and the mind will not be stingy. With faith, one can happily enter the Buddhadharma. With faith, one's wisdom, merit, and virtue all increase. With faith, one will certainly arrive at the ground of the Tathagata."

Avatamsaka Sutra

Faith carried me back to my inner Buddha-seed in strange ways, at odd times. Early mornings on the way to graduate school bicycling down the Berkeley Hills, looking across the Bay at an innocent, sun-washed San Francisco, my eyes would try to spot Gold Mountain Monastery. My thought frequently wandered there before I drew near the place. Student life was more and more the same old tread mill. "Through-put" was the goal, not "truth" or "heart." I read the Buddhist Journal Vajra Bodhi Sea that came from Gold Mountain and the pictures of bare walls and bitter asceticism made my soft insides twitch. But I was growing weary of the aimless bad habits I had dropped into. My life was selfish, covered over with smoke and alcohol and too much sugary food. My heart was not in it any longer. By worldly standards I dwelt in a pleasure-dome. All senses were stuffed to capacity. But the core was hollow and aching. More and more I recognized the poisons I was putting into my body as just that — life-ending poisons. What turned me around were the Buddha's words just like the quote above. I recognized that my life had been all "take" and no "give." I had dabbled in Buddhist meditation enough to know about the words "enlightenment" and "wisdom." No matter how deep I dug into bad ways and unhealthy pursuits, I could not lose that little pure seed. It itched when I felt saddest. "Gee, there must be something better than this to do with my energy." (Itch.) "Yes, you could be an enlightened man," it would say. It would lead me on when I felt happiest. "Wow, if it feels this good to be happy, how does it feel to be happy all the time, like the Buddha?" (Twitch.) "At Gold Mountain you could find out for yourself," said the little seed.

What was it but faith speaking to me? Following the voice, I was lead to happily enter Gold Mountain's door to study the Buddha-dharma. My doubts decreased as my faith grew. Soon I was able to put down my old bad ways gradually as I picked up new, true habits and views. It's a natural, wholesome process, like tending a fertile garden of healthy plants. Faith is the unfailing seed.

**Heng Chau** • January 21, 1978
You can bow with your mind

Morro Bay, 12 miles ahead.

We are heading northwest over the Santa Lucia Mountains. There's a cool, clear wind sweeping down from the north. The hills are green and the land is laughing, with gurgling creeks, birds, and spring buds.

I had a dream last night that we were at the last hour of the final day of Guan Yin Recitation session. People were very sincere and working single-mindedly. Guan Yin Bodhisattva came and people's voices pitched up. The hall filled with an awesome energy and immense light. Everyone felt like one body. Guan Yin Bodhisattva manifested in a huge and magnificent form. People were bowing and kneeling down in joy and awe. Their faces were full of compassion and a deep reverence. It was totally real and electrifying. All beings are Guan Yin Bodhisattva; Guan Yin Bodhisattva is all beings.

Some says, "Guan Yin Bodhisattva has been here all the time, just as real and life-like as you and me. But this is incredible!" This didn't feel like a regular dream. Waking up I was left with a feeling that although such a thing seems inconceivable, we all had "let go" enough to experience it and know it was possible and only the beginning. There was no turning back after this state. The unbelievable and impossible was within our own hearts and within reach. Everyone was very happy and full of light. If you have faith and concentration without let-up, there can be a response. So it's said:

> "One who takes the Buddha's sutras as his own and concentrates his mind without rest, this person will get to see Buddhas equal in number to his thoughts."
>
> Avatamsaka Sutra

Bill Ireland stopped and told us he made arrangements to have our car fixed at a local garage. "You know, when you're young like you fellows, you can get down and bow like this everyday. But when you're old like me, you just can't do it." observed Bill.

"Not with your body, maybe, but you can bow with your mind. Your mind doesn't get old. It's as strong as ever."

"Hmmm…" said Bill, "Maybe so."

There's a section from the Ten Conducts Chapter of the Avatamsaka Sutra where the Bodhisattva contemplates all living beings and the inevitable impermanence of their bodies.

> Again he thinks, "How strange living beings are! How ignorant and lacking in wisdom! Within birth and death they get countless bodies which are perilous and fragile. Without let up they hastily go bad gain. Their bodies have already gone bad, are now going bad, or will soon go bad and yet they are unable to use these unstable bodies to seek a solid body."
>
> The Bodhisattva then resolves to study what all Buddhas have studied and get all-wisdom. He vows to get the Dharma-nature body which does not go bad like conditioned dharmas do, and to then teach all living beings this path.
>
> "I will cause them to obtain eternal peace, security, and happiness by harmonizing with the still tranquility and indestructible Dharma-nature."
>
> Avatamsaka Sutra
> Ten Conducts Chapter

The land seemed dead and withered. Now with spring's rain everything is alive and supple again. The grass, trees, and creatures were just dormant or hibernating. The winter drought works like our false thoughts and attachments. They cover over our Dharma-nature like the cold frost covers the earth. The spring rain and sun revives the withered roots. The Dharma revives our minds in the same way. Birth and death are just five-letter words. Our original nature is "still, tranquil, and indestructible." Our Dharma-nature body never falls apart.

We were bowing on a narrow ledge going up the first ascent of mountains. A man appeared. He was moving quickly and had a racing energy about him. As he handed me some money he said, "If there's true veneration, then even a dog's tooth emits light." He paused to see if I got it, then said, "Have a safe journey," and walked back up the mountain road.

Let no dust alight.

As the sun sets, a long beam of light angles through the tall pines. Within are countless tiny dust particles swirling and tumbling in the air. They are always there but can't be seen until there's sunlight to illumine them.

My false thoughts are the same. At the end of the bowing day there's a certain light gathered within that shines on the mind. All the senses are tuned razor-sharp. Every false thought can be seen. Too many to count, they are just like the motes of dust in the sunbeam.

False, defiled, upside down thoughts created from beginningless time by greed, hatred, and stupidity, they pile up and follow you in life after life. In the Shurangama Mantra preface Ananda recites and wishes the mantra to

> Melt away my deluded thoughts
> gathered in a million kalpas.

A kalpa is an extremely long period of time. (Roughly a million years). A million kalpas is incalculable. That's how long I've been collecting false thoughts and confused karma. I may have – I don't know for sure how long it's been...

Heng Sure and I are becoming very conscientious about the precepts and even the smallest transgressions. It all comes back to obstruct you, sooner or later.

The body is a Bodhi tree,
The mind like a bright mirror-stand.
Time and again brush it clean.
Let no dust alight.

Great Master Shen Hsiu<br>
Sixth Patriarch's Sutra

A California Highway Patrol officer stopped to see if we needed anything. He asked if "He's the silent one" pointing to Heng Sure and then apologizing for trying to talk to him. He was very friendly and helpful and looked after our safety now and again as we bowed through his patrol area.

---

**Heng Sure**
We're going to serenade you

"Faith causes all roots to grow pure and clean and sharp. Faith's power is solid. Nothing can destroy it. Faith extinguishes the roots of afflictions forever."

Avatamsaka Sutra

We left the highway where the sign said, "Pedestrians Prohibited." We took Quintana Road, the access route to Morro Bay, two miles north. Lunch was uneventful; we tried a new pot herb — mallow, a common roadside plant on top of rice. Not bad. Free and fresh. Like the Dharma it grows on all sides. But you have to look through your attachment to names and labels before you recognize its true value. Once a weed, now fuel for enlightenment.

Bowing again after lunch. Just finished reciting a vow to end all sexual desire, a vow I make each day. As I reached this line "I vow that all bad karmic seeds planted in this life through sexual misconduct will come to fruition in another way so that I will not have to endure sexual embrace in order to pay my debts and resolve my negative affinities" — just at that point a pick-up truck skidded up and stopped, one foot from my nose. Five women jumped out carrying Bibles and guitars. "We're going to serenade you," they said. "Praise Jesus." And so they did. For ninety minutes as I slowly bowed up Quintana Road, they sang and danced in a circle around me, now clapping, now passing the Bible and reading scriptures at top volume in my ears. Heng Chau says they looked like bees swarming for honey. I knew this was a special response, not an ordinary encounter. The women were my "good advisors" come to test my patience and resolve. They were my good friends who would help me erase some of the bad karma I had made by selfish indulgence in sexual misconduct.

The women pranced back and forth inches from me on all sides. One planted her feet before me, daring me to knock against her as I bowed. I did not change pace and she yielded. Another moved along in my line of vision making seductive gestures and trying to hold my gaze with flirtatious expressions and pouts. I bowed on steadily, not changing my pace or my expression. My heart was light and happy. I felt concentrated and at ease. I was grateful for this rare chance to really test my "patience gung fu." Their leader, a thirty-year-old man with a fine singing voice joined them and brought along a small boy. He had been talking with Heng Chau but like the women, after exchanging a few words, he joined the buzzing group circling me. It was all my show this day. "I know where you're at, man. I've been there. Look at you: dirty, ragged, sweating, working so hard. You don't need to do all that. You should rest. I can see you're really tired. We love you. You just come up to the commune and give up this bit. It's not really you. There are lots of women up there who will listen to your story. We'll give you a meal. It's a nice set-up. I used to be a rock and roll singer in a band and I took all the dark roads that you're on. I tried everything. This isn't going to make you free. You're just heading into trouble. You know there are a lot of bad dudes up ahead who aren't going to like what you're doing and they're going to come and beat on you. I know it. In fact I love you now but before I saw the light I would have been the first one to kick your rear end, because I used to hate guys like you. It's a tough world. One of these semi trucks is going to roll off the road and squash you flat. You'd better stop right here." I went on bowing.

"And this silence bit. Here I am giving you my whole afternoon of ministry and you won't even give me any feedback. You say you want to help? How can you help people if you don't talk? Just give me a word about where you're at. You can open up right here. Your friend back there won't care. He's as messed up as you are. Come on now. We love you… Well, I'm tired of talking but I'm not tired of singing." Out came the guitar again "I know you're lonely. Why don't you let it down? Why don't you cry a little tear and let us in your heart?" and so forth. He left in mid-song.

I felt clean and light inside as I bowed on. Faith had crossed the rough water and delivered me in a state of peaceful concentration. I felt solid and energized, exactly like the feeling you get at the end of a hard ch'an meditation period after enduring and overcoming big pains in the legs.

The Venerable Abbot had this to say of my experience, "Ha! You subdued them! You might say you had a response to your vow. They wanted you to talk. One word and you would have blown the whole thing."

**Heng Sure**
The road back to the forgotten city

> "The wonderful principles of the Buddhadharma originally were not spoken. After awakening, even one word is too many. Only because living beings are confused and so heavily obstructed does the Buddha come with skillful means and talk and talk."
>
> Master Hua

Arthur Waley tells us that Buddhism brought many new words into the Chinese language. The same process is going on in the West. We can all take part in history and move people's higher consciousness along with the important words of Buddhism, such as Buddha, Dharma, Bodhisattva, samadhi, ch'an. Other words already in English have new meaning: cultivation, transference, precepts, merit and virtue. These words and ideas will change the world as they become familiar and meaningful to Westerners. Use one today!

Our work as disciples of the Buddha is to bridge the gap between the old and the new. The Dharma is a true principle; it already lives in our hearts. First we must uncover it, realize it through cultivation, and understand it ourselves. Then we must look to our guides and our maps to label correctly what we discover within. The purpose is not to fix it – the Dharma is not fixed; it is elastic. There is no limit to the meanings the Dharma symbolizes. Our work is to show ourselves and our Western family how the Buddha traced the route back to his original home 3000 years ago and how he opened his doors wide, wide, to make room for all beings beneath his roof. No matter what language we are used to, we all can speak the Dharma. It's the language of the heart. We learn to identify the principles and words within by applying the methods in our daily lives. With hard work, the words naturally come true, come to life. On the road that appears beneath our feet as we walk and bow once every three step, the road back to the "forgotten city," we notice many footprints. Footprints of Buddhas and Bodhisattvas! A broad, level open road starts from right beneath your own feet.

**Heng Sure** • January 21, 1978
Back to the wheel to smelt anew

Dear Shr Fu,

San Luis Obispo is now behind us. Morro Bay is twelve miles ahead and then, nothing but miles and miles of winding coast line to San Francisco. The San Luis passage felt special, rather like a gateless toll-gate. Many big tests of resolve and concentration. We were very aware of the Ch'an session going on at the City of Ten Thousand Buddhas and felt like our work was a highway Ch'an. Ch'an sessions mirror our cultivation. If the daily work has been carelessly done, you find out right away in a meditation intensive. The pressure reveals the cracks and flaws. Instead of a harvest, the session becomes a trip to the repair shop. City-bowing is the same. All the bad habits that we overlook or fail to smelt out appear as we bow in the city. The false and the hidden aspects of our minds suddenly appear in the spotlight. The verse goes:

> In the country, smelt it down.
> Test its temper in the town.
> Pass or fail we still go on
> To contemplate the noumenon.

When cultivators truly use effort, tests are constant, both in the country and in the city. As Shr Fu's disciples we know that, "Everything's a test to see what you will do. Mistaking what's before your face, you'll have to smelt anew."

Heng Chau related a test he faced: in Pismo State Park, with not a soul around, he looked for several seconds too long at a beautiful double rainbow in the eastern sky. In a flash his head was filled with images of old desires and habits. In that single glance, he "fell back on the wheel," as in the verse:

> When you see things and understand
> You transcend the world.
> When you see things and are confused,
> You fall onto the wheel.

Off by a hair's breadth at the start, D.M. Chau missed the mark by a thousand miles in the end and had to resmelt anew.

I faced and failed a similar test. In this case, it was more like being off by a whale's breadth, but the result was the same confusion.

One evening, near Vandenberg Air Force Base, a familiar van swung over and parked ahead. It was the Gold Mountain Chevy van. I didn't have my glasses on, but I'd know that car anywhere. It was at the end of a long day of bowing and my ego was looking for any excuse to leak out. "How wonderful! A surprise visit from our family," I thought. I projected that it was a Bhikshu bringing new Sutra, or food, or maybe a message from Shr Fu. I had the whole greedy scene worked out in my head in no time. "Funny that no one has come out of the van, though; I wonder what they're waiting for? How come Heng Chau hasn't walked by me to greet them? Oh well, just finish this day's work and then take your reward. There, the van door's open. Who is it?" I thought. "Howdy fellows, have you accepted Jesus as your personal Savior?" Oh no! A Christian preacher who happens to drive a green Chevy van! Back to the wheel to smelt anew.

The smelting process is just like the daily work in the monastery. Be on time, don't rap, eat just enough and no more, stay mindful of your method, walk the Middle Way at all times, subdue your self at every turn. If the smelting has been patient, vigorous and sincere, when the city streets appear below our knees the intensity and temper of the metal is measured. The strengths pass the test; the weak spots go back to the furnace for another round. Just as in a meditation session, cultivation goes on as usual, only more so. With the focus on reciting and sitting, the fruits of daily work roll into the storehouse. The barren trees must be pruned back for the next growing season.

This is an example of an inner dialogue that arises during the smelting. "Have I subdued my desire for fame? How's my concentration as reporters from two local papers click, click, click their cameras for hours? Do I move off my center and start to pose? On to the wheel I go. How about food? Am I still attached to flavor and getting full? Let's test it out. Here come Shramanera Kuo Yu's grandparents, Bill and Pat Ireland, with a tray of hot, home-cooked cornbread. All six organs move at once and the mind is filled with clouds of false thoughts. Back to the foundry. Say, what am I cultivating, anyway, besides greed for hot cornbread? How about sleep? It's 8:30, the Sutra's been recited and I am exhausted in every fibre. My bad habits make me impatient; I'm right on the edge of taking a deep dive into sleep. It's time to meditate, but what's the use? I'll only nod out. Shr Fu! What am I gonna do? I'm at the end of my rope. The deeper I go into my mind, the more muck and garbage I turn up. There's no lotus here; there's just mud. Well, I can't go wrong asking my teacher, even if I'm a hopeless case. His compassion is deeper than my stupidity. Try him again. I'm working to stand on my own feet, but this is a time of need. Here's the Forty-two Sections Sutra; just open it up to see what it says":

> "Shramanas who study the Way should get a hold on their minds and be vigorous, courageous, and valiant. Not fearing what lies ahead, they should destroy the hordes of demons and obtain the fruits of the Way. Having the strength of precepts, samadhi, and wisdom in order to break through and destroy your beginningless habits and your beginningless pretensions, and all your other faults is analogous to destroying the multitudes of demons... Don't turn back halfway. Go forward vigorously and with courage. Only go forward; never retreat. Only advance; never retreat."

Amazing. It's just as if the Master were sitting right here! Then I heard in my inner ear the Master's voice say, "Kuo Chen, you lazy bug. How can you possibly think of sleeping when you haven't done your homework? Do the work just like you wear clothes, just like you eat. Did you skip lunch because you were too tired? No! Well, how can you not meditate? Everyone else is working hard in the Ch'an session, what's your excuse?"

I sat upright, folded my legs into full lotus and sat. My fatigue and my doubts vanished bit-by-bit, like the valley fog before the morning sun. "Pass or fail we still go on to contemplate the noumenon." Who can doubt that drawing near to a wise advisor is 100% of the Way?

| | |
|---|---|
| Morro Bay | 13 miles |
| Monterey | 135 miles |
| San Francisco | 249 miles |
| City of Ten Thousand Buddhas | one single thought |

Disciple Guo Chen (Heng Sure)
bows in respect

---

**Heng Chau** • January 22, 1978
All the karma created is never forgotten

There's a saying, "All the karma created throughout a million kalpas is never forgotten."

Some people from San Luis brought out warm clothes and a thermal blanket. The temperature dropped and they were worried we might be cold.

Disciples from Los Angeles drove up to offer food, gas and supplies. They left at 2:00 A.M. to arrive in time to bow with us all morning.

A young man named Richard came riding by on his bicycle. He stopped, watched for awhile and then joined in behind us all as we bowed past a large prison facility. The L.A. people invited Richard to stay for lunch.

"I just saw you and felt real sincerity and a bond. So I decided to quietly join in. Is it O.K.?" he asked.

Richard said he did a little yoga, *tai ji*, and meditated (ch'an) and, "somehow this bowing looked and felt the same." He made an offering and left to go back to work. He's a gardener. "I'd like to ride my bike up to that City of Ten Thousand Buddhas this spring when I can take a month off of work."

During lunch under some oak trees by a little stream, a man walked up. He folded his hands and did a half bow. Then he reverently offered a bag of fresh fruit and a bunch of long-stemmed red roses. Big smile on his face, no words. He bowed again and left.

When things go bad we try to keep it to ourselves. On the good days, like today, we try to spread it around for others and not keep it for ourselves. It's called "transferring good roots."

> All of the worship, praise and offerings,
> Requesting the Buddha to dwell in the world,
> And turn the Dharma wheel, rejoicing and repenting.
> All good roots that come from these deeds,
> I transfer to all beings that they may reach
> the Buddha's Way.
>
> Avatamsaka Sutra

This is what the Bodhisattva Path is all about: constantly benefit others, don't be selfish. Benefiting others is benefiting yourself. The Avatamsaka Sutra is so important to us for this very reason. Left to myself I too easily drift into being stingy and self-centered. I forget all about others, their sufferings and longings. The Sutra never leaves this theme of compassion, just as the Bodhisattva never turns his back on living beings. If I never leave the Avatamsaka Sutra, then I won't get so lost and confused in this sea of suffering and will eventually cross to the other shore. This Sutra is to our souls what the North Star was to ancient mariners. The Bodhisattva sets his mind and never retreats. So many things come up on the highway.

It's easy to get turned and lose sight of what really matters. After a long hard day, words like these set us straight and raise our spirits.

> "The Bodhisattva saves and protects all living beings and his mind is not wearied. Because he is not wearied, in all worlds, if there are beings somewhere who have not been brought to accomplishment or have not been subdued, he goes to that place and expediently transforms them and takes them across… Among all these beings he lives in peace to teach and transform them. Nothing can cause his mind to move or retreat, nor does he have even a single thought of attachment. Why not? Because he attaches to nothing and relies on nothing. He benefits himself and benefits others. He is pure and fulfilled."
>
> Avatamsaka Sutra
> The Conducts Chapter

"Sufficiency"

> Taking two when enough is one,
> is for sure too much when enough is none.

A woman approached us as we bowed outside the California Men's Colony (a prison). "Will you accept an offering?" she asked very sincerely.

"You may need this for your family," I said.

"Well you know, the Lord provides," she insisted giving them to us. "In your prayers, could you include my husband? He's in there" she said pointing to the prison. "God bless you."

A man stopped who had read about the pilgrimage and the City of 10,000 Buddhas in a local paper. He made an offering. "I'm really excited! I never knew any place like your monastery existed in California," he exclaimed.

Heng Chau • January, 1978
Off an inch in the beginning

Dear Shr Fu,

Sunday, 3:45 a.m. Up for morning recitation, scramble for sweaters to keep out the morning chill. The highway's deserted and quiet, only the sound of the moon and a softly gurgling creek before we start with the Shurangama mantra.

5:00-6:30 a.m. We write and read Sutras, fill up the kerosene lamp. Sit in meditation.

6:30-7:00 a.m. Do *tai ji* – slipping and sliding on eucalyptus-tree berries.

7:15 a.m. Drive to bowing site on mountain pass in Santa Lucia Mts. Cold, clear, and light wind. Sun rising over the mountains.

8:00 a.m. Four disciples from Los Angeles come out bundled up and ready to bow.

9:00 a.m. A man named Richard quietly joins the bowing procession in front of state prison outside of San Luis Obispo. "I just saw you and felt sincerity and a bond. So I decided to join in. Is it okay?" Richard said he did a little yoga, *tai ji* and some Ch'an meditation, "and this bowing looks and feels like the same." He made an offering and then left about 10:00 to go back to work. He is a gardener. He's planning to come to the City Of Ten Thousand Buddhas this spring when he has a month vacation.

10:30 a.m. Stop bowing, transfer merit. Drive to field off freeway for meal offering.

10:45 a.m. Run out of gas (no gas gauge).

11-11:30 a.m. Meditate.

11:30-12:15 Meal offering and meal. During the meal a stranger reverently walks up and with folded hands, does a half-bow and offers a bag of fruit and long-stem red roses.

1-2:00 p.m. Guan Yin praise, Great Compassion mantra and Avatamsaka Sutra, translated by Heng Sure. (Tushita Heaven Chapter).

2-6:00 p.m. Bowing. On the way back to the bowing site, I am in a false-thinking samadhi about how to get the extra food offerings to the City of Ten Thousand Buddhas. I spot a turtle right in the middle of the freeway, craning its neck, bewildered. By the time I woke up and thought to liberate it, we'd gone too far. Had to turn around and drive back. We got back just in time to hear and see the turtle popped and splattered by a big, pink Cadillac that ran over it. We feel the turtle's life end right in our stomachs. There is a big lesson here: "Off an inch in the beginning, off by a thousand miles in the end." Had I been according with conditions and not in one place with my body and in another with my mind, I would have been decisive and stopped the car as soon as I saw the turtle stranded in the road. Instead, my false thinking "samadhi" about food caused me to be off by a few seconds and that made all the difference. Bodhisattvas are supposed to liberate and rescue living beings, says the Bodhisattva Precepts. Lesson: broken precepts begin with false thinking and cause disasters and sufferings.

3:00 p.m. A man walks across the heavy traffic to make an offering, saying, "I never knew such a place existed in California (referring to the City of Ten Thousand Buddhas). I want to help out."

4:00 p.m. A woman stops her car outside the prison gate and approaches. "Will you please accept this?" she asks humbly handing me her book of food stamps. "And could you in your prayers include my husband? He's in there," pointing to the prison. "Bless you, God bless you."

5:30 p.m. "Go home you bald-headed farts," from a passing car.

5:40 p.m. A man walks up to us on a narrow and tricky ledge. He almost falls but keeps coming. Handing me a money offering, he says, "When there is veneration, even a dog's tooth emits light." He turns and leaves.

6:00 p.m. We transfer merit, bow to the Triple Jewel and the Master.

6:30-7:30 p.m. Sit in Ch'an.

7:30-9:30 p.m. Recite Amitabha Sutra and praise. Translate Avatamsaka Sutra.

9:30-10:30 I do some shao lin exercises and then do standing meditation outside to wake up and to chase out the cold.

10:30-11:15 p.m. Recite mantras and bow to the Patriarchs.

11:15-12:30 p.m. Read Vajra Bodhi Sea and sit in Ch'an.

12:30 Blow out kerosene lamp, hear a "who, who" from a solitary night-owl, and fall asleep.

Much peace in the Dharma,
Disciple Guo Ting (Heng Chau)
bows in respect

---

**Heng Sure**
Until you've memorized it

> Just like a host of embroidered images
> Are the works of a Master Artisan
> So too do all Buddhalands
> Come from the Master Artist in the Mind.

Avatamsaka Sutra
Flower Store World Chapter

A night in the Plymouth we read the Avatamsaka Sutra. In eight months we've recited through four volumes – many volumes remain. It's a sublime book: a vast collection of transcendental wisdom lives just beneath those covers. Most of its principles are so lofty that the limits of our minds leave us on the first rung of the ladder, staring open-mouthed and wide-eyed as the brilliant lights and flowers in the Sutra's world pass up and expand to fill the clear sky.

People who regularly attend the Avatamsaka Assembly where the Venerable Abbot of Gold Mountain explains the Sutra, have noticed an uncanny marvel: things that happen in the lives of those in the assembly are often predicted or commented on in the Sutra text. The Sutra was spoken by the Buddha 3000 years ago but time and again, like a daily newspaper, it mirrors with astonishing clarity the important events in our lives today. There are too many examples to mention but the phenomenon has struck most of the regular listeners. The best way to investigate it is to attend the assembly yourself and find your name in its timeless texts.

We have just finished the "Ten Practices Chapter." I was so delighted by its clear summary of how a Bodhisattva, Mahasattva, behaves and thinks that I went back and translated the chapter into English, working for half an hour each night. Something in the chapter caught my heart's ear – inner bells rang. I mentioned it to no one – not even Heng Chau. At Gold Wheel Temple this past weekend the following conversation took place:

Disciple: "Master I'd like to begin reciting Sutras as a regular practice. Would you instruct me in the proper method?"

Venerable Abbot: "Light incense, chant the Incense Praise, recite the Verse for Opening Sutras, be sincere and reverent. In general, one part of respect yields one part of response. Ten parts yields ten parts."

Disciple: "Should I chant quickly or slowly?"

Venerable Abbot: "What I do is memorize the text a chapter at a time. Until you've memorized it, it's still in the book. It's not really yours yet. That's how I do it. Sutras are not just for reciting one time; you should go over them again and again."

Disciple: "I see. Fine. I can't decide which text to recite. The Dharma Flower Sutra is wonderful, the Shurangama Sutra is the sutra for opening wisdom and the Flower Adornment Sutra, the Avatamsaka, is the core and substance of our bowing trips. I feel the Flower Adornment Sutra would be the best one to recite."

Venerable Abbot: "Fine. Recite the Flower Adornment Sutra."

Disciple: "Which chapter should I start with? Should I go from the top? Or how about the 'Worthy Leader Chapter' or maybe the 'Pure Conduct Chapter.' Both of them are fundamental, solid Dharmas."

Venerable Abbot: "You can start with the 'Ten Practices Chapter.' How's that?"

Disciple: "Fantastic! Shih Fu, did you know I've just been translating that chapter? It really caught me up as we read it at night, and I went back to it."

Venerable Abbot: "Oh really? Well, good. Any more questions?"

That's the way it goes all the time around the environment of the Flower Adornment Sutra and the Venerable Abbot of Tathagata Monastery.

---

*Heng Chau • January 23, 1978*
Money confuses people

We took the car in for a fix-up in San Luis. The car just keeps going and holding together despite a lot of doubts and predictions to the contrary. We are half way to San Francisco.

"Seeing Through it"

Strange and unpredictable things happen per force on a trip like this. I often feel like a stupid young fish – the 10,000 things of the world are all baited hooks. Without true wisdom, mistakes are many; understandings are few.

Today a young woman returned to see us. She was very emotional and sticky and wanted to "sit and talk." Novice monks are not supposed to even be alone with women, how much the less sitting on the grass talking. But I'm the Dharma protector and so it's my job to explain the trip and accept offerings if people want to make them. She wanted to talk about our practice of never lying down to sleep.

"We let our bowing talk and keep our mouths closed. We have no wisdom to be talking," I explained.

"I don't believe that. Ever since I saw your faces, my heart has been full of joy," she said. She was very sincere, I believe, and deeply moved by the situation was not completely on the straight and narrow. I can't break precepts.

"Do you want anything?" she asked. "I'll get you *anything* you want."

"Whatever people want to offer is all we want. Our needs are simple."

"Will you take money?" she asked, handing me some cash. I accepted and went to bow. She followed and kept inching closer. Then she ran to her car and returned. She stood in front of me.

"I made a mistake. I gave you my husband's money, not *mine*. Here!" she said with a big expectant look, and lays a large amount of cash in my hands. I hesitate to accept. She keeps waiting for me to do something.

"Oh, it doesn't matter... oh wow!" she shouts putting her hand on top of her head. Then she turned and left.

> "Money confuses people. It turns them upside down. Don't be greedy. Money is basically dirty. Everybody is controlled by it."
>
> Instructions to the bowing monks
> From Ven. Abbot, 1978

I really don't know what it was all about but I do know that money and sex turn people upside down. These two things are really hard to see through and put down. The Master's verse came to mind as I stood on the side of the road wondering if I passed or failed this test.

The affairs of the world are impermanent,
　　don't be attached to them.
Like dreams, like illusions, however,
　　in samadhi one roams freely.
The playful sport of spiritual penetrations,
　　accord with changes and transformation.
In stillness contemplate all things,
　　how their glory fades and withers all by itself.

Verse "Seeing Through It"<br>by Ch'an Master Hua

This woman showed me my weaknesses and attachments. Good and bad alike, we learn from all the people we meet. They are a wonderful, perfect mirror that reflects our flaws and wrinkles, reveals our pretensions and potential.

And in the end it's all impermanent and not one thing can be held. Everything passes. The last line of the verse kept echoing in my mind.

　　...In stillness contemplate all things,
　　　　how their glory fades and withers all by itself.

---

**Heng Sure**
Cultivators transcend them

Unmasking the Wizard.

As an at-home layperson I practiced astrology. My approach to reality depended on it. I saw personalities and forces of nature as one large whole with real divisions and types that could be named and therefore controlled. Basically astrology is just a language. When you can speak astrology, you have access to information about people and their changes. Anyone can learn it and it makes you appear wise and powerful. Thus it is easily and frequently misrepresented and abused. I hid behind this mental power-tool, used it as a mask. If people saw me as a planet-wizard, well let them, it was all right with me.

After leaving home this role became less attractive. The Buddhadharma can take one out of the world. Astrology can only identify it. I asked the Master about it. "It's just life," he said. "I used to study all those arts. You should know that common people are ruled by the heavens, but cultivators transcend them. When you get enlightened, you know all of that information anyway, without having to check the tables and charts. Just don't get attached to it."

I carried my planet books with me on the bowing pilgrimage and spent the first few months mapping the changes in the heavens in advance. As the layers of personality wore thin, I realized gradually that I didn't want to wear any more masks. I didn't want knowledge and mundane truths to come between me and the direct perception of reality. Most of the impulse to check the planets came from fear of harm. We bow through everything: good and bad weather, "tough towns" and "smooth sailing" stretches and our experience of them is that all dharmas are uniform and equal. It all tastes the same here in the Saha: bitter and empty. The only thing to fear is being lazy. There's nothing to hang onto. Whatever you rely on will turn and bite you and may even hold you here and prevent your ultimate independence from birth and death. Who needs to know the weather in advance?

I saw this in terms of astrology with Heng Chau's help. I decided that it was time to take the "wizard" shingle down from my door and give up seeing the world through planetary glasses. The space in my mind that was jammed with aspects, signs, houses, and planets was huge. It felt much better thrown open to the peace and silence of the unconditioned. I made room inside for Dharma-wisdom to take root and grow by stopping each astrological thought as it arose. I imagined quitting smoking feels the same. Once you've got a reason to change and a resolve, it's just a matter of practice and patience before the old habits give way to the new.

Shih Fu makes it real. I offered up my ephemeris, my planet table, which bears my whole identity as an astrologer. It's like a carpenter hanging up his hammer and saw. "I'm through with it, Shih Fu, I hope you'll accept this book."

"No, you keep it. I can't read it. Why do you want the easy way out? If you keep it and don't use it, that's what really counts. If you give it to me, that's forcing it."

Ho! Ho! And you see why he's the Master.

---

**Heng Chau** • January 24, 1978
All beings are created equal

Cold and quiet day. Friends from San Luis drove out with some hot tea to chase the early morning chill. Later they stopped with a hot meal and encouraging words.

A businessman came up to us while we bowed on the road shoulder. "This is a small offering from my mother-in-law who died a year ago. Thank you." he said softly.

Bowing Thoughts.

"Why are you doing this thing?!" so many people ask. We answer, "We are trying to turn back disasters and calamities in the world. We are trying to purify our bodies, mouths and mind and thus neutralize some of the bad, black energy that's polluting the earth. Suffering is the result; greed, anger and ignorance are the cause. Our hearts have gotten off the track. Our minds aren't straight and clear. So it says, 'go back to the source, return to the root.'"

If we want to do right things in the world and in our homes, we have to straighten out our hearts and purify our minds. Turn our greed, hatred and ignorance into kindness, compassion, joy and giving. This is returning to the true Nature.

Originally everything's okay. There's no problem. We just forget and get lost in the dust and the shuffle of the world, chasing rainbows and running from shadows.

> The more things change,
>     the more they remain the same.

French Proverb

Our footprints, the gravel and asphalt, even the crows and clouds above are the same as yesterday. In the final analysis, nothing changes. Even the changes are the same. So it's said,

> "He obtains the level equality of all dharmas because he universally knows the nature of all dharmas does not change."

Avatamsaka Sutra<br>Ten Transferences Chapter

Almost all of my energy goes into making false and arbitrary discriminations among things whose basic nature is the same and doesn't change. This discriminating mind is the very heart of our Western intellectual tradition. Split and divide, separate and dissect everything from mind and body, heaven and earth, to skin color and molecules.

Now we are splitting atoms and things have really gone haywire. Soon the atoms will be splitting us. "All men are created equal" is being nudged out by the ever-growing horror that "all men could be cremated equal" by nuclear weapons.

**Heng Sure**
We eat it with our eyes

> He does not want the five desires or a king's throne.
> He wants not wealth or success or amusement or fame.
> He wants only to end for eternity
>     the suffering of living beings.
> He makes his resolution to benefit the world.
>
> Avatamsaka Sutra

This is the heart of it. Take a look at what people really value. Turn it, whatever it is, just a little bit and look again. Is it still valuable? A color T.V. gives amusement only if it's plugged in to the wall socket and then only if it's properly adjusted. Another condition: the program must satisfy one's interests. Turn it slightly: unplug the set. Increase the green or red until the faces turn purple. Put re-runs of yesterday's weather on every channel. Where did the pleasure go? It was thin to begin with. When the value is placed on impermanent, external things, what was once bliss can quickly turn to suffering. It's all in how we view it.

Everyone enjoys looking at a well-made platter of food. The pleasure comes from anticipating the flavor. We eat it with our eyes, so to speak. We congratulate ourselves for deserving good food. We eat it with our minds before it reaches our mouths. What if someone were to announce that there was a tiny speck of human excrement – no bigger than a fingernail – mixed with the other fragrant delicacies? Oh, no, take it away! No one will dare taste even a mouthful. Excrement is just yesterday's delicious food, slightly turned. Even the thoughts of a small piece of impure ingredients can change our bliss to suffering. What then do we value? Valueless goods? Where is the real quality?

When we take a long look, material goods and fame, sex and sleep, power and food are not the goal; they are only a means to a goal. We all want to be free of pain, free of fear, free of desire. More than that, we want happiness and peace for others as well. Isn't this the real reason why we keep on looking, keep on reaching for quality in life? Ultimate quality has no price tag because it's in the heart. How do you tell when you find ultimate quality? Look at it straight in the eye. But how can I do that unless it's looking at another person? That's it! That's the secret. Benefit others. Work for others, give them the best you have and before long you'll see something really valuable in their eyes, a look that has real quality. It's priceless happiness. Stop then for just a moment, before you continue with your new job. Check your own heart. Don't you feel better than ever? That's a real quality feeling you can learn to value over anything you can buy. Wealth or success, amusement or fame – these are common, half-way diversions. People who have a true sense of value go for the heart of things: help living beings end their suffering. If you give and give and give until you have nothing left to sit on but the cold ground, no king ever sat on a finer throne.

---

Heng Chau • January 25, 1978
I was speeding on the inside

We bow about one time each 30-40 seconds. I finished writing apiece and went back to bow. "Heng Sure has slowed down to a turtle's pace," I thought to myself impatiently. I clocked his pace only to discover he was holding steady at 35 seconds per bow. I was speeding on the inside and nothing outside had changed at all. An instant lesson on how "Everything is made from the mind alone."

So subtle, the mind and all its states. We can only trust precepts, vows, our teacher, and a small thread. There's an indestructible thread of faith that keeps us on the path with true heart. It never breaks.

Faith's power is solid, nothing can destroy it…
Faith can grow a Bodhi tree.

Avatamsaka Sutra

Question: "Are you boys brothers? Your noses are alike."

Answer: "That's a monk's nose. We keep them on the same grindstone."

Simon, a man from South Africa, brought an offering and good wishes. "I've been looking for you. I think it's good what you're doing. I wish you well. We need this in the world."

---

### Heng Sure
We have to want it

Faith is the indestructible seed of merit and virtue. Faith can grow a Bodhi-tree. Faith can add to the most victorious wisdom. Faith can reveal all Buddhas. Therefore when speaking of reliable practices in their proper order, the bliss of faith is the victor.

How powerful is faith in the Buddha?

> The Tathagata's power of self-mastery
> Is difficult to encounter in measureless aeons.
> If one produces a single thought of faith,
> He will quickly realize the supreme Path.
>
> Avatamsaka Sutra
> Verses in Praise in the
> Tushita Heaven Palace Chapter

The Sutra promises so much goodness, so much strength. How can we make it real in our own lives? Take an honest look. How do we approach life? Do we take the easy way out when the road ahead looks hard to travel? Is the attitude correct that says, "Whatever I want I can buy on credit now and pay for later. When I get tired of it I'll sell it or throw it away?" Do we see reality as a big television? When the show is not pleasing, just change the channel?

These approaches will not deliver the faith the Sutra talks about, faith in the Buddha and his teachings (the Dharma), and in the Sangha of men and women who have left the home life to concentrate on keeping the Dharma going. This faith is real. We have to recognize its true value. We have to want it and be willing to make some changes in our lives in order to realize it. Change comes hard to most of us but look at it this way: we change every minute of every day. Change is natural, normal. We are not the children we once were. We aren't yet the old people we will become. Further, we aren't the moldy corpse and the moving transforming spirit we will be when the big change of death comes to us. So why fight change? The illusion of permanence rises from the little attachments we make to physical comfort and convenience. Buying on credit, throwing away what we don't like, turning the channel. This is the easy road, the road of attachment. The turning point of faith is right here.

"The Buddhadharma arises out of difficulty."

Difficulty does not necessarily involve pain and suffering. However, difficulty does mean change, and if the attachments are really heavy, change can involve saying "no!" and meaning it, until the old habits disappear. Is it worth it? How much goodness do we want? How much strength? Let's face it: if you can't put down what's false, you'll never pick up what's true.

Example: (Heng Sure to himself) "Are you going to write that note to Heng Chau or are you going to sit back and recite and let it go? Recite. Don't bother him. He's cultivating." (10 minutes later) (Heng Sure to himself) "How do you feel? Just fine. Calm and clear." All right.

---

**Heng Chau** • January 26, 1978
If you know the right tool, there's no trick

A sheriff's deputy circles us as we eat lunch. We're parked on a quiet farm by a small creek off the highway. Slowly he pulls alongside our car. He watches us do dishes with a tough, straight face.

"People giving you a hard time out there on the highway?" he asks.

"No. People have been really good to us," I answer. He smiles slightly and says,

"That's what counts." — gives a nod of approval, a hat tip salute, and drives off.

> "And yet there is no self and nothing which belongs to self. There is nothing done, and no one who receives it."
>
> Avatamsaka Sutra
> Ten Grounds Chapter, 6th Ground

The self is an illusion, an entity that can't be located and has no substance. But just as the earth was the unmoving, unquestioned center of the universe to the Medieval mind, the self or ego is the center of our world. We have no way to accept this truth and we have no way to avoid it — there is no self. It's a dilemma.

The despair and emptiness that pervades our society is just the inevitable breaking apart of a culture built on "me and mine." But in Buddhism, seeing the falseness of the self is waking up, not the dark end. Understanding and accepting the emptiness of self and dharmas (things), is wonderful existence, not the void of nihilism. Knowing there is no self is the Buddha's wisdom.

> All disciples of the Buddha, in this way know;
> The nature of all dharmas is forever empty and still,
> There is not a single dharma which can be created.
> And just like all Buddhas, they enlighten to no self.
>
> Avatamsaka Sutra
> Ten Transferences Chapter

Our car is old, and someone who offered to fix it couldn't get the wheel cylinder off. So we drove it to a garage. The mechanic popped it off in a second using a special kind of wrench. The man with us said,

"See, for everything there's a trick!" But the mechanic calmly turned and replied,

"No. For everything there's a *tool*. If you know the right tool, there's no trick."

Why haven't I busted through the abyss and attained ultimate wisdom? Why do I still flounder in greed, anger, and stupidity, despite the presence in our midst of great spiritual leaders and sages who can lead people to perfect enlightenment and transcendental truth? Because I've been using the wrong tool. I false think too much. I avoid the direct experience of truth through cultivating morality, concentration and wisdom. I don't know how to walk the Way. I just know how to talk. But cultivation slowly transforms you.

People wonder why two young men with good college educations would be bowing along the open highway, living out of a car to seek the truth. "What do you hope to find by doing this?"

Heng Sure and I both feel that we're too smart for our own good. It's said,

> Extreme intelligence becomes stupidity.
> Extreme stupidity becomes intelligence.

It's possible to become too clever to the point that the simple becomes a mystery and the obvious seems a secret. Our classroom now is the Highway of the Avatamsaka Sutra. We rely on a good and wise advisor and our own hearts trying their best. Our educations were good but not the right tool. They didn't do the "trick."

The whole world is becoming like a big Humpty Dumpty. The slightest tremor and it falls off the wall. "...and all the kings horses and all the kings men, couldn't put Humpty Dumpty back together again." It's our minds that go bad, not the world.

Heaven and earth are unhappy. Why?

Too many people have been killed, children are taking drugs, old people are being neglected, and the environment is polluted. All the result of this made dance of false thoughts of discrimination and greed. "Everything is made from the mind alone."

To turn back this hard rain of bad karma that's going to fall, we need only turn back to our original minds. When the mind repents and changes, then 10,000 disasters are eradicated. In Buddhism it's said,

> "I now repent of all bad deeds which I have done with body, mouth and mind, all based on beginningless greed, hatred and stupidity… Offenses arise from the mind, yet the mind is used to repent. When the mind is forgotten, offenses are no more. When both mind and offenses are eradicated, both are empty. This is called true repentance and reform."

That's our work: to forget the mind. Simply stop discriminating you and me, us and them, past, present and future. Then the fragmented pieces return to the one, the whole is reclaimed. So it's said,

> "With one thought not produced, the entire substance manifests."

Does it sound esoteric and far fetched, not normal talk for everyday regular folks? Not true. This is who we *really* are. Anyone can do it. It's simple.

Disciple: "Master, that's an incredible state."

Master: "Anybody can do it. That's why so few actually do."

The true is so simple and natural we pass it right by in our cleverness and worldly confidence. Tonight we read verses from the Avatamsaka which said clearly what I was trying to get at during the day in these thoughts:

> All dharmas are not produced, nor are they destroyed.
> Moreover, they neither come nor go.
> They don't die here and get born there.
> One who understand this,
>     enlightens to all the Buddhadharma.

> Understanding all dharmas' true, real nature,
> And yet regarding their nature,
>      not making discriminations.
> Knowing that all dharmas
>      are without a nature and distinctions,
> This person skillfully enters all Buddha's wisdom.
>
> Avatamsaka Sutra<br>Ten Transferences Chapter

All places, all beings, all countries, and all time are one, not two.

> "…He knows that all dharmas are just an ordinary view, he enters into the proper stance, and discriminations are no more."
>
> Avatamsaka Sutra<br>Ten Transferences Chapter

---

**Heng Sure**
Don't ask me, ask yourself

More Conversation:
The Buddhist and The Skeptic – Working For The Good:

Skeptic: What are you doing?

Buddhist: Bowing, praying. Trying to work towards the good.

S: What for?

B: We want more good people in the world. With more good people there will be more peace and happiness and fewer disasters and suffering.

S: Are you a good person?

B: I used to be totally selfish and small. Now I've recognized my mistakes and all that wasted time. I've taken the coverings off in public. I've admitted my past errors, my falseness and I'm doing my best to work towards the true.

S: This bowing is true?

B: Yes, it's a start. If you don't do hard work, you're certain not to change.

S: Bowing is going to change you for the better?

B: Yes, but it's just one of 84,000 methods. The point is to use effort to purify your heart and reduce your selfish ways. When you are clean and happy then your family and your circle of friends absorbs the good energy. When the family is happy then the cities are peaceful, then the nations and the whole world can come together. It starts right here with you. With the good thoughts in your mind.

S: That's your goal, all good people in the world? It will never be. You're dreaming.

B: No, I'm working. Even if perfection is far away you've got to take the first steps from where you're standing right now. As for our goals, Buddhism doesn't talk about people being all good. Buddhism doesn't distinguish between good and evil. It's people who make that distinction in their own minds. When we stop making false differences between people, that's what's natural and free of duality. That's where we all began. We want to go back to the source. Then we can all know true peace and harmony with nature and with all living things.

S: How do you realize this dream? It sounds pretty nebulous.

B: Not at all. If you take a complete view it is a matter of doing the ten good acts which means you don't do the ten evil acts. No killing, stealing, or lust, that's the body's share; no lying, harsh speech, duplicity, no frivolous talk, that's the mouth's share; and with the mind you avoid greed, hatred, and stupidity. Ten evils avoided, ten goods accomplished. Keep those rules and you've got a better world right now.

S: Hmmm.

B: If you take a brief view, it means don't pick on the other guy. Stop knocking other people around and have compassion.

S: Am I a good person?

B: Don't ask me, ask yourself:

> Truly recognize your own faults,
> Don't discuss the faults of others.
> Other's faults are just my own faults.
> Being one with everyone: that's great compassion.

To sum it all up you could say we're doing something about what most people feel you can't do anything about.

---

**Heng Chau • January 27, 1978**
We hope to lose something

A young woman out delivering vegetables came running down the road from her van.

"I talked with a man who talked with you and I said, 'I would really like to see them,' and suddenly I see you. I'm pretty lucky."

She filled our bags with vegetables, bread and carrot juice. "When you get to Cambria there's a health food store with a lot of people who are very happy about the energy you are sharing with this area. They will give you anything you need."

Our needs are simple. We want everyone to be really happy. If everyone is truly happy then our needs are met.

"Thank you good brothers," she shouted.

I am full of greed and arrogance. I would like to be really pure and innocently stupid. How fine to have a quiet, cool mind and to be content with what comes. Where is such purity?

> "The nature of people is basically pure. It is because of false thinking that the True Suchness is obscured. Simply have no false thinking and the nature will be pure itself."
>
> The Sixth Patriarch

It is not that we hope to *find* anything by bowing; rather, we hope to *lose* something. We basically have all we need. It is in seeking and trying to find more that we obscure what is naturally ours. By bowing we hope to lose some of our greed, anger and confusion. Cultivating the Way is subtraction – the more you take away the richer you become.

"Learning consists in adding to one's stock day by day;
The practice of the Tao consists in subtracting day by day,
subtracting and yet again, subtracting till one has reached
inactivity. But by this very inactivity everything can be
activated."

Lao Tzu

A man named Antoine stopped to make offerings and say, "I hope you come back and open a place in this area."

"Come to the City of 10,000 Buddhas and get enlightened and open one yourself."

"I'd like to but I don't have enough time," replied Antoine.

Three men in a pick-up truck, full of questions. Finally the driver leans over like he's going to whisper a secret and says with intense sincerity,

"Listen, tell me straight. I mean, really level with me. It won't matter. We'll probably never see each other again. Nobody will ever know... Are you *really* happy? I mean, is it for real!?"

Before I could answer, his friend turned to him in amazed disbelief and said, "Jesus, Jesse, do you think they'd be out here crawling around on their hands and knees for almost *two* years if they weren't for real!? Jesus, Jesse!"

As the sun set we bowed nine times together to transfer the day's work to all living beings. I felt a gentle tugging on my shoulder bag. I turned around to find a smiling man stuffing it full of food.

"All organic... thanks brothers for all the inspiration you're bringing to all our lives."

Ahead is the coastline highway again. We'll turn and head north up into the Big Sur from Morro Bay. Our route from here on is uncertain.

"Precepts can open up the root of Bodhi."

Avatamsaka Sutra

"You should know that the mind is like an illusion, and therefore there is nothing to which you can become attached."

The Sixth Patriarch

---

**Heng Sure**
I must learn to give

> The first vow is to worship and respect all Buddhas.
> The second vow is to praise the Thus Come Ones.
> The third is to cultivate the giving of offerings...

Came back full circle today. Like coming home after wandering a dark, winding road. Like another chance after the last chance.

It can't be entirely grasped in words. The beauty of it is a perfect wholeness and stillness. The change is coming around to seeing it the way it has been from the start. Through the compassion of teachers and wholesome spiritual friends, I've found the road home. Still got to walk it but I'm ready. I've got the heart to do it right, all the way.

The journey began with a method, a bowing technique. It has remained constant from the first bow. My heart has been inconstant. From the purity of the basic method I've experimented and rambled all over the world inside my mind. All the problems with concentration I've had came from my not truly faithfully using the method right before my eyes.

"Buddhism cultivates what is simple, ordinary and basic. Don't forsake the near for the distant."

"You say you have cultivation but you still haven't gotten rid of your greed, hatred, and stupidity. Impossible."

Master Hua

My illness? Selfish greed. Seeking and calculating for benefit. Making plans for myself. The cure? Cultivate the Dharma. Take it and hold it. Treat it as slow, sure, healing medicine.

Today the truth came home. Eleven months of instructions meshed with my experience. I must learn to give. My heart is small. When I give myself away, my meditation will merge with the True Suchness Nature. Selfish desire will vanish in the light of giving.

How to make my heart grow? Enter the Dharma-door my teacher gave me. Don't use other methods. Put it all right here. What is that? Bow and praise the (Avatamsaka) Hua Yen Sutra. Bow and praise the Hua Yen Assembly. Take three steps and praise the Triple Jewel. With all your heart bow and praise the City of Ten Thousand Buddhas. Return the light and give your work away to all living beings. Don't wander. Don't seek. Concentrate on it. Your heart will grow.

Cultivate the giving of offerings. How? What can I give? Give single-minded, whole-hearted bowing, just as you started out to do in the beginning. Cultivate the near; let the distant take care of itself. Give the Dharma-realm a City of 10,000 Buddhas. It feels like waking from a bad dream. It feels like recognizing that I've been sick for along time and then finding right in my hand, the very medicine that will slowly, naturally, bring me back to health.

As I stand and walk from my sick bed, I pray that my vigor will grow and overcome all doubts and confusion. I vow to vigorously cultivate precepts, samadhi and wisdom, and rest forever all greed, hatred and stupidity. I return and rely on the Eternally Dwelling Triple Jewel of all Directions. I'm happy.

**Heng Chau** • January 28, 1978
Happy and satisfied

A quiet, peaceful day. Cool winds, clear skies. Having so little; happy and satisfied. Bow until dusk. A red sky sunset lit up the mountains. We walk back to the car under the stars. After washing up, we cover our legs up in a blanket and sit in meditation.

> Give them simplicity to look at,
>     the uncarved block to hold,
> Give them selflessness and fewness of desires.
>
> Lao Tsu

**Heng Sure**
The big riddles cannot be solved in thought

The Bodhisattva Mahasattva in the Ten Practices Chapter of the Hua Yen Sutra gives away the flesh of his body to feed starving beings who come to beg from him. Not only can he satisfy their hunger, but he is very happy to give in this way.

> Ten Thousand things are born of the Tao.
> One who obtains it connects with the magical.
> Enlightened to the original substance,
> When one connects, all connect.
>
> Ch'an Master Hua

Everyone loves magic and riddles. Birth is magic; death is magic. Most of the natural world is a riddle, a mystery. For all of our human history until the last few decades, magic has been out of the reach of most of us. Only the shamans of each tribe had access to the heart of Nature's mystery. Only medicine men had a way to influence the unknown. The rest of us were too busy keeping ourselves fed and dry, to use effort to solve the big questions.

The modern world has changed all this. Now a common magic has come into being. Now anyone can turn a switch and defeat the dark; dial a telephone and defeat distance and space. Televisions bring us information we never had before. Automobiles take us places we never thought to go before. Surely this is magic, but common magic. The magic of the heart is uncommon magic. Common magic reaches out, changes natures, and stops. It depends on gadgets and things to work its wonder. Common magic does not return to the heart. There is no further riddle to solve, no mystery, no work involved; the heart is left out.

I came to Buddhism because I was bored with small riddles. Buddhism is the teaching of the heart. It looks at birth and death directly and says "the real magic lives inside us all, but you've got to unravel the mystery for yourself." "Nature's magic is there right now inside your heart. If you work hard, the secret can be known."

On the bowing pilgrimage we are using methods handed down to us by our teacher. What does it mean to "have no false thinking?" How do you penetrate this state: "The eyes see shapes and forms, but inside there is nothing. The ears hear mundane sounds, but the mind does not know"? How do you realize, "With one thought un-produced the entire substance manifests. When the six organs suddenly move, you're covered by clouds"?

How do you bow single-mindedly, without that second thought?

When we find out, we will be on our way to understanding the heart of Nature's changes.

The answer depends on solid, sincere, constant effort. The clues to the riddle are faith, vows, and constant, patient, practice. And as a further twist, only when we stop seeking the answer, does the answer naturally, spontaneously manifest. This is a puzzle without pieces, a seamless sphere.

Our false thoughts are the mind's attempt to handle the wholeness of Nature's magic. The head interferes and tries to turn the circle into a straight line. It does not work out. This "truth" is hard to accept. My mind continues to turn and work and worry after ten months of bowing. The big riddles cannot be solved in thought. The whole body must go inside and live the riddle. It takes heart. It takes all you've got to realize that's all you need.

> "There is no knowing and no attachment. Because there is nothing to attain, the Bodhisattva's heart, through relying on the Perfection of Wisdom, has no impeding obstructions. Because he is not hung up, he has no fear. He has left behind all upside-down dream-thinking. In the end he attains to Nirvana."
>
> Heart Sutra

---

**Heng Chau** • January 29, 1978
There is just great wisdom

Open country. The Plymouth, parked under a lone palm tree on an abandoned road, is the only sign of human life for miles. It's a crisp 30 degrees and the moon lights up a few tall mountains. Once in awhile a bird cries out, breaking the silence. For miles in all directions it is this way. Solitude.

We have a skillful and compassionate teacher and firm vows to help see us through all obstacles. They make up for some of our personal weaknesses. But in the end, one takes oneself across. A good teacher can only show the way. You have to walk it yourself. So it's said in the Dhammapada,

> No one saves us but ourselves,
> No one can and no one may.
> We ourselves must walk the Path,
> Buddhas can only show the Way.

It's 12:00 midnight. We are warming up for meditation. On these solitary cold nights on a barren stretch of road, the truth of those words sinks in loud and clear.

There is no way around it. "All beings have the Buddha-nature; all can become Buddhas." Cultivation is like eating, sleeping and wearing clothes. We just do it because it's natural. It's part of being a person.

At some point cultivation ceases to be suffering and becomes a lot of fun. Conversely, the good life and "easy living" becomes suffering and no longer any fun. When this happens, things start to get ineffably wonderful and mysterious.

> "Cultivation! How could there be anything more esoteric or wonderful?"

A man on a bicycle, who saw us back in June, stopped and asked for handout about the pilgrimage. Later he came back.

"Hey, that paper was blank! There wasn't a word on it," he said. He apparently got one that missed the copier.

"When you get right down to it, that's what it's all about," I answered.

"I thought so. But I figured I couldn't read it because I didn't believe it," he replied. We all had a good laugh.

The Patriarch Seng Tsan wrote,

> "In it there is no room for words or speech. It has no present, past or future."
>
> Hsin Hsin Ming

In the Avatamsaka it says the Buddha is nowhere, and nowhere he is not. Basically there's not one thing that can be obtained, not enlightenment and not the Buddha. There is just great wisdom. The ultimate state of wisdom is non-attachment. So whatever you're seeking you'll never find because nothing can be found. There are no fixed dharmas.

"In all the three periods of time you can seek, but there is nothing at all which exists."

Tushita Heaven
Chapter 24

We had cereal and roadside "weeds" for lunch. The wild greens are excellent food – nutritious, clean and simple. In the small field next to us were enough edible plants to feed us for a week. But more revealing than this natural food discovery is the revelation of yet another world.

We have been walking, sleeping, eating and bowing on and through this veritable garden of perfect pilgrim-food and we never "saw" it. They were just weeds to us until a couple of people woke us up to this new world. It says in the Avatamsaka that there are,

"...lands in variety beyond thought, worlds without limit"
and that,

"In a single dust mote and lands as numerous as dust motes."

Avatamsaka Sutra
Flower Store World Chapter

"When living beings thoughts are pure, the lands they see are fully purified."

Avatamsaka Sutra
Flower Store World Chapter

Right before our eyes are worlds within worlds "without limit" but we only see them to the number and measure of our own minds. Looking out the car door at the weeds and grasses we ate for lunch, swaying and shimmering in the waves of wind, was a new world. The highway with all its noisy energy and metal speed falsely drew all my attention to it. I failed to notice all the lands in variety beyond thought "right under my nose."

The five organs are just holes. We *see* with our mind. According to what we think and how we live, our visions of lands follow suit.

This is the heart of cultivating the Way: return the light to illumine within. When the mind is pure and unobstructed, then what we see is pure and unobstructed. Pollution and purity come from our thoughts, as do all the measureless number of lands.

---

**Heng Sure**
It took forty-nine more days

> "The mind is like the artist. It can paint an entire world. The Five Skandhas all come from it. There are no dharmas it does not create...
>
> "If a person knows the actions of the mind as it universally creates the world this person then sees the Buddha and understands the Buddha's true, actual Nature."
>
> Avatamsaka Sutra – Praises from the
> Suyama Heaven Palace Chapter

To get enlightened you have to be a full-time meditator. Anyone can do it – on the highway, on the cushion, in the bank-teller's line, anywhere. But most of us who left the home life did so because we found it easier to meditate in a pure environment. People with dedication, pure faith, and good roots can meditate no matter where they are. However, even the Buddha with all of his merit, virtue, and blessings from each lifetime of cultivation over the past three great aeons, in this life time, had to work hard for six years in the mountains. His seclusion didn't succeed. It took forty-nine more days of pure concentration to open his wisdom storehouse and perfect his enlightenment.

Most of us who don't have the Buddha's head-start in good roots have to work many times harder and longer to realize the Path. But when cultivating the Dharma, effort bears fruit. Enlightenment is available to all living beings. But like the Buddha, we have to meditate hard all the time.

The Buddhist Sangha are full-time, "professional" meditators. Meditation is the heart of the Buddha's experience. Everything we do has the purpose of aiding our concentration. Concentration leads to meditative trance or samadhi, and samadhi produces wisdom. Every part of Buddhism from reducing worldly attachments, to ascetic practices, from precepts to the splendor of Sutras, come as a response to what happens when we meditate.

As monks, our eating, our sleeping, our rules, our clothes, our exercises, our prayers, all come from a central principle: at all times be with "one heart unconfused" – the state of meditative concentration. Everything a monk or nun does reflects and facilitates full-time meditation. Vows and practices are like the scaffold that holds the painter. What the painter creates with his brush depends on how well he or she uses energy in concentration.

The bowing pilgrimage provides an ideal way to focus on moving meditation. Absolutely everything extraneous to the work has been removed from our world. An extra spoonful of food at lunch shows up in the afternoon's bowing. Heng Chau stared at a rainbow for an instant too long and lost his concentration fuel. I wrote a needless note to another monk and broke four vows within ten minutes. Why such picayune details? These seemingly small mistakes reflect a lack of concentration. Consider the archer who holds his bow and arrow at full draw. If he steals a quick glance at a passing flock of birds, he's likely to miss the target entirely.

A driver traveling at high speed cannot afford to take his eyes off the road for even an instant. Although we travel only a mile each day, our insides often feel like jet planes because of our practices: bowing, exercise, sitting Ch'an, Sutra study, ceremonies, and just enough sleep and food. This is the meditator's way of life at its finest. Our teacher makes it possible for us to cultivate as the Buddha did. Are we extremists? Yes, but then again the matter of birth and death is great. Enlightenment is eternal delight. We don't go to extremes, we work to return to the Middle Way that we left so long ago – and it's a full-time job.

Heng Chau • January 30, 1978
Talking makes it harder to get by

Outside: The Irelands bring fruit, thermal shirts and laughter. The car is leaking oil.

Inside: quiet day, long, steady bowing with the wind clearing the mind. Sometimes I can feel past karma exhausting itself as we enter totally virgin ground. We enter only on vows and faith.

> The Buddhadharma is like a vast sea,
>     only on faith can one enter.

Conversation overheard between two people watching from the road:

"How can he not talk!? How does he get by?" asked one.

"When you get down to it, there's probably not a whole lot that needs to be said. Mostly talking makes it harder to get by," answered someone.

> For it is the way of heaven not to strive
>     but nonetheless, to conquer.
> Not to speak, but nonetheless, to get an answer.
> Not to beckon; yet things come to it of themselves.
> Heaven is like one who says little,
>     yet nonetheless has laid his plans.
>
> Lao Tzu

It's true. The less we strive and seek, the easier it is to get by. The less we speak, the more answers we get.

## Heng Sure
Grab for all the gusto you can get

> "The Bodhisattva... gains peace and security for himself
> and causes others to gain peace and security. He can leave
> defilement himself and cause others to leave defilement."
>
> Avatamsaka Sutra<br>Chapter II

"You only go around once in this life so grab for all the gusto you
can get." (Beer advertisement)

I've reflected on where I stepped off the path of purity in this
life. I want to prevent it from happening again. We plant seeds now
that ripen into fruit in the future. How long ago did I set up the
causes for my bad karma in this life? How deep are those bad roots?

Ignorant sayings like the beer ad above fooled me into tasting the
fruits of evil. "That's life," was all we could say the morning after a
binge with drink and dope and sugar and sex. All our body signals
were shouting "Hey! Quit taking this stuff! Why do you do this?" But
I bought the idea that good times meant high living and high living
meant indulging in intoxicants, excessive eating and careless promis-
cuity. Boy, was I stupid. I knew it wasn't any fun – it didn't last, it hurt
others. Did I stop? Not until I met my teacher's purity and virtue.

No one advertises how good it feels to be pure. The happiness of
being clean, strong, unpoisoned and chaste is wonderful, but who
believes it until they try it? What is the difference? Being pure takes
effort. Being polluted is easy. You don't fall; you have to *climb* into
purity. What is the number one most useful tool to staying clean?
One sentence: "No thank you."

As for the karma patterns that tug at us, the Dharmas of
repentance and reform in Buddhism are like the sun shining into a
gloomy hall. Open the shutters and chase the darkness. I'm sorry for
the bad I've done. I vow never to do it again!

"(The Bodhisattva) can purify himself and cause others to be purified. He can enter Nirvana and causes others to enter Nirvana. He becomes happy and he can make others happy."

Avatamsaka Sutra
Ten Practices Chapter

---

Heng Chau • January 31, 1978
No hassle is great happiness

The car fixed itself, somehow. No more leaking oil or falling apart noises from rear axle.

We leave Highway 1 and will take Quintana Road on an alternate route through the City of Morro Bay. The highway is closed to pedestrians for the next 3-1/2 miles.

Bob, a Cuesta College, Art History Professor, came out with offerings and asked permission to film the bowing for his class. He asked to hear a "Buddhist chant" but just then his tape ran out.

"Oh, darn," he said. "My tape all ran out. There's nothing left. I won't be able to record a Buddhist chant."

"It's okay. When your mind tape runs itself out and there's nothing left, that's the original Buddhist chant," I said.

I don't know why I said that. The words just popped into my head. Bob really liked it though and said,

"Boy, that's it, isn't it!? When your mad tape finally runs out, then you're almost home... I mean, just being as it really is, huh?"

When the mad mind stops,
that very stopping is Bodhi.

Shurangama Sutra

Two pick-up trucks full of "Jesus people" from a nearby commune drove down from the mountains. They spent 2-1/2 hours stomping, singing, reveling and preaching to convert us to rebirth by bathing "in the blood of the lamb." They took turns reading biblical scriptures, exhorting us to stop bowing and praise Jesus instead of the Buddha. It was pretty noisy.

Everyone had a guitar or tambourine and was clapping and hooting. They encircled us for most of the afternoon as we bowed down the road.

Heng Sure took the brunt of their mission. The vow of total silence somehow made him a special target. He held firm in not talking. One by one they got hoarse and weary and drifted away. One young man, who said he used to be a star lead singer in a rock n' roll band, stayed behind to "give it all I've got to make you believe," as he put it.

For 45 minutes, he yelled, pleaded, wailed and threatened trying to get Heng Sure to talk. He clung to Heng Sure's side strumming a guitar and singing Jesus songs at the top of his voice. He was pretty uptight. Finally, he too gave up and left.

> "All Dharmas are empty and unreal. They arise quickly and as quickly disappear. They are unstable. Like dreams, like shadows, like illusions and transformations."
>
> Avatamsaka Sutra
> Ten Practices Chapter

How strange. Minutes before there was just the sound of the wind and a rooster crowing in the distance. After they all left, it was the same, silent and empty. Everything at root is "level and equal, still and extinct," as the Avatamsaka says.

Tonight we read a passage from the Avatamsaka that spoke directly to our experience with the "Jesus people."

> Their minds are equal with the Buddhas
> of the three periods of time.
> They are blessed with the Tathagata's
> measureless strength,
> Which arises from Dharmas

which are not upside-down, and
They reveal the path of peace and security
to all living beings.

Bowing in repentance and reform is wholesome and solid Dharma. And because it isn't the least bit upside-down, a special kind of strength is built-up in one's mind and will. Living right and squarely in line with true principle brings "measureless strength."

Heng Sure was calm and happy in the middle of an all-out group conversion attempt. They were unpleasant and impolite. There was a lot of mocking and harassment. He took it. He remained quiet and peaceful, secure within the "bowing heart" – a heart that is without anger, fear or fatigue.

A little boy watched intently from the sidewalk. He was absorbing the "path of peace and security" apart from words and all the noise. Praising the Tathagata is pointing to the best qualities in each of us. In not getting upset or angry, Heng Sure, without speaking a word, was praising the Buddha "like it really is." Because "like it really is," is just, "everything's okay, no problem." What is there to argue about or fight over? Basically there is no "you" or "me," so who is there to contend with? Being kind and peaceful to people is praising the Buddha. No hassle is great happiness.

Their minds show no fear,
They produce great happiness.
Using inexpressible, measureless, inexhaustible
numbers of dharmas of praise like it really is:
They praise the Tathagata
without ever growing weary.

Avatamsaka Sutra

Tomorrow, Morro Bay. We reached the city limits by nightfall.

**Heng Sure**
It's because they don't concentrate!

Go All The Way Through One Gate.

Before lunch, I learned the basic turn of Shao Lin meditation. Heng Chau praised my practice, "It was right. It was concentration. There was no self, just pure heart and form combined." His comment helped me connect the Master's instructions in my mind. The last pieces of a puzzle fell into place. A puzzle I'd been working on all my life. How come I did the turn right? Pure motivation: I wanted to learn it so I could give it away. It was selfless and not seeking. It had to do with concentration and will power and heart.

> "Why do cultivators work back and forth within the Buddhadharma for several great aeons and never get anywhere? It's because they don't concentrate! You should go all the way through one gate. Concentrate your mind and fix your will. Whichever method you use, use it with a *single mind*!"

I've heard this instruction from the Master many times. Only now has it begun to appear in my practice. What is the difference? Heart and pure motivation.

Further connections: why had I wasted so much time on my pilgrimage doing false thinking? The Master pinpointed my problem – no concentration. After hearing that lecture, I returned the light on my cultivation practices and took an honest look. What had I done with the Dharma tools I learned? Same as ever: I collected them and stacked them neatly in a tool chest. I would use three of them at once, all with half-hearted resolve. The tools designed to clear the mind were choking me. Tools like the vajra sword, "who?", "return the light," quotes from the Sutras, the wisdom in verses. Any one of these was a first-rate path to enlightenment. Heaped together and used all at once, they simply confused me and allowed the false thoughts to continue as I bowed.

"Study what is close at hand. Don't be greedy for quantity. In cultivation, it's like eating. If you are greedy for a lot, your teeth can't chew it all. You are forgetting the near and being greedy for what's far away. You have a supreme treasure at home but you can't use it. You just go out and shuffle through garbage. This is wasting time. Practice as much as you know," said the Master.

Where to begin? I realized that motivation was the problem. Before I left home I worked for these goals: love, approval, fame, control of the world and expansion of self through knowledge and climbing on conditions. All of these goals are based on a lie: the lie of self. None of them lead to satisfaction, because they were false goals to begin with. When they carried over into cultivation, my energy system kept blowing fuses. Cultivation aims to end love, to stop all seeking and climbing. Cultivation works to reduce the self. How could I concentrate when my heart was confused about the purpose of the work?

The Bodhisattva works from a true heart, a big heart. He has no thoughts of self. He needs no approval or recognition at all. He works only to give to others and to get them to liberation.

The Master's instructions last month confirmed my discovery and tied together all the pieces of new awareness that began with the Shao Lin turn. He said, "Don't seek for anything. Seeking is greed. It comes from the self."

On the road again using this basic truth, concentration began to flow from my heart. I found that what I really wanted was exactly the method I began the trip with. My goals were the very goals I had vowed to achieve at the beginning. By concentrating on these basics and letting the rest go, I will be able to penetrate my self and enter all the way through one gate into the Flower Store World.

* * * * * * * *
## February 1978

Heng Chau • February 1, 1978
As much value as King Tut's Tomb

Morro Bay, California...

A high school student named Dave watched for a long time and then came up at the end of the day.

"It's really amazing! Well, I don't know how to say this, but, well... ah, we have a group of friends that get together and sort of talk things through – try to get the truth and past all the phoniness, you know? Well anyway, we are sincerely interested in what you're doing."

He wanted more information about Buddhism to share with his friends. He asked a question they had all wondered about:

"What's the core of Buddhism?"

"Anybody can do it."

> All beings have the Buddha-nature.
> All can become Buddhas.
> It's only because of false thinking and attachments,
> That they don't attain the fruit.
>
> Shakyamuni Buddha

A well-dressed man on his way home from work, "I think it's great what you are doing. I really believe in it." He made an offering and wished us luck.

Woman: "I really honor your life. I wish I could do it."

Monk: "Anybody can do it."

Woman: "Oh, no... it takes real... real something to be able to do..."

Woman's husband: "I guess you can do anything if you set your mind to it."

Woman: "That's what it's all about, isn't it? Set your mind and never retreat."

The Avatamsaka Sutra is in the minds of people. Everyday we hear the wonderful Dharma. Each person along our way speaks their own chapter, in their own way. These people were reciting from the "Ten Transferences Chapter" in their own hearts.

> "In thought after thought his wisdom increases. It grows full and perfect and he does not retreat. He cultivates Bodhisattva practices with wholesome, skillful means and never rests."
>
> Avatamsaka Sutra
> Ten Transferences Chapter

In the early morning, young people jog past and the old folks stroll by briskly in groups of 3's and 4's. They do it every morning. Everything is a question of habits. Cultivating the Way is trying to get into the habit of no-habits.

> "The enlightened Dharma King sees the true, real Dharma, and within it he is not attached or bound up. In this way, he is independent and his mind unobstructed. And he never sees the arisal of a single Dharma."
>
> Avatamsaka Sutra
> Ten Transferences Chapter

It is by attaching to things that they spoil; holding on turns them sour. Why does the Bodhisattva "never see the arisal of a single Dharma?" Because that's how it really is: there's not one thing that is fixed. Everything is in flux.

Not attached to the soft comforts, we aren't defeated by hardship or afraid of difficulty. Not bound up in pleasure, we don't suffer extreme pain. Not falsely clinging to life, how could we fear death? That's why it's said,

"True emptiness is just wonderful existence."

Empty means no attachments. No attachment is ultimate freedom and comfort. The Buddha was called the "Patient Immortal" in lives past, because he cultivated to the state where he saw that everything is impermanent and un-produced. And facing this awareness, he didn't freak out. He just patiently smiled and returned his life to the "true, real nature." The Buddha is the "Dharma King." It's all a question of habits.

Fritz, an engineer with the San Luis Fire Department, stopped by. He heard about the pilgrimage from fellow firemen who had watched over us in San Luis. "Well, I just stopped to say hello and let you know I'll be helping you out, kind of protecting you for awhile," said Fritz. "I grew up on the edge of the desert and always feel close to home when I'm out in the open, empty spaces and my mind's got room to spread out. I feel we got a lot in common somehow," he said.

"In all worlds, his mind is like empty space, without any attachments."

Avatamsaka Sutra
Ten Transferences Chapter

Sufficiency:

"Be content with what you have and are, and no one can despoil you."

Lao Tzu

"Our business in life is to know suffering."

Master Hua
from "Admonishment Verse"

Being content with what you have is knowing sufficiency. Insufficiency comes from having too much, not too little. The more I acquire the less I am satisfied. Sometimes even a little is too much, and, almost always a lot is too little. That is, there's "never enough" to bring satisfaction because the mind of greed is like a bottomless pit. I am a greedy person. I never feel I have enough. This pilgrimage is teaching me that I have all I need to be content. True satisfaction is in seeking nothing, not in getting what you seek.

A middle-aged teacher sat with us in the tall grass alongside the road and reflected on his life.

"You know the time, the *only* time, I was really happy... yeah, satisfied... was when I had everything I owned and needed in a pack on my back and was hiking around the country alone," he said.

It's said,

> "To be content with what you have is to be rich."
>
> Tao Te Ching

An older man in a pick-up truck stopped. He said his name was George. He got right to the point.

"I'm an atheist, I don't believe in anything. I read about you and saw your pictures in the papers and you've been in my thoughts for 3 weeks. I haven't been able to get you out of my mind!"

"Oh?" I said.

"Yeah. I figured I had to come out and see you. I can see you're different; otherwise I wouldn't have bothered at all. I mean you're really simple. You're not out for yourselves. Do you know how rare this is!? There's probably only a handful of such people left on the entire messed-up planet that are *really* out to help the lot of human kind!" said George.

He walked along and talked as we bowed in the grass.

"You're Buddhists, right?"

"Yes. We are Buddhist monks from Gold Mountain Monastery."

"What you're doing has real value," said George mildly sarcastic. "– about as much value as King Tut's Tomb! It's totally futile! A waste! How are you two going to change anything?"

I explained how we are starting with the small and close at hand. We're trying to get rid of our own greed, hatred and ignorance. If our small world can find peace, then there's that much more peace for the big world. If we want to improve the world we must start by straightening out our own minds. George listens carefully and replies,

"Hmm. Okay. But *show* me. I mean just show me how bowing does anything?" he persists. We talk back and forth for awhile, then I say,

"After awhile, talking is useless. You've got to actually bow to find out how it works. It can be experienced but not explained." I tell him about children who come out and just bow along to find out what it's all about instead of rapping.

"No way!" snaps George. "I'm not going to do that! No way... I just couldn't."

"There are a thousand ways to purify the mind and to do good. Bowing is only one of them," I try to point out.

"Well, you just name me one thing I could do, just name *one* that would make any sense or work. Name one!" shouts George, challenging and skeptical.

"Don't get angry." The words just popped into my mind without thinking. "No matter what happens, be kind and happy and never get angry." I felt the words come through me, not from me.

George stops cold and just stares. He looks me straight in the face, steady and sincere for the first time since we've been talking, and slowly says in a subdued voice.

"You know, mister, for 45 years I've been trying to get a throttle on my anger. Boy that's it! That's really it! I figure I'm just a little guy and can't even touch all the suffering and problems in this crazy world. But if I could not blow my top all the time... well, that would be something."

George relaxes and quietly walks with us. The sun is setting. Rush hour traffic has died down.

"Einstein says we are all the same substance," reflects George. "Just think, if all your 'molecules' were mellow and you never got angry, what an effect that could have on all mankind. I'm glad I stopped. Really glad! God bless you, God bless you!"

We shook hands, like old friends, and then George drove off waving and smiling from his old truck.

> He clearly sees the Dharma Realm.
> How it is vast, big and peacefully set up.
> He understands the entire world as well as all Dharmas.
>> are level, equal and non-dual, and
> He leaves all attachments behind... and to the very end,
>> he hasn't the slightest thought of anger.
>
> Avatamsaka Sutra
> Ten Transferences Chapter

An older woman, weeping softly approaches. "Thank you. Thank you. Will you take this please," she says holding out some money. Everything about her was honest.

A local vegetarian family who does yoga together, made a "pure food" offering. "Thank you" said the mother. "There are lots of vegetarians in the area and many others who send a lot of light and energy to your journey. This is a holy area and we are happy you are passing through."

A young man named Steve wanted to help out but didn't know how. "All I got is some cans of motor oil in my car. Can you use it?"

Strange. I had just checked the engine. The Plymouth was bone dry. We needed oil badly. A few hours later, Steve shows up to offer 3 quarts.

**Heng Chau** • February 2, 1978
Jewels to adorn the throne

I don't trust my own mind. I've neglected it too long. It's full of bad habits and selfishness. I trust the Sutra. I trust my teacher. I trust the bowing with a single mind.

> Each of the Bodhisattvas,
>     upon reaching the Buddha's place,
> Bowed at the Buddha's feet,
> Using the Buddha's spiritual power,
> Then and there by transformation
> They made a lion's throne
>     from a treasury of wonderful jewels.
>
> Jeweled nets were festooned
>     and draped everywhere above it.
> All the Bodhisattvas assemblies
>     in accordance with the direction they came from,
> Set upon the throne in full lotus.

Avatamsaka Sutra
Praises in the Tushita Heave Palace

We read this passage last night. Today while gathering wild greens under a tree by the freeway, the words came to mind. Suddenly they made sense. The daily work of bowing and keeping the precepts is preparation for listening to the Sutra at night. We are building a "throne" inside for the Dharma, a pure vessel to hold the Buddha's wisdom light that pours from the Sutra. The harder we bow in repentance and reform, the emptier we get. The emptier we become, the more we can hold. The fewer false thoughts we strike up, the more jewels there are to adorn the throne.

The principles of the Sutra are in our own minds. Cultivation is simply the work of getting rid of the junk that covers them over. The "Buddha's place" is within, but it's all boarded up and grown over with weeds. So we cultivate and adorn it by "bowing at the Buddha's feet."

The "jeweled nets" and "treasury of wonderful jewels," are just the wisdom light of each person's self-nature. It spills forth and radiates as we go towards the good. Our light shines from holding pure precepts, cultivating the 6 paramitas, and taking the 4 unlimited minds (kindness, compassion, joy and giving), as our substance and function. All of these adorn our throne.

The palace from where the Buddha speaks Dharma is located within our own hearts. The Tushita Heaven Palace is made from one's mind. The throne is the "jewel within," and all beings universally possess it. But until the mind jewel is rubbed and polished, it's just an ordinary rock. And until we cultivate the Way, we're just ordinary people.

An elderly and stately woman in a black limousine drove up. "You'll need gas, won't you?" she said smiling and dropping money into my bag.

---

Heng Chau • February 3, 1978
While in the middle of it

Morro Bay...

Virginia McKenzie came out to welcome us to Morro Bay on behalf of a group of citizens and local ranchers who believe in the principles we are bowing for. They wanted to support us as we passed through their area.

"It's no trouble. It's not work, it's joy," she said. "You are doing us *all* a great service."

Reminder to myself:

"Giving isn't tiring. Taking wears you out. Repay the kindness of your parents and go towards the good. Treat all beings with kindness, compassion, joy and giving. No matter what happens, anger is never okay.

"Truly recognize your own faults and don't fault-find others. Don't let a day pass without correcting your mistakes and knowing shame. Purify your mind and be happy. Whatever you have you can't take with you past the grave. Give big and break all attachments."

A man invited us to spend the evening in his home. We declined and explained our vow to stay outside or in the car for the pilgrimage.

"Yes. Everyday is a new day, happy and wonderful when your life is not so burdened. I can understand your wanting to stay away from residences and homes... so you don't get tangled up in and tied down with the stuff as we all are," said the donor.

Afterwards I thought to myself, "If one could stay free and untangled while in the middle of it, that's even better." There's nothing intrinsically defiled or enslaving about the world. It's all made from the mind. Things (dharmas) don't tie us down, our own thoughts do.

> If you are able, while in the mundane world,
> To leave behind all your attachments, and
> Be happy with an unobstructed mind,
> Then you can become enlightened to the Dharma.

Avatamsaka Sutra
Verses in Praise in the
"Tushita Heaven Palace Chapter"

Lots of people ask about stamina and endurance. "Isn't it hard on your body," and "Are you stiff and tired?" or "You must get a lot of injuries and sickness living such a difficult life."

We've never been healthier. False thoughts and attachments are exhausting and hard on your body. Sickness comes from greed. "Accidents" are the retribution of anger. All suffering is born from ignorance. However much greed, anger, and stupidity we have, that's how much we suffer. Whatever we can't put down puts us down. Attachments wear us out; false thinking makes us old. Precepts keep one young and light. Concentration guards health. Wisdom cuts through ignorance and makes "everything okay, no problem."

No Fatigue:

Giving makes you lighter.
Desire ties you down.
Floating in samadhi,
Affliction makes you drown.

The Avatamsaka describes a state of total mind/body, light ease and comfort. It is the result of mental concentration to the point of no attachments. Attractive or ugly, good or bad, no longer exist. Inside and outside merge, and without feelings of love and hate, one is light as the wind. It says,

He saves all forms, up to and including
    all objects of touch,
And be they attractive or ugly,
He knows neither love nor disdain.
His mind achieves $dz\ dzai^2$

The Bodhisattvas inhabit the world, and
They are not attached to any Dharmas
    either inside or outside.
Like the wind which travels through space unobstructed,
The Great Knight's concentration is also like this.

Avatamsaka Sutra
Bodhisattvas Ask for Clarification Chapter

As we gathered herbs and wild greens in an empty field, a woman out walking her dogs stopped. She came to convert us.

"This last year, Jesus gave me so much. My car, my house, my dogs... What has the Buddha done for you?"

---

2. lightease, comfortable freedom

In the world if you're true,
    people say you're false.
If you're false,
    people say you're true.
It's upside-down.

Instructions en route from Ven. Abbot

I didn't answer because we never argue. Sometimes saying nothing at all is the kindest thing to do. It's not fixed, though. (The Master later offered an answer that was very simple, yet full of principle. The Abbot said, "The Buddha gave me Jesus.")

"What do you hope to gain," asked the woman.

"We hope to lose. If we can lose a little, then others gain."

Bowing is just learning to be a person. Cultivating the Way melts the false coverings and pride I've layered over my true face. There are no tricks, no secret teachings. There's just hard work and patience. Hold precepts, concentrate the mind, and eventually wisdom opens by itself.

A waitress stopped on her way home from work. She saw us bowing on the road and gave us all her tips for the day.

"It's not much. This is the slow season. But it's from my heart," she said.

**Heng Chau** • February 4, 1978
Like a hamburger or girlfriend or something

Morro Bay.

> "Moreover when a person's life is over, nothing follows one into the grave. At the last instant of life all the organs scatter and one departs from all his relatives. All status and power is lost. Nothing survives: neither servants, nor ministers, palaces or cities, nor elephants, horses, cars, or chariot, neither jewels nor treasures. At the last moment of life only these kings of vows do not leave one. At all times they guide one forward along a road. In a split second one is reborn in the land of Ultimate Bliss."
>
> Avatamsaka Sutra, Chapter 40

Bill, a photographer from the local newspaper, has been trailing along for the last two days doing a story. He stopped to say goodbye.

"I've come to the conclusion that a lot of what's wrong with the world – the reason there's so much suffering and trouble – is because of insecurity. People are insecure about their station, possessions, jobs, friends, death… it's endless," he said. "You two men are the most secure people I've ever met. I had to say this. I envy you very much."

"Anybody can cultivate, we're not special."

"It takes a real man to have shame – to be able to say 'I'm wrong' and change. That's *real* strength and security. I'm afraid I don't have the guts to do what you're doing," he said sincerely.

"If you have the courage to say what you just said, then you have the guts to do anything you want," I answered.

"Maybe so. I want to thank you, and I hope our path cross again someday and I am more ready to join you." He shook hands and left a bag of fruit on the car.

Security:

> Nothing left to lose,
> Nothing hoped to gain.
> Heroic vajra strength,
> In yielding and from shame.
>
> Repaying parents kindness,
> By ending "me" and "you."
> Find your face before you're born,
> And everyday renew.

Morro Bay, February 4, 1978<br>Written for a photograph

Bill, the photographer, was speaking the Sutra. He felt the freedom and power of repentance and reform, one of the ten great vows of Universal Worthy. The fourth vow is to "repent of karmic obstacles and reform." This is what Bill meant by "to have shame, to say, 'I'm wrong' and change." Anyone who cultivates these ten vows "with a heart of profound faith" will quickly gain *real* security.

> "All of the bitter grief arising from the mundane illness of body and mind will be wiped away up to and including as much bad karma as there are fine motes of dust in a Buddhaland... he will move freely through the world like the moon in space appearing through the clouds."

Avatamsaka Sutra<br>Chapter 40

Jack (Hanneman), a 70 year old retired man, walked up with an offering and said,

"I've been around awhile, enough to have seen the world get more topsy-turvy everyday. My wife and I wish you the best of luck, and hope you help make things right again."

The world starts to go bad in small, close-to-home ways. The practice of filiality, respecting, taking care of and repaying the kindness of parents, is a small thing at first glance. But its influence is immeasurable. When filiality is honored and cultivated there are few disasters and wars. Where filiality is neglected, calamities and strife flourish. More than any single principle of Buddhism we have presented to people on this pilgrimage, filiality stirs the deepest response and enthusiasm.

"You don't know how happy I am to hear and see this (filiality). We all seem to have forgotten today in this crazy world what really matters. I thought such notions were gone forever. It was a real boost to hear you Buddhists talking of 'repaying kindness of your parents.' There's still hope," said a man yesterday.

An elderly gray-haired couple approached us as we bowed down Main Street. They were happy and excited to find us.

"We've watched you with deep interest for days. Will you accept this small offering?" They asked, handing us a bag full of home-cooked food and fresh fruit.

We sat meditating and writing under a palm tree by a road culvert next to a mobile home park. A young paperboy leaned over the handlebars of his bike to listen in as Bill, a college student, sat on the curb and talked to us about his life.

"I've read a bit and feel close to Taoism and Buddhism. My favorite book is Sayings of the Buddha. But you know, leading a spiritual life is really going against the grain."

"Oh?" I said.

"It seems that when I try to practice the things I read and know inside, I get a test. I mean, just when I get my desires low and a little control, I get a test – like a hamburger or girlfriend or something."

The paperboy leans his bike against the tree and squats down next to us. Bill goes on.

"A lot of my friends start on the Way, but then turn around because it gets so hard to go against the grain and still be in it all."

"We use this verse a lot on our trip. It helps," I answer.

Everything's a test,
To see what you will do.
Mistaking what's before your eyes
You'll have to start anew.

Master Hua

"That's good. Nothing is really good or bad. I guess it's what you do with it that matters... Well I'm glad I stopped. I'd like to check out that City of 10,000 Buddhas." he said getting up to leave. "You know, it's really incredible what you're doing."

"Anybody could do it."

"I suppose, if you set your mind to it... What are you going to do when you get there?" he asked.

"Keep setting our mind to it."

Route #1 – The Coast Highway.

We are bowing ocean-side again. The air changes. The weather, people, all conditions change, and turn unpredictable and raw. We never know what to expect. Most highways just go from one place to another, but this road goes in all directions, especially within. Highway 1 has a contemplative spirit and whoever travels it "travels far." Some find this uncomfortable, some a relief, but everyone finds it. The road is ideally suited for a pilgrimage – something about it mirrors the emptiness of things and life's impermanence. The road and the ocean seem to merge into a timeless expanse that can turn the mind back on itself like the shore turns the waves back to the sea. Thought after thought washes over and echoes inside like wave after wave on the sand.

We are on our way out of Morro Bay bowing on always-damp, sand-swept beach roads through rows of look-alike, faded pastel houses. Ahead are Cayucos, Cambria, and San Simeon.

**Heng Sure**
Level and uniform

Making Lunch Level.

Sitting in the dragon car after lunch I glanced at the tall green grass blowing in the breeze and felt in my heart a new peace and quiet. The bowing, the eating, the sitting, the ceremonies, all of it is life. I care for it equally. Like life, it is clear, timeless and without a flow or a seam anywhere. It is level and uniform.

**Heng Chau** • February 5, 1978
Sometimes within minutes of each other

In Morro Bay a Park Ranger and his family watched over us. Nearly everyday one of the family brought out food, water, gas and other necessities. They were always cheerful and supported us for weeks.

Yesterday, by contrast, we received the instant protection of two young boys named Dave and Bobby. They first appeared to test our temper and challenge our sincerity by skidding and buzzing us on their bicycles. One would block the sidewalk, while the other squealed rubber within inches of heads bowed to the ground. After a few questions, they left.

But, later when a gang of tough youths gathered to throw rocks at us, Dave and Bobby came speeding up and sent them running. When the crisis had passed, the two young boys returned and did a half-bow from their bikes. They flashed a proud grin and gave a head-nod of allegiance.

"How can you do good?" asked Bobby.

"Take good care of and respect your parents," I answer.

"That won't help anything," snapped Dave.

"They take care of you. That helps you, doesn't it?" I asked.

They smile. "Yes. We'll come back tomorrow, okay? You won't have any more trouble today."

> "He vows that all living beings get good and wise advisors who constantly follow them, cover them and protect them."
>
> Avatamsaka Sutra

Dharma protectors are traditionally laypeople who support the left-home monks and nuns enabling them to cultivate full-time by providing the necessities of life. Heng Sure and I have noticed that from the very first day of the pilgrimage, in every area we pass through, Dharma protectors have appeared to take care and watch over us. We have never been alone. A particular individual or family will introduce themselves one day, and then just start showing up daily checking our needs and supplying food, fuel, maps, clothes and encouragement. One almost seems to sign in as another signs off, sometimes within minutes of each other. We have watched this with gratitude and surprise.

They vary and we never know who might come next, but someone always seems to come. Our Dharma protectors have included: a housewife, farmer, fireman, retired couple, park rangers, policemen, a waitress, college student, nurses, teachers, a medic, a minister, wanderers, a soldier, a tortilla maker, doctors, mechanics, cowboys and children. Often they are Buddhists, but just as often they are not.

Sometimes they provide "instant protection" as with Dave and Bobby. Emergency Dharma protectors have appeared the couple of times when serious accidents were imminent. In those cases no harm came to us, and the Dharma protectors left immediately after. They have shown up when we get lost or take a wrong turn to guide us back. They've arrived in the "nick of time" to thwart thieves or cool down a gang of local toughs all set to give us a hard time. In times of sickness or water shortage, suddenly someone will appear with medicine and fresh water. They unselfishly stand by our side through difficult times and then leave. The "long term" Dharma protectors in contrast, support and protect us for weeks, some for months.

These Dharma protectors are different somehow from regular people – like the difference between a plain Christmas tree and one that's lit up. They seldom meet each other, yet share the same clear, bright eyes and pure field of light. They bend over backwards to help the pilgrimage and never ask for anything in return. They delight in giving. We seldom talk, but a mutual feeling of "old friends" pervades – like we have all known each other before. We have learned to listen carefully to their advice and follow their suggestions. They keep the pilgrimage alive.

On Silence.

A woman cautiously approaches to ask, "Can I look at his face?" Heng Sure's vow of silence stirs a mixture of responses from carnival curiosity to deep respect.

"Won't he flip out from not talking for so long?" asks one.

"I really admire that. I wish I could do it for even a day," says another.

"Can he hear us? Is he blind too? Someone says he forgot *how* to talk, you know, like his tongue got stuck and he can't use his voice box anymore. Is that true?"

"You don't need to say a word. What you're doing says it all," remarks an elderly man offering some gas money.

We ate lunch in an empty field turned sandlot baseball diamond on the edge of town. Three or four young couples and their families made a meal offering. They've been coming for the last few weekends to recite the Great Compassion Mantra and listen to the Avatamsaka after lunch.

During the meal a man named Mark drove up and joined us.

"I saw you bowing and sitting in meditation on my way to and from work. It looked natural, part of it all, not above or below common things. And I said to myself, 'It's spring and there are the monks. Of course, good! It felt so natural, like I was expecting you or something. You fit right in with the plants and the road.'" Mark got some food from his car and returned.

"A lot of people who pass through are into selfish things, and they give off bad vibes. You look of the earth and the bowing struck me as spiritual, like it included everybody. It does not seem selfish. It appeals to me. Bowing and sitting seems real, you know? It's level and equal."

Mark then told of an experience he had. "While driving past, back near Cuesta College, I bowed slightly. I don't know whether you saw me or not. I felt you did. After I bowed I felt a tingling – as if I went through walls – and something gentle and pleasant came over me. I don't know how to say this exactly, but, you are sending an energy wave ahead of you and leaving one behind as you go. I also saw or sensed that one of you is deeply involved in the bowing and the other is surrounding the act (the other monk), watching over everything."

Vicky, a young mother, said, "Buddhists only give energy and don't take anything is how I see it. Everyone *talks*, but you never meet anyone doing what is honest."

Everyone stayed to recite and listen to the Sutra. We made an altar in the grass and sat in a circle on blankets and jackets. We read,

> "When the Bodhisattva, Mahasattva, contemplates his good roots in this way, his way of faith is purified. His Great Compassion is solid and durable. He uses profound thoughts, happy thoughts, pure thoughts, most victorious thoughts, soft and pliant thoughts, kind and compassionate thoughts, thoughts of gathering in and protecting, thoughts of benefiting, thoughts of peace and joy, and, universally for all living beings he truly and really transfers. He does not merely mouth the words."
>
> Avatamsaka Sutra
> Ten Transferences Chapter

As people were leaving Mark commented, "I don't know much about Buddhism, but the little I've been able to pick up I like. We all suffer and the idea of compassion and equality appeals to me. It gives me a good sense of location and frees me from lots of fears of spirits, demons and gods."

Ray and his wife retired and moved to Morro Bay from Idaho. He's a solid man, 6'5", who still wears his plain wool work shirts and likes straight, no-nonsense talk.

"My wife and I want to invite you for dinner. We greatly admire what you are doing. We are interested when anybody does this kind of work. We need more, lots more of it in this country," said Ray.

I explained our vow to stay outside and that we didn't go to people's homes. Ray understood.

"The country needs more men like you. *This* is what makes America strong. Good luck!"

A mother with a motley crew of six or seven bright faced children stopped with questions and offerings.

"Do you bless children?" she wondered.

"The blessings are in the bowing, not in us. You bless yourself by doing good for others."

"What a great idea!" she exclaimed. And then they all bowed while their mother said, "and just think of giving a gift to everybody so they will be happy."

"Producing a wholesome joy and desire the Bodhisattva ever-enjoys cultivating the practice of vast, great giving... 'I should give the thought of happiness to all beings.'"

Avatamsaka Sutra
Ten Transferences Chapter

In cultivation, peace of mind is not being confused when facing a situation. Not being confused comes from digging out all the ignorance. What is ignorance? Ignorance is just emotion. Without emotion you're free, and even crises can be turned into good advisors. Without emotion the mind naturally comes to focus and illumines every state. So it's said,

> If, in the place of tuning
> Emotion is not kept
> You always and forever dwell
> In Naga concentration.

Sixth Patriarch Sutra

Dragons have a great deal of concentration power. But they don't keep the precepts, and so end up being dragons. Even with great concentration strength, when one does not hold precepts, ignorance cannot be destroyed. When a crisis comes up you'll panic and lose your temper and peace of mind. And so,

> A hundred days of wood gathering
> Can go up in a single blaze;
> A year of sincere cultivation
> Can be destroyed in a single burst of anger.

---

**Heng Chau** • February 6, 1978
Misery is created as if out of nothing

"People's minds are just like the Buddha's mind."

Master Hua

High winds and rain clear to blue sky by bowing time. Bobbie and Dave, the little Dharma protectors on bikes, return with an offering of fresh carrots. They stare at the picture of Guan Yin Bodhisattva hanging in the car.

Boys: "Who's that?"

Monk: "Guan Yin Bodhisattva who helps all living beings when they recite her name."

Boys: "Can Guan Yin hear you?"

Monk: "Can *you* hear us?"

Boys: "Sure can."

Monk: "Then Guan Yin Bodhisattva can hear us too."

> With a thousand eyes to see all;
> A thousand ears to hear all;
> A thousand hands to help
> and support living beings everywhere...
>
> Verse in Praise

Highway road conditions sign says the road is closed 50 miles north at San Simeon. We decide to keep on rather than change routes. San Simeon is nearly 2 months away for us. We clip along about 1/8 mile per hour.

Sign on a bag of fruit left on car, "When I told them at the food store who I was buying this for, they wouldn't take my money. Good luck."

"Doesn't it get boring?" asks a passerby.

"Does it make you happy?" wonders another.

No. Heng Sure and I are realizing happiness and affliction are made within, not from externals. Happiness is already ours. True bliss is originally existent in the self-nature. But I turn my back on the true and unite with garbage. And so misery is created as if out of nothing.

I cover over my original bright-share with false thoughts and grasping. The Buddha's methods are just a wonderful bag of tricks designed to help us forget the false so the true can return by itself. Bowing is a trick.

Peace and happiness, understanding, and freedom sneak up when least expected. That's just our nature as people, maybe. We need to be tricked out of suffering into bliss. If we aren't tricked we don't believe. If it's so easy we don't do it. That is why the Buddhas appear in the world.

"The wonderful principles of the Buddhadharma basically can't be spoken. After awakening, even one word is too many. Only because living beings are confused and so heavily obstructed, does the Buddha come with skillful means and words and talk."

"Speaking Dharma" verse<br>by Ch'an Master Hua

Two young men in a car,

"Man, we saw you guys out here bowing and it stopped our minds cold. It was like we entered another world – India or China or some place thousands of years ago… like it had never changed. It really made me look at my life."

Buddhism is one of the oldest things on the planet. Basic, unchanging, and universal, it is the teaching of all living beings. It is not of this world, and yet it's right in the middle of it. The Buddhadharma cuts across time and countries, leveling all differences. The Buddhadharma is our natural and original home and when we meet it, it's as if "nothing changed."

"The Buddhadharma is not different from the dharmas of the mundane world. Mundane dharmas are not different from the Buddhadharma. The Buddhadharma and mundane dharmas are not mixed together, nor are they distinguishable. He understands that the substance and nature of the Dharma Realm are level and equal. Universally he enters into the past, present and future…"

Avatamsaka Sutra<br>Ten Practices Chapter

The McKenzie, the Park Ranger's family, drove out with fresh water, food supplies, towels and bedding.

"There's a big storm coming. The roads are washed out ahead by big mudslides. They hope to have them open soon, maybe by the time you get there. For some reason we didn't get any of the bad storms here. Yesterday's rain was just a dribble. But there's a stinker of a storm coming in tonight! New York is buried in snow, we're lucky," said Mrs. McKenzie as they emptied portable gas cans into our tank.

They bring out a huge 25-gallon glass bottle full of fresh water and funnel it into our 1-gallon jugs.

---

**Heng Chau** • February 7, 1978
The difference between success and failure

Big storm. A long sit in meditation "clears the air" like a storm in the morning leaves clear sunny skies in the afternoon. The car is dead. We are camped on the city limits of Morro Bay by an offshore oil dock. Mammoth oil tankers unable to enter port and unload because of the storm, drift offshore in rough seas at $750.00 an hour.

High tide breakers crash 10 feet from the highway shoulder. A rancher leaves walnuts and oranges and good wishes.

The storm inside is the impatience and "fire" that cultivators occasionally catch. I barely have it under control when I go to sleep. But in my dreams for the last six nights the Master has appeared to calm me. I wake up relaxed, cool and smooth. A sense of humor is back and I'm ready to go again.

> "He vows that living beings be delighted with their Good Knowing Advisors and never leave them. He vows that all beings unite their good roots with their Good Knowing Advisors..."
>
> Avatamsaka Sutra
> Ten Transferences Chapter

A good teacher (a "Good Knowing Advisor") literally can mean the difference between success and failure in spiritual practice. Uniting with a kind and accomplished teacher can turn big obstacles into little bumps and pull you over the hump when your own power is insufficient. A beginning student related this story to us.

"I attended my first meditation session. It was difficult for me. The teacher was very kind and solicitous saying, 'Don't worry, don't worry.'

"Later I went out to my truck to sleep, but was really upset – I'd been working pretty hard in the session and all kinds of emotions, doubts and fears were pouring over me and out of me at once.

"I lay in the truck thinking how I really needed the Master's help in getting out of this one.

"I pulled myself together enough to recite the Great Compassion Mantra, when who should come walking along the road but the Master with another person.

"He asked me if I was sleeping. Was I crying he wondered.

"Then he sat down on the back of the truck and talked to me while holding my hands and patting me on the head.

"He said he'd help me wake up."

"He vows that all living beings be gathered in by Good Knowing Advisors. That they cultivate great kindness and leave all evil behind... That they thoroughly are able to accept and hold the dharmas of Good Knowing Advisors and attain all samadhis, states, wisdom, and spiritual powers."

Avatamsaka Sutra
Ten Transferences Chapter

**Heng Sure**
All dharmas as equal

> Buddhalands are not distinguishable.
> They are not longed for or loved,
> But only according to beings' thoughts,
> Do the divisions appear to view.
>
> Avatamsaka Sutra
> Bodhisattvas Ask for Clarification Chapter

No more edges: no more "good parts" (resting or vacations), and no more "hard parts" to endure (hard work or bad weather). It always begins and ends in my heart. Pain comes from standing apart from the Dharma realm, slicing it into chunks and putting values and price tags on it. These divisions don't exist outside of my mind. Reality is originally one big happy, quiet piece of on-going wonder.

> "As long as you practice seeing all dharmas as equal, none more important than others, then slowly, bit by bit, they will be. As long as you pick out certain dharmas and make them special, for whatever reason, then you will always fall beneath the wheel."
>
> Master Hua
> at lunch at Gold Wheel Temple

By allowing my mind to want lots of food, I put a big obstacle in my path to even-mindedness. Buddhas see all dharmas, including lunch, as uniform and level. I resolved to study and cultivate what the Buddhas practice. I finally got tired of stumbling over my own obstacles. Encouraged by the Gold Mountain Bhikshus who took up the practice of eating one bowl of food per day, I resolved to limit my intake. The purpose is not to force suffering through starvation. The purpose is to take the little juicy kick out of lunch, to make eating like a fuel stop, a necessary part of being a human. Lunch is not a vacation, not a chance to stop cultivating.

**Heng Chau** • February 8, 1978
All of its troubles I alone make

Cayucos, California.

Storm continues, heavy rain for 2 days. We entered Cayucos, a small settlement of new houses and commuters by the ocean. The car is still stuck and won't start.

> "All in the world with the many different kinds of karmic retribution, none is not completely brought about by the power of deeds. If one takes away the doing, then all in the world ceases to exist.
>
> Avatamsaka Sutra
> Ten Transferences Chapter

Trouble Maker.

Making a beginning, I fear an end. Attaching to forms, I dread emptiness. Making a "me," I grasp after "you." Creating time, I become its slave. I think so much about the past and the future, and now and today aren't real until I can call them yesterday and tomorrow.

Life is truly a dream. All of its troubles I alone make. When I stop "making," the trouble stops. With a single mind, with an unbound heart, we can wake up the wonderful existence in true emptiness that we are in the middle of right now. When "all in the world ceases to exist," only the wonderful remains.

> Give without seeking: perfection of giving.
> Giving 'til empty: wonderful living.
> Fools waste riches adorning the skins,
> The Sages in rags hide the jewel within.
>
> H. Sure and H. Chau

**Heng Chau** • February 9, 1978
It is made to eat the flesh of men

"Stuck."

Pouring rain and heavy winds continue. We are camped on a grassy shoulder alongside the highway. The engine still won't turn over. Everything's wet and soaked. We need to find a laundromat, but there is no way to move. Service station can't fix the car. Road North of here is closed and getting worse.

The homes on the hillsides around us are endangered by mudslides. They could fall into the ocean any second. So other people have it worse than we do. Construction emergency crews and equipment are hustling around like ants trying to control and contain the earth. I think of the ancient saying, "The earth is made to eat the flesh of men."

What is there in life that one can attach to? Not one thing is solid and lasting. Non-attachment is truly the natural state of affairs and our basic "place."

The streets are deserted. Traffic is light, with only emergency vehicles. Last night, during a break in the storm, three men came knocking on the window inviting us to "dry off at our prayer gathering" down the street. We declined.

We bow as always and walk back to the car for the noon meal and ceremonies. Even when you're "stuck" you're still moving and not dwelling. It's when the minds gets stuck that all the problems begin. I remember the verse the Venerable Abbot gave us last month at the airport,

> Seek movement in stillness,
> Seek stillness in movement.
> Movement does not obstruct stillness,
> Stillness does not obstruct movement.
> When you concentrate your mind,
> Movement and stillness are one.

**Heng Sure**
Stories of heroes like never before in the West

> The Great Knight travels throughout the world.
> He brings all beings to peace and security.
> Universally causing them all to be happy,
> He cultivates the Bodhisattva's practices
>     without feeling weary.
>
> Avatamsaka Sutra
> Ten Transferences Chapter

I have always been a hero-worshipper. As a child, I emptied the local library of biographies: Daniel Boone, Jim Bridger, astronauts, explorers, inventors, and pioneers. I read the stories and dreamed of heroic courage. It was the real spark of my imagination. Most admirable were free men who lived by principle. Men who were happy and big hearted. No matter what troubles they faced, they were fearless and unmoving. Men like King Arthur's Knights, Cochise, Admiral Farragut, Marco Polo, the monk Hsuan Tsang.

When I entered the world I found that true heroes are rare. Most of us compromise our freedom for security. Our desires chain us to unhappiness. Selfless people are happy but most of us drift in a state of constant discontent, anchored by the ego that we prize. What happened to all those heroes?

In college I found it again – real heroes to wonder at and dream about! The enlightened Buddhist monks of history starting with the Buddha himself were the freest, happiest men to walk the planet. The stories of the Buddhist Patriarchs sent my heart soaring. I had to know if such men still existed.

"He eradicated all the poisons in the mind. In his thoughts he cultivates the highest wisdom. He does not seek peace and happiness for himself. He only wishes that all beings leave their suffering."

Avatamsaka Sutra
Ten Transferences Chapter

There they are! In Vajra Bodhi Sea. Stories of heroes like never before in the West. Men who are totally fearless. All my childhood favorites had to lie down when the time came to die. Enlightened monks defeated even death! To the Bodhisattva, death is a tool for teaching others to sever their attachments. Bodhisattvas see the body as a gift, to help beings end their suffering. In a past life the Buddha threw himself into a pit to feed a mother tiger who was trapped and unable to nurse her two cubs. It's said that in every mote of dust, a Buddha has given up his life to save living beings. Wow! That's truly heroic!

Buddhist heroes had another unique aspect that caught me by the heart. A Bodhisattva is kind and compassionate, virtuous and pure. Frankly it blew my mind to conceive of a real he-man cultivating the qualities of virtue and purity. As I understood it, men were supposed to be hard and fierce, but here was Guan Shi Yin, the Greatly Kind and Compassionate Bodhisattva Who Regard the World's Sounds. Here was the Buddha "Adorned With Ten Thousand Virtues." Clearly I had a lot to learn.

When I finally found Gold Mountain Monastery, there inside was an entire hall of great heroes, and to my unending delight, each night the Abbot introduced us to the tales of world-transcending *gung fu* in the Hua Yen, Flower Adornment Sutra. Absolutely beyond compare, the Oceanic Assembly of Buddhas and Bodhisattvas of the Flower Store World does the deeds of superheroes but they never stand apart from common people.

How wonderful to meet the Dharma, the high road to wisdom! How vast is the Dharma! Anyone can become a Bodhisattva. When I heard the Ven. Abbot proclaim the path to Bodhisattvahood, I was entranced, gathered in for keeps. My heart belonged to the Dharma. I felt like I had returned to my true home.

"If one seeks to eliminate one's measureless evil deeds, then one must be a courageous and vigorous hero within the Buddhadharma."

Avatamsaka Sutra
Bodhisattvas Ask For Clarifications Chapter

How does heroism and courage translate in to real life terms? For a cultivator of the Way, the chances to practice the vigor of heroes are always present. For example, cultivation is work to subdue the ego to stillness. The ego resists its death and fights for survival. Cultivation becomes a constant practice of staying on edge, using effort all the time, learning to deal with steady, grinding pressure. It's not glamorous but it is heroic. To not grasp at needs and desires when the chances arise takes solid will power. Sitting still when the legs hurt in meditation takes the stamina and will-power of a great being; sitting on when the pain subsides is even scarier and harder to handle.

Basically cultivators know how to do everything right to quiet the mind, but very few dare do it all the time. Very few dare to stay on the edge. It takes courage to stop eating before desire is satisfied. It takes gung fu to not talk or socialize and still be happy. The hero says no to his self and yes to others. The hero puts down his dependence on women (and women for men). This is not easy. To leave the Triple World one must put an end to all seeking outside, stay in the middle all the time. One must bring forth the resolve for enlightenment, the resolve of a great hero.

This is the stuff of true courage. What counts is doing it today and tomorrow and again and again without expecting a thank you or a reward or a song of triumph to honor your work. Then when the fruit of works comes full, your effort will not have been in vain.

"The Bodhisattva gives in order to take delight in fundamental practices cultivated by all Buddhas... He causes all beings to leave suffering and to attain bliss."

Avatamsaka
Ten Practices Chapter

**Heng Chau** • February 10, 1978
I turn the key – varoom!

I look up from meditation this morning to see bright golden Buddhas sitting upright in a VW bus that's pulled up behind us. It's a young disciple on his way to Gold Wheel Temple in L.A.

"Good thing you're right in this spot. I had no idea where to look for you. If you had been any other place I would have never found you. I've come to take you to L.A. The Master told me to bring you."

I had worked on the car that A.M. so we could drive to a laundromat, but it was dead cold, wouldn't even groan.

"Well, give it one more try," says the young man. "We should get it off the road and push it to a safe place for the weekend."

"Hopeless," I answered. "We've tried to get it going for two days. Even the service station can't fix it."

I turn the key – varoom! It starts up immediately, running smooth as a top. After stashing the Plymouth in a secure spot, we pile into the VW with the golden Buddha images and drive through the worst storm I've ever seen. All the way there's flooding, high winds, roads washed out and buried under oozing mountains of mud. Cars are stuck and abandoned everywhere. Trees, furniture and dead animals float by in a muddy river that goes where it pleases. It feels like we're riding in a boat at sea. It occurs to us that had the car not broken down, we would have missed a chance to meet with the Master.

We barely make it over the last set of mountains before dropping into the L.A. basin. An entire mountain has melted into mud covering the highway. We plough through minutes before the whole road is closed by the CHP as impassable. When we arrive at Gold Wheel, it's sunny and blue skies. The Venerable Abbot is standing on the front porch smiling, "How's everything going?"

Gold Wheel Temple, L.A.

The Mayor of L.A. declared a state of emergency. Flooding and high windstorms continue to pound the city. The disciples at Gold Wheel Monastery sponsor a three-day Medicine Master Repentance mini-session. Throughout the day and night people bow and recite the name of Medicine Master Buddha (Akshobhya), "Who dispels calamities and lengthens life." They are very sincere and on the first day of the session, reports of responses appear.

Even though there are trees fallen, power lines down, gas pipes dangerously leaking and deaths in some places, the monastery seems to be blessed. A huge front of black clouds lines the sky above the monastery where the session is being held. The half-black with half-pure blue sky is overhead. The sidewalks are dry.

A number of the participants tell how their own homes have been spared, as if "protected," in neighborhoods where houses all around have been hit with damage and calamities. One woman relates waking up to loud crashes. Large trees and a telephone pole uprooted by 100 mph winds ripped through the roofs of houses on both sides but her house was untouched.

The merit and virtue of the session isn't only for the participants. The idea is to transfer the blessings to seek aid and protection for all beings undergoing disasters and suffering. So it's said,

> "All the disasters and multitudes of suffering in the world, are deep and vast without a shore just like the ocean. And sharing these with living beings, being able to bear it all, they cause them to obtain peace and happiness."

> Avatamsaka Sutra
> The Ten Transferences Chapter

Sunday evening someone rushes in with the latest news report. A tidal wave and windstorm disaster headed right for the city from the ocean, unexpectedly veered off course and fizzled out. The crisis is over.

Everyone was extremely happy and relieved. The Master, moved by the vigor and sincerity of the assembly, composed this verse to commemorate the auspicious event.

> Medicine Master's Dharma meeting ushers in good luck.
> The City of Los Angeles avoids calamities.
> Good and faithful donors alike are vigorous.
> Human and divine protectors are busy, busy all.
> Sincerity brings responses
>     of more blessings and long life.
> Joy and giving, kindness and compassion,
>     insure a peace to come.
> Shocking heaven and shaking earth,
>     like springtime thunderclaps.
> The sounding drum and ringing bells
>     alter the ten directions.

That night the Abbot expressed some of the Buddhist thinking about averting disasters and universally benefiting all living beings.

"People are a mixture of good and bad. The same combination exists in Los Angeles. Sometimes good people have to suffer what is due to the bad people, and sometimes bad people can reap the benefit due to the good. So the good had to suffer a disaster, but by the same token, due to the good people, the disaster has diminished in its proportions, and the bad people enjoy that effect as well. The same principle applies to earthquakes: severe earthquakes turn into minor tremors, and minor tremors vanish before they appear...

"With this bowing of the Medicine Master Repentance, there is certain to be a tremendous response."

Instructions - Bits or Pieces For the Bowing Monks.

"No matter what it is, if you fear it, you'll never successfully complete it. Concentrate on bowing and studying sutras, but not too much. Too much reading will cause you to scatter. Studying sutras is not an end in itself. When you get a bit, go practice it. That's what matters. You don't want to know so much. If you know too much you'll scatter your energy. Go find out for yourself directly… Gather in your body and mind; don't have so many false thoughts. The reason for writing is to keep busy so you won't have time to false think!"

"You two understand very little principle now. As you understand more, your problems will be easy to resolve. Especially as you understand the Flower Adornment Sutra – it contains all of it. How to handle any situation."

"I get uncomfortable when I have too many things (material possessions). It's too much like greed. The less stuff you have, the better."

"Cultivators should not pay special attention to which food and drinks supplement their cultivation and which do not. Cultivators don't need to mind their bodily health that way. Keep to the natural, stay where you are. Don't be so concerned with your body. Once you add some sort of supplement, you're out of balance. Excess leads to deficiency and your troubles begin… Basically if your conduct is pure, you've got all of your need inside for balanced health. If you eat some rich nutritious food, the fire will rise up until you can't take it."

"Practice simplicity. The Buddha-dharma cultivates ordinary matters. Purify your mind. If you claim to have cultivation but you haven't purged your bad habits, then this is impossible. Don't forsake what's near and seek what's far."

Heng Chau • February 13, 1978
No pedestrian traffic beyond this point

A layman took us to a store for raingear. En route three multiple car accidents occurred. In each case we escaped without a scratch. In one collision on the freeway, the car ahead, behind, and on both sides wiped out, but our car was untouched. We slid right through.

This happened to me a couple of times as a layman. In each case I was reciting the Great Compassion Mantra at the time.

"To recite this mantra is to wipe away all offenses, keep one free of demons, and prevent natural disasters."

Dharani Sutra

Not falling into emptiness
Not clinging to existence.

After picking up the Plymouth in San Luis Obispo, we drove back to the bowing sight we had marked with a rock on the side of the road. I dropped Heng Sure off and drove ahead ½ mile to park the car. All the time I had been reciting mantras on my beads, convinced I had entered a state of proper mindfulness, a light and constant samadhi like,

Walking, standing, sitting, lying down,
never separate from this.

Master Hua

But when I walked back, Heng Sure was gone. I couldn't find him anywhere. I climbed a hill looking for miles in all directions. Nothing. The ground was still soft from the rain and I was able to follow his tracks, but they ended at a bridge overpass and steep ravine.

Fear and worry crept in. "Maybe he fell and is lying injured or unconscious in the ravine" or "maybe he was kidnapped by some maniacs, or was hit by a car and left to die." Anxiety turned to anger. "Stupid! He doesn't wear his glasses. He's practically blind without them. He may have taken a wrong turn and bowed up one of these mile-long ranch farm driveways or right into the sea, for all I know." Or, "he entered samadhi" and is sitting under a tree someplace totally oblivious.

I drove up and down the highway for miles in both directions, checking the ditches, looking for tracks. Nothing. After 2 hours of futile searching, I was desperate. I was just about to call the police when I thought, "No, call your teacher first, in your mind."

So I said aloud as I drove, "Help this novice. I've lost my monk!" Then I got a strong intuition, almost a nudge, to turn down an obscure, narrow side road. I took it on the impulse. Rounding the first curve I found Heng Sure, peacefully bowing through the tall flowers on the side of the road.

First relief: "Boy, am I glad to see you. I'd just about given you up for lost. You're okay, huh?" He nods, looking a little perplexed. Then anger, "Stupid! You really had me worried. Why didn't you tell me you were going to change the route? You just took off on this pastoral side road on your own while I was out there scouring the ditches and ravines thinking you were hurt, maybe dying…"

Heng Sure wrote a note: "I took the only route possible. There's a sign just past the point you dropped me off reading: 'No Pedestrian Traffic Beyond This Point' and an arrow pointing to this by-pass road. Didn't you see it? It was plain as day."

I didn't believe it. I drove back and forth covering that ground all morning. Had there been a sign I certainly would have seen it. I hopped in the car and drove back. Right in the middle of the road was the sign:

"No Pedestrian Traffic Beyond This Point," and an arrow pointing to the road Heng Sure took.

I pulled over and parked the car. Time to do some figuring. The Abbot's instructions started crystallizing. "Be alert. Be careful. Don't enter samadhi. You're the Dharma-protector. The cars won't enter samadhi. If you do they'll run you over and smash you to bits." I remembered the airport lesson last month where I miscounted the plane fare because I was spaced-out, convinced I had entered samadhi. *True* samadhi is bright and alive, totally in tune with conditions yet nowhere attached. It is emptiness without a thought of emptiness. Like it says in the Avatamsaka Preface:

> "Although emptiness is emptied and the traces are cut off, still the sky of mornings' stars glitter and blaze."

My state was stiff and frozen, a piece of wood, a lifeless rock. I fell into emptiness, but this was as wrong as clinging to existence. Why? Because both are attachments, false states to keep the view of self-intact.

I remembered back to L.A., as we were preparing to go to the airport, outside the monastery a young boy listened to directions. I watched his alertness and thought, "That's the way to be, right here and now. Alert and unattached. He won't get lost." Then en route, the Master said, "Be very careful. You have to break attachments to both self and dharmas. No attachment to self; no attachment to dharmas. Then everything's empty; even emptiness is empty." I reached over my shoulder and pulled the Avatamsaka from the top of the car seat and read,

> "All Tathagatas whatsoever, in all directions understand all dharmas with none left out. Although they know everything is empty and still, towards emptiness itself, they do not have a single thought.
>
> "The Bodhisattva contemplates the mind as not outside. Moreover, it cannot be gotten at inside. He knows the nature of his mind does not exist at all. Self and dharmas are all left behind, forever still and extinct."

## Heng Sure
So don't write that note to Heng Chau

Doing *tai ji* in the morning after sitting Ch'an meditation, my whole body feels exhilarated, alive. After 18 years (of "reading 10,000 books"), my practices ("walking 10,000 miles") are breaking through old barriers. Flexing, popping, stretching, new life in old joints, warmth and lightness spreads and energizes. How wonderful to feel good all over, all the time! And it comes from holding the Buddha's precepts, returning the light and doing Dharma work.

> "Where was there ever a man of wisdom who got to see
> and hear the Buddha, without cultivation of pure vows and
> walking the same path the Buddha walked?"
>
> Avatamsaka Sutra – Praises in the
> Tushita Heaven Palace Chapter

Don't do anything that hinders the cultivation of others. If you are real you can inspire them instead of blocking them. They might get enlightened. How wonderful! So don't write that note to Heng Chau. It is unimportant and might disturb his concentration. Return your own light!

## Heng Chau • February 14, 1978
Live outside and laugh in the rain

Norman and Fritz, two firemen from San Luis, bought out a lunch offering. We sat together on grass mats under a wind-bent cypress tree on a small plateau overlooking the ocean. They were all tense and fired-up inside over hassles with their jobs and the world.

"Fritz got grilled for some minor errors in judgment by a new boss, and I got socked for back taxes on my teaching job," said, Norm. "You know one of these days I'm going to put it all down and live outside and laugh in the rain..."

"How's your fantasy trip coming, Norm, to hike the coast and live off the land?" asked Fritz as he slapped a sandwich together.

"Still in my mind," answered Norm.

"I don't want the almighty buck" declared Fritz. "My wife is on me to get new clothes and get more 'things,' but I'm happy with these old beat-up hush puppies and jeans... You ruin your insides trying to look good outside."

Fritz told stories about the peregrine falcon, a nearly extinct species, making its last stand on the huge rock in the Morro Bay. We can see the rock behind us.

"So many of my friends get all tied down to their jobs, homes, kids..." he observed. Norm gathered some edible herbs and wild plants and showed us how to prepare them.

"Boy, this is home for me out here" said Fritz. "You know Norm, when I came, how tense I was? My stomach was just a big knot. It's all loose now. One of these days, I'm just going to turn around and... Hey Norm, how does that verse go you read me, you know, 'if you can't put down the false...'"

Norman had copied a verse of the Master's on his last visit. He recited it for Fritz:

> If you can't put down death,
> You can't pick up life.
> If you can't put down the false,
> You can't pick up the true.

"Wow! That really says it," exclaims Fritz.

After lunch Norman borrowed another Sutra. They both expressed pleasure over the tasty vegetarian leftovers from Gold Wheel Monastery.

"Boy, if I could learn to make this, I could easily put down meat. I never knew..." says Norm.

They warn us of big storms coming ("worse than last month"), and want to come back out to fix our car. They're in no hurry to go back home.

"The Bodhisattva is not attached to the householder's life. He leaves behind all contemplations of the family. He renounces the karma of the householder and all material objects. He is not greedy for it, he has no taste for it, and his mind is not bound by attachment to it. He knows the home-life easily falls apart and in his mind, he despises and forsakes it, and amidst it he feels no love or delight...

"He only wants to leave the home-life to cultivate the Bodhisattva Path and adorn himself with all the Buddha's Dharmas."

Avatamsaka Sutra
Ten Transferences Chapter

"You guys going to read from the Sutra today? I really like listening," says Norm.

The McKenzies stopped, "We've been keeping watch every day. Happy to see you back."

A pair of wool hiking socks and a note hanging in the car door at end of the day. "Your presence brings holiness to this land. Thank you."

---

**Heng Chau** • February 15, 1978
Producing the mind that doesn't seek or reject

Leave Cayucos. Ahead is Cambria.

Samadhi is a Sanskrit word meaning "proper reception" or "proper concentration." The incident of losing Heng Sure yesterday prompted me to take a closer look at my samadhis. How "proper" is my concentration?

I'm finding that a lot of states I took for samadhi are just attachment-trances, or "deviant samadhis." Proper samadhi is difficult to enter. The ego resists. The mind rebels with urges to sleep, richly detailed dreams, and bizarre fantasies, and non-stop yak yak static.

In a single day of bowing, proper mindfulness is abandoned to thoughts of food, clothes, shelter, and doting over my body's moods and feelings. My eyes chase after flying birds and rainbows, or fix and stare at cats and grazing cattle. My ears eavesdrop like a spinning radar scope. My mouth casually raps out whatever it feels like saying. Nose and tongue run wild at lunch grasping at smells and tastes. My mind is always dwelling on yesterday, tomorrow – anywhere but the here and now. Cravings pull me around and emotions move me like a dry leaf in a gust of wind. It's all a deviant samadhi and none of it brings enlightenment or opens wisdom.

> "He reverently contemplates the five skandhas, the eighteen realms, the twelve places, and his own body. In each and every one of these he seeks for Bodhi, as their substance and nature ultimately cannot be obtained."
>
> Avatamsaka Sutra

The 18 realms, 12 places and five skandhas are the "places" for entering an improper samadhi. The six organs of eyes, ears, nose, tongue, body and mind, unite with the six dusts of sights, sounds, smells, tastes, tangibles, and dharmas. These are the 12 places. The six consciousnesses arise between the six organs and the six dusts, and together they make up the 18 realms. The five skandhas or "heaps," are form, feelings, perceptions, activities, and consciousness. They are what are commonly taken for the "self" or "personality."

These dharmas and their states all arise from false thinking and attachments. They are false discriminations covering the originally pure and mark-less self-nature. So the Bodhisattva sees through them all and never leaves proper concentration.

Proper concentration is producing the mind that doesn't seek or reject, that doesn't cling to what is or fall into what is not. True samadhi is just not discriminating among dharmas because one knows "their substance and nature ultimately cannot be obtained." This is to be free and easy and nowhere attached.

Traveling with the Master: The layman in charge of the luggage and passports was daydreaming as we arrived for customs inspection. As a result luggage was lost and the group unnecessarily delayed while a mass of confusion got untangled.

Later: "What happened?" asked the Master. "I don't know," answer the layman. "You were false thinking about pretty stewardesses."

Layman blushes and is quiet. The Master goes on, "People who have no samadhi power make other people nervous and then they get angry. A lot of trouble is caused in this way."

Lesson: In proper concentration there are no hassles and no mistakes.

> He makes no mistakes.
> His mind is vast, big and pure.
> He is happy, blissful,
>     apart from all worry and vexation.
> His mind and will are soft and flexible.
> All his organs are clean and cool.
>
> Avatamsaka Sutra
> Ten Transferences Chapter

Rain lifts. Quiet and clear. Big blue skies, white waves and cool winds that make your feet want to run. Good bowing.

**Heng Sure**
Returning the light to shine within

> The Tathagatha's power of self-mastery
> Is difficult to encounter in measureless aeons.
> If one produces a single thought of faith,
> He will quickly realize the supreme path.
>
> Avatamsaka Sutra – Praises in the
> Ten Tushita Heaven Palace Chapter

Kuo Chou told of an old college roommate. A philosopher who has read all the books, literally read several entire libraries. Now the poor fellow is obstructed by his own knowledge. He's experimenting with chemical hallucinogenic states and he writes, "How can we know that what we know is true?" My heart goes out to this man. There but for the Buddhadharma go I. I left graduate school for this very reason. All his knowledge does not bring him peace. He lacks the heart of faith. Dharma doctor? Prescribe! One wholesome Dharma method. Recite the Buddha's name without pause. Don't think of anything. Have no doubts; don't seek understanding. Simply recite with all your heart. Amitabha!

While sitting I practice "returning the light." Literally pulling back on the energy that flows out of my eyes, ears, nose, tongue, skin and mind – the six organs. I practice pulling it back to the energy center and watching the gates of organs, plugging the leaks. When I'm concentrating, I keep this practice going all day.

On Returning the Light:

> Truly recognize your own faults,
> Don't discuss the faults of others.
> Others' faults are just my own.
> Being one with everyone is called Great Compassion.
>
> Master Hua

At first we don't know a good path from a bad path. Then we meet the Buddhadharma and seek the good road. We resolve to walk it to Buddhahood, our faith in the Buddha's enlightenment is born. We begin to cultivate and obstacles arise. Frustration comes with the obstacles: How come I'm more confused than ever? I really want to succeed but I'm getting nowhere. Faith is tested. Return the light and shine inside. Review your teacher's instructions. Keep on walking.

Ah! The principle connects. It is my own bad habits from beginningless time past, my endless pretensions and delusions that hold me back now. The will to change, the heart of transformation is here. Go for the yang principles of the Supreme Dharma. "Forget your self for the sake of the Dharma."

"The self is as tall as Mt. Sumeru and just as hard to knock over." But the Dharma is the best medicine going. When resolve to change is real then constant success is sure. The Dharma is so good and clean it makes you want to do anything to penetrate it; then it even shows you how to trust your Good Wise Advisor. He wants you to succeed. "Offer up your conduct according to his instructions."

> The Bodhisattva constantly cultivates the Dharma of patience. He is humble and respectful. He has this thought only: "I should always speak the Dharma for beings and cause them to leave evil behind and to cut off greed, hatred, and stupidity."
>
> Avatamsaka
> Ten Practices Chapter

> "He will certainly become the Supreme Honored One. Do not doubt it for an instant."
>
> Avatamsaka Sutra
> Chapter 24, Eulogies in The Tushita Palace

Past Cayucos. Few buildings, light traffic. Strong N.W. wind.

**Heng Chau** • February 17, 1978
Just do the work that needs to be done

Wrestling in dreams with demons with elastic-rubber bodies that can't be bent or broken. They wrap around me like a boa constructor and laugh at my futile resistance. I caught them, I am sure, by staring at cows in a pasture we bowed past yesterday. We just read in the Preface of the Handbook for Daily Vinaya on how we lose our original clarity of mind because of false thinking, and for aeons turn in the 6 paths of rebirth, climbing and falling back into the pit again and again.

I was able to break the demons' hold in the dream by reciting some lines from Shurangama Mantra, but woke up weak and trembling. I was feeling low and discouraged. I'm not all careful about cause and effect.

> "He protects the pure precepts without violation. With heroic courage he is vigorous, his mind unmoving."
>
> Avatamsaka Sutra
> Ten Transferences Chapter

A car pulled up. An old, white-haired couple with happy, twinkling eyes shouted,

"We believe and support you in what you're doing. Don't worry; you'll make it. Just try your best, that's all that counts."

They made an offering and said, "Wish we could do more." They did a lot.

> "And so it is that he never has a thought of fatigue or retreat. Courageous and valiant, he decisively and constantly transfers merit."
>
> Avatamsaka Sutra
> Ten Transferences Chapter

We often feel we are climbing a steep mountain. As we near the summit we slip and fall, tripping on our past karma of broken precepts. When your own debts for past wrongs are paid up, then you can stand in for and help others exhaust their bad karma. It's endless because living beings are endless and our offenses are endless. Just do the work that needs to be done. This is filiality: All beings are my parents; all beings suffer. I've got to find a way to help.

> "I will stand in for beings and receive all the extremely severe and bitter suffering they bring on with their evil karma. I will liberate all these beings and ultimately bring them to accomplish unsurpassed Bodhi."

> The Bodhisattva cultivates transference in this way: "The realm of empty space could be exhausted, the realm of living beings could be exhausted, the karma of living beings could be exhausted, the afflictions of living beings could be exhausted, but my transference is inexhaustible. It continues in thought after thought without cease; my body, mouth and mind never weary of these deeds."

> Avatamsaka Sutra
> Universal Worthy's Conduct and Vows Chapter

The McKenzies stopped to fill our tanks with gasoline. Strong winds, cold clear nights. Very little talking.

> "...by day and by night he practices what he studies. The Proper Dharma is the only thing he reveres."

> Avatamsaka Sutra
> Ten Grounds Chapter

Heng Chau • February 18, 1978
Borrow the false to discover the true

When we began the trip the world seemed real and full of excitement. The Avatamsaka seemed dull and like a dream. Now the Avatamsaka is real and exciting; the world seems like a dull dream and illusion.

> "...and at this time he leaps for joy and happiness to receive the Tathagata's profound (deep) Dharma Flower."
>
> Avatamsaka Sutra
> Ten Transferences Chapter

Studying the Avatamsaka at night is the best part of the day. More than food, clothes, and the shelter of the car, the Sutra is our means to survival. The mind is basic. The "soul" (8th consciousness) is the first thing to come and the last to go. The Avatamsaka is "soul" food. We would be lost without it.

"States."

States are states. They are unreal, impermanent, and unreliable. To discriminate good and bad, pleasant or unpleasant, pure and defiled is adding a head on top of a head. To compare and compete with someone else's state is even more stupid and dangerous. States often are demons in disguise. As soon as I try to "understand it" and hold on or reject it, the state backfires and suddenly I'm strapped with a big, grinning demon.

The Master advised us,

"Each one cultivates his own way and takes himself across. There are no fixed dharmas. Your method and all the variety of states are a personal thing and in the end, you have to put it all down. You simply borrow the false to discover the true. Don't compete or obstruct others."

Ultimately the nature of all dharmas and living beings is empty and still. They don't exist in that they cannot be obtained. They neither exist nor don't exist. They are apart from all such discriminations. States are the same. Made from the mind, they are like, "illusions, like a flame, like the moon's reflection in water."

I constantly have to remind myself: don't be turned by *anything*. Don't be turned by being turned. Don't go up; don't go under. Keep to the Middle where it's perfectly balanced and even. If you do the work, states are bound to arise. Sit back and watch them come and go with a free and easy unattached eye. They are "like a dream, like a shadow, like an image in a mirror." Nothing belongs to you. It's all borrowed and you're just passing through. Use the light of wisdom to see it like it really is.

> Another light comes forth called Wisdom Lamp.
> This light is able to awaken the masses,
> Causing them to know the nature of living beings
>     is empty and still.
> And that all dharmas are empty without a host.
> They are like an illusion, like a flame,
>     like the moon's reflection in water.
> They are also like a dream, a shadow,
>     like an image in a mirror.
> For this reason this light shines forth.

Avatamsaka Sutra

---

**Heng Sure**
Mr. Morgan's gift of fearlessness

I was the starting pitcher for the McKinley Frogs Little League baseball team. Games were held on Saturday mornings. Always had nervous butterflies in the stomach before each game. The umpires stand behind the pitcher on the mound in Little League. The umpire's disposition had a lot to do with the pitcher's concentration during the game. I'll never forget one umpire. I recall his name was Mr. Morgan. He called balls and strikes for two of my starts – both were winning games. His disposition was totally open, friendly and frank. He liked boys and he liked baseball. As the game progressed, he would talk over your shoulder. His words were skillful; they went right in the ear and down to the heart as the pitcher worked. Mr. Morgan had the manner of a good and wise advisor. He gave like a Bodhisattva – the gift of fearlessness.

He'd speak in a low voice so the infielder couldn't hear him, "Okay, son. Now's the time to work hard. Concentrate and relax. You're going to give this batter your best pitches, throw the ball right past him. Don't worry about whether you win; just make this your very best pitch, give it all you've got. Steerike One! Take your time now, bring your energy together and show them what you're made of. They're a little scared of you on the other bench 'cause you're looking really strong today."

He would take all the butterflies away with his soothing words and before you knew it, you were pitching the best game of the season. When it was your turn at the plate, you could see Mr. Morgan giving the same encouragement to the other team's pitcher, but he was so clean and kind in his giving, that it didn't matter a bit. No one could feel selfish attachment to his big heart – there was enough light there for everybody.

> …(The Bodhisattva's) constant wish:
>     to help others and make them happy.
>
> Avatamsaka Sutra<br>Worthy Leader Chapter

A tough inning: two men on base and no outs. Mr. Morgan would say, "Now's the time to bear down and try your best. This is good baseball, son. There's nothing fixed here – it's a test of your skill and your courage. Have you got what it takes to pull your team out of the hole? I know you do and so do these eight other guys out here – they are all pulling for you and giving you their support. Let's see you fog it by this old grandmother at bat. See, he swings like a rusty gate. Steerike! There you go. Set your mind on it and then relax your body. Don't tighten up. Just give your best all the time and win or lose, that's what counts. When you work hard right to the end, then no matter how strong the other team is, and sometimes they're gonna be stronger, you can go home feeling like you played a good game no matter what the final score was. Say, that was a good curve ball! I saw Dizzy Dean throw curves like that back when I was about your age. Steerike three! That's good pitching, son."

**Heng Sure** • February 1978
Twenty miles of awesome rocks

> "As the nature of earth has a unity, and yet all livings beings dwell on it separately, still the earth has not the slightest thought of differences, and all the Buddhadharma is the same."
>
> Avatamsaka Sutra – The Bodhisattvas
> Ask for Clarification Chapter

We came around the steep curve and there, before us, unrolled the next three weeks of work; twenty miles of awesome rocks. In the slanting afternoon sun, the sheer green cliffs and the vast azure ocean looked fearsome. The first sight of it took my breath away. Sinewy, twisting towers fell straight down to the rolling surf. We could see tiny flecks of sun glare on glass – cars and campers in the distance following a tiny thread of highway, ridiculous and insignificant, stuck up there halfway between oblivion and nowhere. We were going to bow this road? I got scared and started to dive down into my old defenses – to take refuge in a daydream – avoid reality. Then I could not do it. A new yang energy kept my spirits high.

Heng Chau • February 19, 1978
Hot diggity!

Brad, Cliff, Vicky and their crew came out with a meal offering and to recite Guan Yin Bodhisattva's name and listen to the Avatamsaka. ("What's your Dharma body?" asked Vicky last week.)

Cliff said, "I've tried to fit into a lot of different religions and groups, but they were never for me. But Buddhism is different somehow, you know? It feels like home."

Brad told a story about how he was caught in a bad storm and heavy winds last week. "I was driving a small car. It was very dangerous. Tree limbs were falling and the road washed out in places. Then I hit a bird. I saw it in the mirror roll on the highway and die. I felt real remorse and empathy. For some reason without thinking I said, 'Namo Guan Shi Yin Pu Sa' about 5 or 6 times. It felt like the right thing to do. I remembered that Guan Yin helps in times of suffering and disasters. Suddenly the winds died and the sun came out. The skies cleared. I felt sorry for killing the bird, but now everything was okay."

"When he got home," said Vicky, "Brad was all glowing and happy. I've never seen him like that before. Strange, huh?"

> Always practicing great kindness and compassion,
> He constantly has faith as well as reverence.
> He is replete with the merit and virtue
>     of repentance and reform.
> Night and day increasing wholesome dharmas.
>
> Avatamsaka Sutra
> Ten Grounds Chapter

Brad had never recited Guan Yin's name before. Out of faith and "feeling of compassion and reverence" for a dying being, he repented while driving down the highway. He felt a change and added something wholesome to his life.

A family on a picnic outing stopped as we were writing alongside a small creek on the land. "Oh, you're the *monks*. Will you accept some food?" They opened their picnic basket and offered some cheese, bread and fruit. "Stay as long as you like. It's very peaceful here."

The McKenzies drove out with food, gas and water. Someone asked if there's anything we "would like." We explained that the offerings are not for us but made *through* us. It's not what we "would like," rather the Sangha is a pure field where people can plant blessings. Making offerings is a chance to support and add to what Buddhism stands for: enlightened wisdom, peace, compassion and ending suffering of all kinds.

> As the earth is all one,
> Yet it puts forth sprouts each according to the seed,
> And it doesn't reject or favor any of them.
> So it is with the Buddha's field of blessings.

> Avatamsaka Sutra – The Bodhisattvas
> Ask for Clarification Chapter

"It's like seeds, huh?" said Mrs. McKenzie. "Like planting good seeds. I don't understand a whole lot; all I think about when I give is *up there* (City of 10,000 Buddhas). I visualize all those faces, land, and fine buildings and what they represent and I 'send it up' to help it grow."

The McKenzies both work to support a family of 4 children. They're moving house and yet take time to drive out to put gas in our "four wheeled friend" as they call the Plymouth, and ask about Buddhism.

"Every day I try to do a little better and learn a little more, and when I saw those pictures and the people at the City of 10,000 Buddhas I said, 'Hot diggity!'"

The McKenzies tell their story:

"We lived in S. Pasadena, had a Cadillac and a color T.V. and all the rest. But it became not whether you had a color T.V., but *how* many. So we sold the Cadillac and moved to the mountains with the kids. We lived near Sequoia for 3 years."

"I learned to save rubber bands and felt like I was in kindergarten again," laughed Mrs. McKenzie.

"But the children needed school and scouts so we moved to Morro Bay. John got a job with the Forest Service. I'm a college graduate hopping tables now." she says.

"We like coming out to make offerings. It's my way of meditation and we appreciate the chance to give," she said.

As the kids filled our gas tank and water jugs, their mother quietly sat staring off through a grove of tall trees off Highway 1. We are all looking for a way out of the long dark night, a way back to the land of eternal brightness. The most breathtaking virgin paradise ever experienced is right in our laps. The wonderful Dharma Jewel is within our own self-nature. What we seek and find outside is just a reflection of what we uncover within. The Flower Store World and Pure Land are produced from our thoughts; the Avatamsaka Sutra is being spoken right now in our own minds. We just forget and get lost sometimes in the shuffle. With a single thought of purity the millions of wonders reappear even on a single tip of a hair. In just sitting still and quieting the mad mind we find the perfect spot.

> Within each and every hair pore
> Are many kinds of adornments and marks
> That have never before been caused to appear…
> Contemplate the nature of the Dharma-realm,
> It's all made from the mind alone.
>
> Avatamsaka Sutra
> Flower Store World Chapter

Harold, a mayoral candidate in Morro Bay, stopped with his daughter.

"I'm happy and surprised to learn there were still some people dedicating their lives to doing good and ending suffering for others," he said.

> I do not seek liberation for my own body,
> But only to save all living beings,
>    so that they all attain the mind of all-wisdom.
> And cross over the flow of birth and death,
> And gain liberation from all their suffering...
> I should stand in for living beings amid all evil paths,
> And cause them to be liberated from those paths.
>
> Avatamsaka Sutra
> Ten Transferences Chapter

## Heng Sure
The developers are me

"Buddhism has always impressed me," said Harold. "Buddhism's not narrow. There's lots of room. I like that. It takes it inside, you know, an inner experience that doesn't leave anything out."

> In the ten directions with nothing left out,
> Measureless, boundless within the Dharma-realm.
> Without beginning or end, neither near nor far,
> Is revealed the independent strength
>    of the Well Gone One.
>
> Avatamsaka Sutra
> Ten Transferences Chapter

"Keep The Developers Out!"

As I bowed, a comment Harold made stuck in my mind. He said, "My campaign is this: Keep the developers out." Who are the developers? They are just my own thoughts of greed and self-seeking, my desire mind that's like a bottomless pit. The developers outside come from the developers inside. In my mind I'm always scheming for a better deal for myself: a bigger hunk of this, a better piece of that. Whether food, fame, wealth, sex or sleep, I never feel I have enough. Not content with what I have, my busy mind runs all over the Dharma Realm, even in dreams, day and night, climbing on conditions and "looking for some action." My body and mind are choking with progress and over-development. And so the world I live in reflects my greed and confusion, because everything is produced from the mind.

It is like Morro Bay: on the edge of the continent with no more room to grow. Outside the land's gone. We are hungry and got the itch to move to greener pastures but the pastures are all gone. We feel like the last Peregrine falcon clinging to the rock in Morro Bay with no place left to fly. "It's the developers' fault" I want to say. But the "developers" are I.

The Sixth Patriarch said:

> "People of the East want to be reborn in the West. So where should people of the West go to be reborn?"

His meaning was "go within" and don't rely on external conditions. Develop the mind ground and return to your original home. Don't forever seek outside and not be able to stand on your own. I don't want to continue frantically developing into outer space. Why not develop inner space? There are men on the moon, but there's still no peace of mind.

> "The further one travels, the less one knows."
>
> Lao Tzu

Heng Chau bowing near Vandenberg Air Force Base

# Buddhist Text Translation Society Publication

## Buddhist Text Translation Society
## International Translation Institute

http://www.bttsonline.org

1777 Murchison Drive,
Burlingame, California 94010-4504 USA
Phone: (650) 692-5912 Fax: (650) 692-5056

When Buddhism first came to China from India, one of the most important tasks required for its establishment was the translation of the Buddhist scriptures from Sanskrit into Chinese. This work involved a great many people, such as the renowned monk National Master Kumarajiva (fifth century), who led an assembly of over 800 people to work on the translation of the Tripitaka (Buddhist canon) for over a decade. Because of the work of individuals such as these, nearly the entire Buddhist Tripitaka of over a thousand texts exists to the present day in Chinese.

Now the banner of the Buddha's teachings is being firmly planted in Western soil, and the same translation work is being done from Chinese into English. Since 1970, the Buddhist Text Translation Society (BTTS) has been making a paramount contribution toward this goal. Aware that the Buddhist Tripitaka is a work of such magnitude that its translation could never be entrusted to a single person, the BTTS, emulating the translation assemblies of ancient times, does not publish a work until it has passed through four committees for primary translation, revision, editing, and certification. The leaders of these committees are Bhikshus (monks) and Bhikshunis (nuns) who have devoted their lives to the study and practice of the Buddha's teachings. For this reason, all of the works of the BTTS put an emphasis on what the principles of the Buddha's teachings mean in terms of actual practice and not simply hypothetical conjecture.

The translations of canonical works by the Buddhist Text Translation Society are accompanied by extensive commentaries by the Venerable Tripitaka Master Hsuan Hua.

# BTTS Publications

**Buddhist Sutras.** Amitabha Sutra, Dharma Flower (Lotus) Sutra, Flower Adornment (Avatamsaka) Sutra, Heart Sutra & Verses without a Stand, Shurangama Sutra, Sixth Patriarch Sutra, Sutra in Forty-two Sections, Sutra of the Past Vows of Earth Store Bodhisattva, Vajra Prajna Paramita (Diamond) Sutra.

**Commentarial Literature.** Buddha Root Farm, City of 10 000 Buddhas Recitation Handbook, Filiality: The Human Source, Herein Lies the Treasure-trove, Listen to Yourself Think Everything Over, Shastra on the Door to Understanding the Hundred Dharmas, Song of Enlightenment, The Ten Dharma Realms Are Not Beyond a Single Thought, Venerable Master Hua's Talks on Dharma, Venerable Master Hua's Talks on Dharma during the 1993 Trip to Taiwan, Water Mirror Reflecting Heaven.

**Biographical.** In Memory of the Venerable Master Hsuan Hua, Pictorial Biography of the Venerable Master Hsü Yün, Records of High Sanghans, Records of the Life of the Venerable Master Hsüan Hua, Three Steps One Bow, World Peace Gathering, News from True Cultivators, Open Your Eyes Take a Look at the World, With One Heart Bowing to the City of 10 000 Buddhas.

**Children's Books.** Cherishing Life, Human Roots: Buddhist Stories for Young Readers, Spider Web, Giant Turtle, Patriarch Bodhidharma.

**Musics, Novels and Brochures.** Songs for Awakening, Awakening, The Three Cart Patriarch, City of 10 000 Buddhas Color Brochure, Celebrisi's Journey, Lots of Time Left.

**The Buddhist Monthly–Vajra Bodhi Sea** is a monthly journal of orthodox Buddhism which has been published by the Dharma Realm Buddhist Association, formerly known as the Sino-American Buddhist Association, since 1970. Each issue contains the most recent translations of the Buddhist canon by the Buddhist Text Translation Society. Also included in each issue are a biography of a great Patriarch of Buddhism from the ancient past, sketches of the lives of contemporary monastics and lay-followers around the world, articles on practice, and other material. The journal is bilingual, Chinese and English.

Please visit our web-site at **www.bttsonline.org** for the latest publications and for ordering information.

# Dharma Realm Buddhist Association Branches

### The City of Ten Thousand Buddhas
4951 Bodhi Way, Ukiah, CA 95482 USA
Tel: (707) 462-0939  Fax: (707) 462-0949
Website: **http://www.drba.org** Email: **cttb@drba.org**

### Buddhist Text Translation Society Online Catalog
Website: **http://www.bttsonline.org**

**Institute for World Religions (Berkeley Buddhist Monastery)**
2304 McKinley Avenue, Berkeley, CA 94703 USA
Tel: (510) 848-3440  Fax: (510) 548-4551  Email: paramita@drba.org

**Dharma Realm Buddhist Books Distribution Society**
11th Floor, 85 Chung-hsiao E. Road, Sec. 6, Taipei, Taiwan R.O.C.
Tel: (02) 2786-3022  Fax: (02) 2786-2674  Email: drbbds@ms1.seeder.net

**The City of the Dharma Realm**
1029 West Capitol Avenue, West Sacramento, CA 95691 USA
Tel: (916) 374-8268  Fax: (916) 374-8234  Email: cdrclasses@yahoo.com

**Gold Mountain Monastery**
800 Sacramento Street, San Francisco, CA 94108 USA
Tel: (415) 421-6117  Fax: (415) 788-6001

**Gold Wheel Monastery**
235 North Avenue 58, Los Angeles, CA 90042 USA
Tel: (323) 258-6668  Fax: (323) 258-3619

**Gold Buddha Monastery**
248 East 11th Avenue, Vancouver, B.C. V5T 2C3 Canada
Tel: (604) 709-0248  Fax: (604) 684-3754  Email: drab@gbm-online.com
Website: http://www.drba/gbm-online.com

**Gold Summit Monastery**
233 1st Avenue, West Seattle, WA 98119 USA
Tel: (206) 284-6690  Fax: (206) 284-6918
Website: http://www.goldsummitmonastery.org

**Gold Sage Monastery**
11455 Clayton Road, San Jose, CA 95127-5099 USA
Tel: (408) 923-7243  Fax: (408) 923-1064

**The International Translation Institute**
1777 Murchison Drive, Burlingame, CA 94010-4504 USA
Tel: (650) 692-5912  Fax: (650) 692-5056

**Long Beach Monastery**
3361 East Ocean Boulevard, Long Beach, CA 90803 USA
Tel: (562) 438-8902

**Blessings, Prosperity, & Longevity Monastery**
4140 Long Beach Boulevard, Long Beach, CA 90807 USA
Tel: (562) 595-4966

**Avatamsaka Vihara**
9601 Seven Locks Road, Bethesda, MD 20817-9997, USA
Tel/Fax: (301) 469-8300  Email: hwa_yean88@msn.com

**Avatamsaka Monastery**
1009 4th Avenue, S.W. Calgary, AB T2P OK8 Canada
Tel: (403) 234-0644  Fax: (403) 263-0537
Website: http://www.avatamsaka.ca

**Dharma Realm Guanyin Sagely Monastery**
161, Jalan Ampang, 50450 Kuala Lumpur, West Malaysia
Tel: (03) 2164-8055  Fax: (03) 2163-7118

**Prajna Guanyin Sagely Monastery (formerly Tze Yun Tung)**
Batu 5½, Jalan Sungai Besi, Salak Selatan, 57100 Kuala Lumpur, Malaysia
Tel: (03) 7982-6560  Fax: (03) 7980-1272

**Lotus Vihara**
136, Jalan Sekolah, 45600 Batang Berjuntai, Selangor Darul Ehsan, Malaysia
Tel: (03) 3271-9439

**Source of Dharma Realm** – Lot S130, 2nd Floor, Green Zone, Sungai Wang
Plaza, Jalan Bukit Bintang, 55100 Kuala Lumpur, Malaysia
Tel: (03) 2164-8055

**Buddhist Lecture Hall** – 31 Wong Nei Chong Road, Top Floor, Happy
Valley, Hong Kong, China
Tel: (02) 2572-7644  Fax: (2) 2572-2850

**Dharma Realm Sagely Monastery** – 20, Tong-hsi Shan-chuang, Hsing-lung
Village, Liu-kuei Kaohsiung County, Taiwan, R.O.C.
Tel: (07) 689-3717  Fax: (07) 689-3870

**Amitabha Monastery** – 7, Su-chien-hui, Chih-nan Village, Shou-feng,
Hualien County, Taiwan, R.O.C.
Tel: (07) 865-1956  Fax: (07) 865-3426

**Gold Coast Dharma Realm**
106 Bonogin Road, Mudgeeraba, Queensland 4213 Australia
Tel/fax: (07) 61-755-228-788  (07) 61-755-227-822

# The Dharma Realm Buddhist Association

## Mission

The Dharma Realm Buddhist Association (formerly the Sino-American Buddhist Association) was founded by the Venerable Master Hsuan Hua in the United States of America in 1959. Taking the Dharma Realm as its scope, the Association aims to disseminate the genuine teachings of the Buddha throughout the world. The Association is dedicated to translating the Buddhist canon, propagating the Orthodox Dharma, promoting ethical education, and bringing benefit and happiness to all beings. Its hope is that individuals, families, the society, the nation, and the entire world will, under the transforming influence of the Buddhadharma, gradually reach the state of ultimate truth and goodness.

## The Founder

The Venerable Master, whose names were An Tse and To Lun, received the Dharma name Hsuan Hua and the transmission of Dharma from Venerable Master Hsu Yun in the lineage of the Wei Yang Sect. He was born in Manchuria, China, at the beginning of the century. At nineteen, he entered the monastic order and dwelt in a hut by his mother's grave to practice filial piety. He meditated, studied the teachings, ate only one meal a day, and slept sitting up. In 1948 he went to Hong Kong, where he established the Buddhist Lecture Hall and other Way-places. In 1962 he brought the Proper Dharma to the West, lecturing on several dozen Mahayana Sutras in the United States. Over the years, the Master established more than twenty monasteries of Proper Dharma under the auspices of the Dharma Realm Buddhist Association and the City of Ten Thousand Buddhas. He also founded centers for the translation of the Buddhist canon and for education to spread the influence of the Dharma in the East and West. The Master manifested the stillness in the United States in 1995. Through his lifelong, selfless dedication to teaching living beings with wisdom and compassion, he influenced countless people to change their faults and to walk upon the pure, bright path to enlightenment.

# Dharma Propagation, Buddhist Text Translation, and Education

The Venerable Master Hua's three great vows after leaving the home-life were (1) to propagate the Dharma, (2) to translate the Buddhist Canon, and (3) to promote education. In order to make these vows a reality, the Venerable Master based himself on the Three Principles and the Six Guidelines. Courageously facing every hardship, he founded monasteries, schools, and centers in the West, drawing in living beings and teaching them on a vast scale. Over the years, he founded the following institutions:

## The City of Ten Thousand Buddhas and Its Branches

In propagating the Proper Dharma, the Venerable Master not only trained people but also founded Way-places where the Dharma wheel could turn and living beings could be saved. He wanted to provide cultivators with pure places to practice in accord with the Buddha's regulations. Over the years, he founded many Way-places of Proper Dharma. In the United States and Canada, these include the City of Ten Thousand Buddhas; Gold Mountain Monastery; Gold Sage Monastery; Gold Wheel Monastery; Gold Summit Monastery; Gold Buddha Monastery; Avatamsaka Monastery; Long Beach Monastery; the City of the Dharma Realm; Berkeley Buddhist Monastery; Avatamsaka Hermitage; and Blessings, Prosperity, and Longevity Monastery. In Taiwan, there are the Dharma Realm Buddhist Books Distribution Association, Dharma Realm Monastery, and Amitabha Monastery. In Malaysia, there are the Prajna Guanyin Sagely Monastery (formerly Tze Yun Tung Temple), Deng Bi An Monastery, and Lotus Vihara. In Hong Kong, there are the Buddhist Lecture Hall and Cixing Monastery.

Purchased in 1974, the City of Ten Thousand Buddhas is the hub of the Dharma Realm Buddhist Association. The City is located in Talmage, Mendocino County, California, 110 miles north of San Francisco. Eighty of the 488 acres of land are in active use. The remaining acreage consists of meadows, orchards, and woods. With over seventy large buildings containing over 2,000 rooms, blessed with serenity and fresh, clean air, it is the first large Buddhist monastic community in the United States. It is also an international center for the Proper Dharma.

Although the Venerable Master Hua was the Ninth Patriarch in the Wei Yang Sect of the Chan School, the monasteries he founded emphasize all of the five main practices of Mahayana Buddhism (Chan meditation, Pure Land, esoteric, Vinaya (moral discipline), and doctrinal studies). This accords with the Buddha's words: "The Dharma is level and equal, with no high or low." At the City of Ten Thousand Buddhas, the rules of purity are rigorously observed. Residents of the City strive to regulate their own conduct and to cultivate with vigor. Taking refuge in the Proper Dharma, they lead pure and selfless lives, and attain peace in body and mind. The Sutras are expounded and the Dharma wheel is turned daily. Residents dedicate themselves wholeheartedly to making Buddhism flourish. Monks and nuns in all the monasteries take one meal a day, always wear their precept sash, and follow the Three Principles:

> *Freezing, we do not scheme.*
> *Starving, we do not beg.*
> *Dying of poverty, we ask for nothing.*
> *According with conditions, we do not change.*
> *Not changing, we accord with conditions.*
> *We adhere firmly to our three great principles.*
> *We renounce our lives to do the Buddha's work.*
> *We take the responsibility to mold our own destinies.*
> *We rectify our lives to fulfill the Sanghan's role.*
> *Encountering specific matters,*
>    *we understand the principles.*
> *Understanding the principles,*
>    *we apply them in specific matters.*
> *We carry on the single pulse of*
>    *the Patriarchs' mind-transmission.*

The monasteries also follow the Six Guidelines: not contending, not being greedy, not seeking, not being selfish, not pursuing personal advantage, and not lying.

---

## International Translation Institute

The Venerable Master vowed to translate the Buddhist Canon (Tripitaka) into Western languages so that it would be widely accessible throughout the world. In 1973, he founded the International Translation Institute on Washington Street in San Francisco for the purpose of translating Buddhist scriptures into English and other languages. In 1977, the Institute was merged into Dharma Realm Buddhist University as the Institute for the Translation of Buddhist Texts. In 1991, the Venerable Master purchased a large building in Burlingame (south of San Francisco) and established the International Translation Institute there for the purpose of translating and publishing Buddhist texts. To date, in addition to publishing over one hundred volumes of Buddhist texts in Chinese, the Association has published more than one hundred volumes of English, French, Spanish, Vietnamese, and Japanese translations of Buddhist texts, as well as bilingual (Chinese and English) editions. Audio and video tapes also continue to be produced. The monthly journal Vajra Bodhi Sea, which has been in circulation for nearly thirty years, has been published in bilingual (Chinese and English) format in recent years.

In the past, the difficult and vast mission of translating the Buddhist canon in China was sponsored and supported by the emperors and kings themselves. In our time, the Venerable Master encouraged his disciples to cooperatively shoulder this heavy responsibility, producing books and audio tapes and using the medium of language to turn the wheel of Proper Dharma and do the great work of the Buddha. All those who aspire to devote themselves to this work of sages should uphold the Eight Guidelines of the International Translation Institute:

1. One must free oneself from the motives of personal fame and profit.
2. One must cultivate a respectful and sincere attitude free from arrogance and conceit.
3. One must refrain from aggrandizing one's work and denigrating that of others.
4. One must not establish oneself as the standard of correctness and suppress the work of others with one's fault-finding.
5. One must take the Buddha-mind as one's own mind.
6. One must use the wisdom of Dharma-Selecting Vision to determine true principles.
7. One must request Virtuous Elders of the ten directions to certify one's translations.
8. One must endeavor to propagate the teachings by printing Sutras, Shastra texts, and Vinaya texts when the translations are certified as being correct.

These are the Venerable Master's vows, and participants in the work of translation should strive to realize them.

## Instilling Goodness Elementary School, Developing Virtue Secondary School, Dharma Realm Buddhist University

"Education is the best national defense." The Venerable Master Hua saw clearly that in order to save the world, it is essential to promote good education. If we want to save the world, we have to bring about a complete change in people's minds and guide them to cast out unwholesomeness and to pursue goodness. To this end the Master founded Instilling Goodness Elementary School in 1974, and Developing Virtue Secondary School and Dharma Realm Buddhist University in 1976.

In an education embodying the spirit of Buddhism, the elementary school teaches students to be filial to parents, the secondary school teaches students to be good citizens, and the university teaches such virtues as humaneness and righteousness. Instilling Goodness Elementary School and Developing Virtue Secondary School combine the best of contemporary and traditional methods and of Western and Eastern cultures. They emphasize moral virtue and spiritual development, and aim to guide students to become good and capable citizens who will benefit humankind. The schools offer a bilingual (Chinese/English) program where boys and girls study separately. In addition to standard academic courses, the curriculum includes ethics, meditation, Buddhist studies, and so on, giving students a foundation in virtue and guiding them to understand themselves and explore the truths of the universe. Branches of the schools (Sunday schools) have been established at branch monasteries with the aim of propagating filial piety and ethical education.

Dharma Realm Buddhist University, whose curriculum focuses on the Proper Dharma, does not merely transmit academic knowledge. It emphasizes a foundation in virtue, which expands into the study of how to help all living beings discover their inherent nature. Thus, Dharma Realm Buddhist University advocates a spirit of shared inquiry and free exchange of ideas, encouraging students to study various canonical texts and use different experiences and learning styles to tap their inherent wisdom and fathom the meanings of those texts. Students are encouraged to practice the principles they have understood and apply the Buddhadharma in their lives, thereby nurturing their wisdom and virtue. The University aims to produce outstanding individuals of high moral character who will be able to bring benefit to all sentient beings.

## Sangha and Laity Training Programs

In the Dharma-ending Age, in both Eastern and Western societies there are very few monasteries that actually practice the Buddha's regulations and strictly uphold the precepts. Teachers with genuine wisdom and understanding, capable of guiding those who aspire to pursue careers in Buddhism, are very rare. The Venerable Master founded the Sangha and Laity Training Programs in 1982 with the goals of raising the caliber of the Sangha, perpetuating the Proper Dharma, providing professional training for Buddhists around the world on both practical and theoretical levels, and transmitting the wisdom of the Buddha.

The Sangha Training Program gives monastics a solid foundation in Buddhist studies and practice, training them in the practical affairs of Buddhism and Sangha management. After graduation, students will be able to assume various responsibilities related to Buddhism in monasteries, institutions, and other settings. The program emphasizes a thorough knowledge of Buddhism, understanding of the scriptures, earnest cultivation, strict observance of precepts, and the development of a virtuous character, so that students will be able to propagate the Proper Dharma and perpetuate the Buddha's wisdom. The Laity Training Program offers courses to help laypeople develop correct views, study and practice the teachings, and understand monastic regulations and ceremonies, so that they will be able to contribute their abilities in Buddhist organizations.

## Let Us Go Forward Together

In this Dharma-ending Age when the world is becoming increasingly dangerous and evil, the Dharma Realm Buddhist Association, in consonance with its guiding principles, opens the doors of its monasteries and centers to those of all religions and nationalities. Anyone who is devoted to humaneness, righteousness, virtue, and the pursuit of truth, and who wishes to understand him or herself and help humankind, is welcome to come study and practice with us. May we together bring benefit and happiness to all living beings.

# Verse of Transference

May the merit and virtue accrued from this work,
Adorn the Buddhas' Pure Lands,
Repaying four kinds of kindness above,
And aiding those suffering in the paths below.

May those who see and hear of this,
All bring forth the resolve for Bodhi,
And when this retribution body is over,
Be born together in the Land of Ultimate Bliss.

Dharma Protector Wei Tuo Bodhisattva